THE
EVERYTHING®
ANTI-INFLAMMATION
DIET BOOK

Dear Reader,

The Everything® Anti-Inflammation Diet Book is an educational journey into the world of silent inflammation, which touches each and every one of us. My insatiable passion and curiosity about how nutrition and physical activity affect the human body has spurred my interest in anti-inflammatory living.

Inflammation presents itself to me via my skin. When my stress level is high and my diet is not up to par, I experience psoriasis and other skin-related conditions. I previously remedied these conditions by obtaining medications from a dermatologist, but over time, I have realized the positive (and negative) impact that food and physical activity (and inactivity) can have on the body. This infusion of knowledge has enabled me to better manage my skin issues and other inflammation-related consequences of suboptimal dietary and lifestyle habits.

I am honored to share with you the knowledge I have gained over the years practicing as a registered dietitian and exercise physiologist. I truly love to help other curious minds obtain proper and productive information about anything related to nutrition and physical activity. I hope you enjoy your journey.

Karlyn Grimes, MS, RD, LDN

Welcome to the EVERYTHING® Series!

These handy, accessible books give you all you need to tackle a difficult project, gain a new hobby, comprehend a fascinating topic, prepare for an exam, or even brush up on something you learned back in school but have since forgotten.

You can choose to read an Everything® book from cover to cover or just pick out the information you want from our four useful boxes: e-questions, e-facts, e-alerts, and e-ssentials.

We give you everything you need to know on the subject, but throw in a lot of fun stuff along the way, too.

We now have more than 400 Everything® books in print, spanning such wide-ranging categories as weddings, pregnancy, cooking, music instruction, foreign language, crafts, pets, New Age, and so much more. When you're done reading them all, you can finally say you know Everything®!

QUESTION

Answers to
common questions

FACT

Important snippets
of information

ALERT

Urgent
warnings

ESSENTIAL

Quick
handy tips

PUBLISHER Karen Cooper

DIRECTOR OF ACQUISITIONS AND INNOVATION Paula Munier

MANAGING EDITOR, EVERYTHING® SERIES Lisa Laing

COPY CHIEF Casey Ebert

ACQUISITIONS EDITOR Katrina Schroeder

ASSOCIATE DEVELOPMENT EDITOR Hillary Thompson

SENIOR DEVELOPMENT EDITOR Brett Palana-Shanahan

EDITORIAL ASSISTANT Ross Weisman

EVERYTHING® SERIES COVER DESIGNER Erin Alexander

LAYOUT DESIGNERS Colleen Cunningham, Elisabeth Lariviere, Ashley Vierra, Denise Wallace

Visit the entire Everything® series at *www.everything.com*

THE EVERYTHING®

ANTI-INFLAMMATION DIET BOOK

The easy-to-follow, scientifically proven plan to:
· Reverse and prevent disease · Lose weight and increase energy
· Slow signs of aging · Live pain-free

Karlyn Grimes, MS, RD, LDN

Avon, Massachusetts

This book is dedicated to my mom and dad, who
gave me the tools necessary to succeed in life.

An Everything® Series Book.
Everything® and everything.com® are registered trademarks of F+W Media, Inc.

Published by Adams Media, a division of F+W Media, Inc.
57 Littlefield Street, Avon, MA 02322 U.S.A.
www.adamsmedia.com

ISBN 10: 1-4405-1029-6
ISBN 13: 978-1-4405-1029-8
eISBN 10: 1-4405-1236-1
eISBN 13: 978-1-4405-1236-0

Printed in the United States of America.

10 9 8 7 6 5 4 3 2

Library of Congress Cataloging-in-Publication Data
is available from the publisher.

The Everything® Anti-Inflammation Diet Book contains material adapted and abridged from: *The Everything® Healthy Meals in Minutes Cookbook* by Linda Larsen, copyright © 2005 by F+W Media, Inc., ISBN 10: 1-59337-302-3; ISBN 13: 978-1-59337-302-3; *The Everything® Guide to Being Vegetarian* by Alexandra Greeley, copyright © 2009 by F+W Media, Inc., ISBN 10: 1-60550-051-5; ISBN 13: 978-1-60550-051-5; *The Everything® Mediterranean Cookbook* by Dawn Altomari-Rathjen, copyright © 2003 by F+W Media, Inc., ISBN 10: 1-58062-569-9; ISBN 13: 978-1-58062-869-3; *The Everything® Superfoods Book* by Delia Quigley, copyright © 2008 by F+W Media, Inc., ISBN 10: 1-59869-682-3; ISBN 13: 978-1-59869-682-0; *The Everything® Whole Grain, High Fiber Cookbook* by Lynette Rohrer Shirk, copyright © 2008 by F+W Media, Inc., ISBN 10: 1-59869-507-X; ISBN 13: 978-1-59869-507-6.

The information in this book should not be used for diagnosing or treating any health problem. Not all diet and exercise plans suit everyone. You should always consult a trained medical professional before starting a diet, taking any form of medication, or embarking on any fitness or weight-training program. The author and publisher disclaim any liability arising directly or indirectly from the use of this book.

This book is available at quantity discounts for bulk purchases.
For information, please call 1-800-289-0963.

Contents

Acknowledgments

The primary people I *must* express my deepest gratitude and love toward are my wonderful family for their unwavering support and copious amounts of patience with my incessant need to create, develop, and work. I am grateful to . . . my husband, Pete, for his dedication to our children and unrelenting focus on the happiness of our family; my only daughter, Olivia, for her unending wit and good humor; my first-born son, Nicko, for his great smile and sensitive heart; my strong-willed athlete, Douglas—thanks for your hugs—and my little sunshine, Lucas, who has added joy to the lives of everyone he encounters. My acknowledgments would not be complete without a special thank you to our cats, Cooper and Sierra, for joining me during my late-night writing sessions.

Finally, to all my readers, may you embrace an anti-inflammatory lifestyle so you can live well, laugh often, and love much.

Introduction

FROM THE FIRST DAY of life and throughout the life cycle, the human body is continually bombarded by toxins, chemicals, viruses, bacteria, and other potentially damaging factors. Fortunately, the body naturally responds to these adverse circumstances by initiating an inflammatory response. During this response, the potentially harmful threats are dealt with promptly and completely. Or at least this is what was once believed.

Years of research has led to the realization that the inflammatory response is not always turned off in a timely manner. As a result, a majority of humans venture through their lives with some degree of "silent" inflammation that can wreak havoc on their bodies. Instead of protecting and healing the body, inflammation becomes the enemy. This can clearly be seen by the increased prevalence of heart disease, diabetes, cancer, Alzheimer's disease, and autoimmune disorders, to mention a few. Now it is proven that these conditions are clearly and intimately linked to uncontrolled silent inflammation.

So what to do when a good thing goes bad? The most common response, especially in the medical world, is to treat the symptoms, diseases, and conditions with medications such as over-the-counter analgesics and often with more powerful, and potentially harmful, prescription drugs. This will quell inflammation temporarily, but is this really a long-term solution? Individuals versed in prevention would answer this question with a definitive no. To properly treat silent inflammation, a few steps need to be taken backward before the patient can move forward and treat inflammation from a preventative and permanent stance rather than with an after-the-fact approach.

There is a desperate need for humans to identify and address their inflammation-producing dietary and lifestyle behaviors in a preventative manner. Luckily, more and more research supports specific behaviors that can significantly reduce the presence of inflammation in the body. Rather than treat the problems linked to inflammation, the focus turns to preventing inflammation in a proactive manner before it spawns an uncontrollable monster that robs years from our lives and life from our years. Humans need to embrace the wisdom that states "an ounce of prevention is worth a pound of cure."

The Everything® Anti-Inflammation Diet Book will educate readers on the inner workings of the inflammatory response so they can get a better grasp on their own personal internal inflammatory environment. This will enable readers to target their inflammatory touch points and vulnerabilities and create a plan for putting out the flames of inflammation. Most importantly, the reader will learn to identify, shop for, and prepare foods to help keep inflammation at bay so they can live a long and fulfilling life.

CHAPTER 1

Introduction to an Anti-Inflammatory Lifestyle

The anti-inflammatory lifestyle is not a fad diet. It is a lifestyle change that can add years to your life and life to your years. Embracing this lifestyle can help treat or reduce the risk of a variety of chronic diseases and conditions. This lifestyle can be beneficial for anyone at any time. Noticeable benefits can occur in as little as two weeks. So come along and jump on the anti-inflammatory bandwagon for the healthiest ride of your life!

What Is an Anti-Inflammatory Lifestyle?

Although inflammation is a natural and essential response to injury, irritation, and infection, too much of a good thing can be extremely detrimental to the body. This is especially true when the inflammation is chronic and overlooked. Chronic systemic inflammation can impose harmful degenerative effects throughout the body, resulting in a variety of diseases. Unfortunately, it is hard to escape inflammation in a world that is moving at the speed of light.

As the population ages and lives longer, silent inflammation is becoming more prevalent and its effects more pronounced. As the immune system ages it becomes less efficient at disarming inflammation. So even though most people generally report feeling well on a day-to-day basis, inflammation may be shortening lives right here and now. So what's the solution to this inflammatory epidemic?

Commitment to anti-inflammatory (anti = against; inflammation = swelling) eating patterns and lifestyle practices is the first line of defense in fighting off inflammation and the disabling chronic diseases that plague humans worldwide.

Cooling inflammation is all about making the right choices, most of the time. These anti-inflammatory choices include consumption of healthy fats, fruits and vegetables rich in phytochemicals (plant chemicals) and antioxidants, lean protein foods, whole grains, and probiotics. Adequate sleep and fluids, weight management, exercise, stress reduction, and dietary supplements round out the anti-inflammatory menu. You can expect to see a noticeable difference in your inflammatory symptoms within two weeks of following the anti-inflammatory diet. Before a discussion on anti-inflammatory eating strategies, it is helpful to gain a better understanding of the biology behind inflammation.

Understanding the Inflammatory Response

Whenever you are exposed to an infectious agent or experience tissue injury or damage, your immune system mounts an inflammatory response. For example, when you cut your finger and it becomes red and swollen, inflammation is working its magic, and it's a lifesaver. During this response, your body releases pro-inflammatory chemicals and hormones that are equipped to deal with any threat to the body. These mercenaries attack unwelcome foreign invaders such as bacteria while tending to harmed tissue. Blood flow increases to places that require healing. Pain intensifies as a signal that something is wrong within the body.

The main hormones that control the inflammatory response are called eicosanoids, also known as prostaglandins, prostacylins, thromboxanes, and leukotrienes. Eicosanoids influence many of the bodily systems and processes. In addition to triggering inflammation, eicosanoids, most notably the prostaglandins, are what promote pain, fever, and blood clotting when an injury occurs in the body.

FACT

The body uses fatty acids to make eicosanoids. Omega-6 fatty acids produce the eicosanoids that promote inflammation and blood clotting, suppress the immune system, and reduce healthy high-density lipoprotein (HDL) cholesterol levels. Omega-3 fatty acids have the opposite effect of omega-6 fatty acids as a result of the eicosanoids they synthesize. Hence the more omega-3 fatty acids consumed in the diet, the more anti-inflammatory eicosanoid generation in the body.

It is important to remember that the inflammatory response is completely normal and is the cornerstone of the body's healing response. It is simply the way the body supplies nourishment and enhanced immune activity to areas experiencing injury or infection. Under normal circumstances, once the threat is under control, anti-inflammatory substances are released to turn off the immune response.

The Overactive Immune System

Sometimes inflammation gets the upper hand and continues to operate chronically. This causes continual secretion of pro-inflammatory chemicals. Chronic release and circulation of these chemicals results in an attack on healthy cells, blood vessels, and tissues.

Damage to blood vessels can promote atherosclerosis, a process that results in narrowing of the arteries. If pancreatic tissue is harmed, an individual may develop diabetes. Injury to joint tissue, when the immune system mistakenly attacks normal tissue, can contribute to autoimmune disorders such as arthritis. Pro-inflammatory chemicals can also alter normal brain chemistry and potentially contribute to dementia and Alzheimer's disease. Over time, chronic inflammation acts like a slow but deadly poison, causing overzealous inflammatory chemicals to damage your body as you innocently go about your normal daily activities.

The list of the negative consequences associated with out-of-control pro-inflammatory chemicals does not end here. Other diseases and conditions thought to be associated with chronic inflammation include, but are not limited to, allergies, anemia, cancer, congestive heart failure, fibromyalgia, kidney failure, lupus, pancreatitis, psoriasis, and stroke.

Free Radicals as Inflammation Activators

Emerging research has demonstrated that chronic inflammation creates an environment that fosters free radical production. Free radicals are continually being produced in your cells and a certain level of free radical production is completely normal, just like the little pockets of benign inflammation present throughout the body. When free radical production exceeds the body's natural ability to impede their production extensive bodily damage occurs. As free radicals take over, mayhem ensues and chronic disease risk rises.

What Is a Free Radical?

Free radicals are chemicals that contain unpaired electrons. In nature, electrons like to exist in pairs. Since free radicals are missing an electron, they travel through the body looking for electrons to steal so they can become stable. Free radicals commonly steal electrons from polyunsaturated fats situated within the membranes of nearby cells. This can lead to cell malfunction or even cell death. They also target DNA within the nucleus of the body's cells. Free radical alterations to the DNA code can lead to uncontrolled cell growth and cancer.

When free radicals steal electrons from other substances in the body, they cause these substances to also become free radicals. This leads to a chain reaction because each modified cell will try to become stable and steal from another vulnerable cell in the body.

Free radical dominance can lead to the following disruptions in the body:

- Alteration in genetic material such as DNA, which can cause cancer and/or promote cancer growth
- Modification of low-density lipoprotein (LDL) cholesterol in such a way that it sticks to artery walls, increasing the risk of high blood pressure and heart disease
- Damage to cell membranes so they cannot communicate properly with other cells
- Destruction of collagen in skin, leading to wrinkles
- Muscle damage and soreness during and after exercise

In the long run, free radicals stimulate inflammation and thereby perpetuate the inflammatory cycle. So management of inflammation is essential for squelching free radicals before they can run rampant in the body.

ALERT

Environmental factors such as pollution, radiation, cigarette smoking, herbicides, and contaminants such as lead can spawn free radical production. Humans have internal defense systems that help to deal with free radicals, but when free radical production is excessive these defense systems can't keep up. This is often referred to as "oxidative stress."

Methods for Identifying Inflammation

All individuals experience some degree of inflammation. Logically, the more inflammatory signs, symptoms, and conditions an individual experiences, the more inflammation they harbor within the body. Physicians can also evaluate certain biomarkers in the blood to determine if inflammation is present.

Biomarkers of Inflammation

Biomarkers in the blood will give you a more definitive idea of the extent of inflammation in your body versus solely relying on symptomatic indicators. Biomarkers provide biological evidence that inflammation is present.

Inflammatory biomarkers are measured when individuals are showing definite signs of inflammation-associated conditions so that possible treatment options can be determined. Unfortunately, most doctors are not searching for silent inflammation. As a result, many of these valuable tests are not drawn upon frequently enough.

Erythrocyte sedimentation rate (ESR) and C-reactive protein (CRP) are the most common tests used to detect an increased presence of protein in the blood indicating that inflammation has gone awry. The ability of these tests to detect inflammation enables them to be classified as "markers" of inflammation. These tests are often administered to patients with inflammatory bowel disease (IBD), arthritis, autoimmune disorders, pelvic inflammatory disease (PID), and coronary heart disease (CHD).

Erythrocyte Sedimentation Rate

To measure ESR, a blood sample is taken and put in a special tube, which is maintained upright. The red blood cells (erythrocytes) in the sample gradually fall to the bottom of the tube, creating the sediment. The ESR measures how long it takes for the red blood cells to fall to the bottom of the tube. When an individual has inflammation, the red blood cells become covered with inflammatory proteins. These proteins cause the red blood cells to fall at a faster rate. A high ESR indicates that there is inflammation in the body.

C-Reactive Protein (CRP)

CRP is an actual protein produced in the liver and found in the bloodstream. Levels of CRP rise as a result of inflammation. High levels of CRP have been linked to an increased risk of diabetes, high blood pressure, and heart disease. CRP changes more rapidly than ESR, at the start of inflammation and as it resolves. Additionally, CRP is not affected by as many factors as is ESR. Therefore, CRP is currently deemed a better marker of inflammation.

FACT

At this point in time, the American Heart Association does not recommend a CRP screening for healthy individuals—only for those with an elevated heart disease risk. But beware: a high reading may be the first clue that inflammation is building up in your body. Tests cost between $25 and $35 and can be performed easily in your physician's office.

Other Biochemical Tests

Although ESR and CRP are valuable tools for monitoring inflammation and how well an individual is responding to treatment, it is important to note that each of these tests is nonspecific. This means they only identify whether or not inflammation is present, but do not tell the doctor exactly where the inflammation is in the body or what is causing it.

Additional tests must be administered to find out the real cause of the inflammation. Here is a list of additional tests that may be performed to better assess an individual's inflammatory status.

- **Fibrinogen** is a protein found in the bloodstream that assists with blood clotting. Some fibrinogen in the blood is critical, but too much can be harmful. Elevated fibrinogen is a red flag that the body is mounting an inflammatory response. It can contribute to atherosclerosis by worsening any existing injury to the arterial walls. Fibrinogen can also cause a clot to form in an artery, resulting in a heart attack or stroke. Factors that increase fibrinogen levels include inactivity, excessive alcohol consumption, smoking, and estrogen administration via birth control pills or hormone therapy.

- **Lipoprotein-associated phospholipase (Lp-PLA2)** is an enzyme produced by the immune cells that is responsible for consuming and destroying foreign proteins, debris, and old cells. Most Lp-PLA2 in the blood is bound to LDL cholesterol. Researchers believe that Lp-PLA2 plays a role in inflammation of the blood vessels and promotes atherosclerosis. Studies have found that people with CHD possess increased blood levels of Lp-PLA2.

- **Interleukin-6 (IL-6)** is a pro-inflammatory regulatory protein made by the white blood cells, the most notable members of the immune system. Chronically elevated IL-6 has been associated with an increased incidence of chronic diseases such as atherosclerosis, diabetes, rheumatoid arthritis, and depression. IL-6 is also produced by fat cells and is the principal reason why CRP levels are elevated in obese individuals.

- **Nuclear factor-κB (NF-κB)** is a pro-inflammatory protein molecule that regulates the immune system's response to infection, stress, free radicals, foreign bacteria, and viruses. When present in excessive amounts over long periods of time, NF-κB may spur autoimmune and inflammatory diseases.

- **Leukocyte count** is a measure of white blood cells circulating in the blood. A high white blood cell (leukocyte) count indicates that there is an increase in disease-fighting cells circulating in the blood. Elevated leukocytes may be due to a bacterial or viral infection or an immune system disorder (such as rheumatoid arthritis), and is highly indicative of an inflammatory response.

Determining Your Inflammatory Quotient

Always keep in mind that one single sign, symptom, or blood test alone cannot determine your risk of developing inflammation-related diseases or conditions, but you can use the following checklist to estimate whether you possess a low, moderate, or high level of silent inflammation.

CATEGORY A: COMMON SYMPTOMS ASSOCIATED WITH INFLAMMATION

- ❏ Frequent body aches and pains
- ❏ Intermittent infections
- ❏ Chronic stiffness
- ❏ Loss of joint function
- ❏ Recurrent swelling
- ❏ Continual congestion
- ❏ Persistent indigestion
- ❏ Regular bouts of diarrhea
- ❏ Unrelenting skin outbreaks

CATEGORY B: BIOCHEMICAL SIGNS OF INFLAMMATION

- ❏ Elevated highly sensitive C-reactive protein (CRP)
- ❏ Elevated erythrocyte sedimentation rate (ESR)
- ❏ Elevated fibrinogen levels
- ❏ Elevated lipoprotein-associated phospholipase (Lp-PLA2)
- ❏ Elevated interleukin-6 (IL-6)

❏ Elevated nuclear factor-κB (NF-κB)
❏ Elevated leukocyte count
❏ Elevated blood pressure
❏ Elevated blood glucose
❏ Elevated blood cholesterol
❏ Elevated blood triglyceride

CATEGORY C: COMMON CONDITIONS ASSOCIATED WITH INFLAMMATION

❏ Allergies and food intolerances
❏ Arthritis
❏ Asthma
❏ Cancer
❏ Dementia or Alzheimer's disease
❏ Depression
❏ Diabetes
❏ Eczema and psoriasis
❏ Heart disease
❏ Irritable bowel syndrome
❏ Overweight and obesity
❏ Periodontal disease (swollen gums)

Evaluating Your Personal Inflammatory Checklist

Use the following table to assess your level of inflammatory potential based on the number of check marks in each category.

▼ **EVALUATING YOUR PERSONAL INFLAMMATORY CHECKLIST**

Low Inflammatory Potential	Moderate Inflammatory Potential	High Inflammatory Potential
Category A	Category B	Category C
Less than or equal to 1 check mark	2 to 4 check marks	5+ check marks
0 check marks	1 check mark	2 or more check marks
0 check marks	1 check mark	2 or more check marks

Quick Fix Treatments for Inflammation

When inflammation occurs, people often choose nonsteroidal anti-inflammatory drugs (NSAIDs) such as Motrin and Aleve to ease their pain. The NSAIDs have been developed by pharmaceutical companies to tame unruly inflammation. They work by disrupting the production of pro-inflammatory chemicals in the body, such as prostaglandins. Two cyclo-oxygenase enzymes found in the body, COX-1 and COX-2, are responsible for producing prostaglandins. NSAIDs work by blocking the COX-1 and COX-2 enzymes, resulting in a reduction in prostaglandin production.

On a positive note, NSAIDs will temporarily help to reduce inflammation, pain, and fever. On the flip side, NSAIDs prevent prostaglandins from producing the mucus that lines the stomach and maintaining adequate stomach acid production. This combination of effects can lead to stomach ulcers. Additionally, inhibition of prostaglandin release reduces the blood's ability to clot, which can contribute to prolonged bleeding after surgery or an injury. Other serious side effects include kidney and liver failure due to reduced blood flow to these critical organs. Common mild side effects include nausea, vomiting, diarrhea, constipation, dizziness, and drowsiness.

Fortunately, there are numerous dietary and lifestyle anti-inflammatory options that can be followed to put out the flames of inflammation. Following an anti-inflammatory lifestyle will keep inflammation at bay and make chronic diseases go away without the unnecessary side effects of NSAIDs and other anti-inflammatory agents.

CHAPTER 2

Disease-Busting Benefits of an Anti-Inflammatory Lifestyle

Unfortunately, you live in a pro-inflammatory world. Toxins such as lead and mercury pervade the environment, processed foods are taking over the grocery store shelves, and you are probably on the go 24-7, which promotes stress and robs you of adequate sleep. All of these conditions have been shown to promote inflammation. Inflammation contributes to multiple chronic illnesses that are costly and corrode the quality of life. If left to its own devices, inflammation can take its toll on the body over time without your even knowing it. It is essential to gain a better understanding of the disease-busting benefits of the anti-inflammatory lifestyle before inflammation gets the best of you.

Obesity: A Root Cause of Inflammation

A study published in the *Journal of the American Medical Association* (JAMA) in January 2010 revealed that in 2007–2008, the age-adjusted prevalence of obesity was 33.8 percent overall, 32.2 percent among men, and 35.5 percent among women. The corresponding prevalence estimates for overweight and obesity combined were 68.0 percent overall, 72.3 percent among men, and 64.1 percent among women. These statistics demonstrate the high incidence of overweight and obesity in America that correlates with high levels of silent inflammation and elevated C-reactive protein (CRP) levels.

Adipose Tissue Joins the Dark Side

Everyone needs some body fat to stay healthy. Adipose tissue acts as an efficient storage site for energy, it protects the body against cold temperatures, and it cushions vital organs to protect them from shock. But adipose cells take on a whole new personality when they grow beyond a certain point. Normal function of excessively large adipose cells becomes compromised, causing these cells to start producing pro-inflammatory substances. This results in a state of chronic low-level inflammation. And studies have confirmed that obese individuals possess higher levels of inflammatory biomarkers in comparison to individuals with healthy body fat levels.

Current research suggests that bloated fat cells may actually burst open. When this happens, white blood cells (WBCs) from your immune system rush to the injured fat cell to try to fix the damage. Once there, the WBCs start churning out unhealthy inflammatory chemicals, causing greater damage and chaos. More WBCs arrive in an attempt to control the pandemonium, but only increase the production of pro-inflammatory substances, which spill over into the bloodstream and affect the whole body.

The Government Takes Action Against Obesity

As the Centers for Disease Control (CDC) puts it, "American society has become *obesogenic.*" This inclination toward excess body fat is due to the availability of unhealthy foods around every corner coupled with physical inactivity. The World Health Organization and the U.S. federal government, including the CDC, the Surgeon General's Office, U.S. Department of Agriculture (USDA), and the U.S. Department of Health and Human Services

(HHS) are committed to halting the upward trend in overweight and obesity prevalence.

The focus now is more prevention-based. The government is presently striving to make changes in the food and physical environment to foster better dietary and physical activity behaviors among Americans. Multiple legislative and public health strategies have been proposed so that the control of obesity reaches beyond individuals and affects larger numbers of different populations in multiple settings, such as in communities, schools, work sites, and health care facilities. These policies aim at environmental change initiatives that make healthy eating and physical activity available, affordable, and downright easy. And don't be surprised if taxes are placed on foods high in calories, fat, or sugar such as soda and snack foods, or if commercial advertising companies start using their marketing skills to promote healthy foods and habits rather than tasty but deadly food options.

Heart Disease

Cardiovascular disease (CVD) is the leading cause of death in the United States. Western lifestyles currently encourage the development of CVD because of the prevalence of high-fat diets, sedentary behaviors, cigarette smoking, stress, chronically elevated blood pressure and cholesterol levels, and excess body fat. All of these behaviors promote inflammation, and there is a very strong association between systemic inflammation and CVD, more specifically coronary artery disease (CAD).

Formation of a Narrowed Artery

CAD is a type of heart disease caused by narrowing of the coronary arteries that feed the heart. High blood pressure or LDL cholesterol levels, cigarette smoking, elevated homocysteine levels, and some viral and bacterial infections are potential sources of arterial wall injury. This damage triggers an inflammatory response, causing the immune system to send out white blood cells (WBCs) in an attempt to fix the damage. Often LDL cholesterol travels to the injury site as well. The WBCs attempt to gobble up the cholesterol, but over time turn into foam cells and, ultimately, plaque. Plaques result in a narrowing and hardening of the arteries, which compromises the elasticity of the artery and constricts and narrows the channels for blood flow. If the cap that forms on top of a plaque bursts like a balloon, the debris may barricade the narrowed artery. A blood clot from elsewhere in the body can also become clogged in the narrowed artery. Both of these situations can lead to a heart attack as the flow of oxygen-rich blood and nutrients to the heart is interrupted. When a similar process occurs in the cerebral (brain) arteries, a stroke can occur.

Individuals with CAD possess elevated levels of CRP and fibrinogen due to an active inflammatory response. Those with higher levels of CRP demonstrate more advanced disease severity. It is proposed that inflammation may make the cap that forms over a plaque more likely to rupture. To make matters worse, the inflamed internal environment found in individuals with CAD promotes free radical production. These free radicals cause modification of LDL cholesterol in such a way that it sticks to your artery walls, thereby increasing your risk of high blood pressure and heart disease.

Shrinking Adipose Cells to Prevent Heart Disease

Anti-inflammatory food choices can significantly reduce the incidence of obesity and subsequently heart disease. Cutting back on red meat, high-fat dairy, trans and saturated fats, and processed carbohydrates while increasing consumption of fatty fish, colorful fruits and vegetables, and fiber-rich foods will inevitably lead to weight loss. And it is this weight loss that can reduce the risk of inflammation and other obesity-related chronic diseases.

Cancer

The role of inflammation in cancer is not as definitive as its role in heart disease, but it is clear that certain organs in the body show a greater risk of cancer when they are chronically inflamed, infected, or irritated. For example, blood samples taken from individuals with colon cancer have consistently demonstrated elevated levels of CRP, which coincide with bodily inflammation. Inflammation is believed to promote cancer by damaging genes, enhancing cancer cell growth and development, and supporting the development of blood vessels that allow cancer cells to thrive. Many researchers now believe that genetic damage is the match that lights the cancer fire, and inflammation is the fuel that feeds the cancer fire.

Free Radicals and Cancer Development

Chronic inflammation creates an environment that fosters free radical production. These free radicals can cause damage to genetic material in healthy cells. As altered cells continue to grow and divide, cancerous tumors can occur. Although chronic inflammation and free radicals will not always initiate cancer, they can establish the ideal environment for cancer cells to thrive. For example, individuals with inflammatory bowel disorders, such as Crohn's disease and ulcerative colitis, have an increased risk of colon cancer, and this risk is believed to be associated with excessive inflammation. The inflammation in the intestines allows free radicals to thrive and alters cell division in a way that allows intestinal cells to multiply out of control.

The numerous anti-inflammatory dietary and lifestyle interventions that can be adopted are essential for halting excessive free radical activity and reducing the risk of damaged cells reproducing uncontrollably.

Alzheimer's Disease

The ravages of inflammation are also linked to chronic diseases of the brain, such as Alzheimer's disease. Research has shown that chronic inflammation can destroy brain cells and attack nerve cells, both of which can contribute to dementia, Alzheimer's disease, and the cognitive and behavioral impairments evident during aging. Neurologists are still trying to figure out the Alzheimer's puzzle, but currently they believe that the body's immune cells mount an attack on the beta-amyloid proteins in the brain. Beta-amyloid proteins are completely normal inhabitants of the brain and generally cause no problems. Cognitive issues occur when inflammation changes the nature of the beta-amyloid proteins so they become plaques. These plaques build up in the brain and are believed to cause progression of this degenerative brain disease.

Tau protein is another brain constituent that is essential for maintenance of normal nerve structure. Researchers have found that individuals with Alzheimer's disease have twisted tau proteins that can ultimately lead to nerve damage in the brain. As the number of damaged neurons increases, brain function becomes progressively compromised.

FACT

It is suggested that the inflammation and resultant plaques associated with Alzheimer's may be the result of common infections that individuals contract. And this inflammatory process can occur years before the onset of any symptoms of Alzheimer's. The plaques concentrate in parts of the brain that are involved in memory, thinking, and decision making. Ultimately, the plaques and inflammation lead to signs and symptoms characteristic of Alzheimer's.

Taking a Bite out of Alzheimer's

Fortunately, you have ammunition in your food supply that can help reduce the incidence of Alzheimer's and dementia. A brain-healthy diet starts by limiting saturated and trans fats, and increasing fruit and vegetable intake. Recent studies have demonstrated that certain phytochemicals have the potential to stop free radicals from causing damage to brain cells and can also help to decrease the production of pro-inflammatory substances in the brain. This leads to a reduction in cognitive deficits that occur as part of the natural aging process. To maximize phytochemical intake, choose fruits and vegetables that make up the colors of the rainbow, such as red, yellow, and orange bell peppers, beets, eggplant, oranges, cherries, and all types of berries.

Foods high in omega-3 fatty acids, such as fatty fish, can also be used as dietary reinforcements against Alzheimer's. Omega-3 fatty acids keep brain cells in tiptop shape. One study showed that eating omega-3-rich fish just once a week may lower a person's risk of developing Alzheimer's by up to 60 percent, a very significant return on investment.

Diabetes

Researchers at Harvard Medical School have identified a connection between an imbalanced, overactive immune system and metabolic abnormalities such as type 2 diabetes. It is now clear that there is a link between excess body fat and inflammation. It has been proposed that fat cells release pro-inflammatory chemicals. These chemicals hamper the body's ability to regulate insulin production. Proper regulation of this hormone is essential for normal blood sugar maintenance and avoidance of chronically elevated blood sugar levels.

Fatal Fat Cells Spur Insulin Resistance

In normal healthy individuals, the hormone insulin allows cells throughout the body, such as those in muscle, the liver, and adipose tissue, to take up sugars from the blood after a meal. This process returns elevated blood sugar levels to normal, but excess body fat interferes with this process. It does not allow insulin to do its job. In other words, enlarged fat cells cause cells to become resistant to insulin. This results in chronically elevated blood sugar levels, also known as hyperglycemia.

Hyperglycemia can result in serious health consequences. The short-term effects include weakness, fatigue, excessive thirst, increased urine output, enhanced risk of infection, and blurry vision. Chronically, hyperglycemia can cause damage to blood vessels throughout the body. This compromises the supply of oxygen and nutrients to vital organs and prevents the removal of wastes. Ultimately, this will increase the risk of heart disease, stroke, kidney disease, and vision and nerve problems.

In a nutshell, where there is excess body fat, there is insulin resistance and blood vessel damage. This combination of factors causes a vicious cycle of inflammation that wreaks havoc throughout the body.

Dietary Modifications to Dodge Diabetes

It is now clear that weight loss is the best defensive move against diabetes. Essentially, all dietary and lifestyle interventions that have been helpful in managing diabetes have also resulted in significant weight loss. Diabetes-friendly dietary and lifestyle modifications include consumption of plenty of the omega-3 fatty acids eicosapentaenoic acid (EPA) and docosahexaenoic acid (DHA), incorporation of low-glycemic-index (GI) foods such as non-starchy or low-starch fruits and vegetables, use of lean meats and low-fat dairy, and regular exercise and stress management.

The GI assesses how carbohydrate-containing foods raise blood sugar levels. Foods with a high GI raise blood sugar levels more than foods containing a lower GI. In general, foods such as dried beans and legumes, non-starchy veggies and some starchy veggies, most fruits, and many whole-grain breads and cereals possess a low GI. Low-GI foods may help individuals with diabetes better manage their blood sugar levels, thereby alleviating diabetes-related complications.

FACT

Many factors affect the GI of a food. The more ripe, processed, and cooked a food is, the higher the GI. When choosing low-GI foods, you must still control the amount you are eating to encourage weight management. Actually, researchers have shown that the total amount of carbohydrate in a food is far more important to consider than the GI of the food. Therefore, it is advised to focus first on the quantity of carbohydrates consumed, and then use the GI to assist in fine-tuning your blood sugar levels.

Autoimmune Diseases

Autoimmune disorders such as rheumatoid arthritis (RA), inflammatory bowel disease (IBD) like Crohn's disease, lupus, and asthma occur when the body's immune system attacks its own cells. This turns on a systemic inflammatory response that can spur inflammation throughout the body.

RA is one of the most wel-known autoimmune disorders. This disorder attacks the joints and surrounding tissues as if they were foreign invaders. Commonly affected joints include the wrists, fingers, knees, ankles, and feet. The pro-inflammatory chemicals present within the joint cause irritation, wearing down of cartilage (the cushions at the end of the bones), and swelling of the joint lining. This causes joint tenderness, swelling, and pain.

A study published in the *Journal of Rheumatology* found that those individuals who cut back on foods high in saturated fat such as meat and high-fat dairy foods experienced less joint tenderness and swelling. The improvement was even more pronounced when fish oil supplements were added to the regimen. Generally, doses of 3 grams or more of DHA and EPA every day have been found to reduce symptoms associated with rheumatoid arthritis, such as morning stiffness and joint tenderness and swelling. A vegetarian diet may also help calm flares associated with autoimmune disorders.

When a person with RA is experiencing a flare-up, she needs to rest and allow the flare-up to resolve or joint inflammation can worsen. When joint pain dissipates, exercise will help to maintain joint flexibility, strengthen the muscles that surround the joint, prevent joint deformity, and reduce stiffness. Exercise also helps individuals to maintain a healthy weight, which is crucial because excessive body weight can lead to stiffer joints and more pain.

ESSENTIAL

Most individuals, whether they are in the early stages of an autoimmune disorder or later stages, have "flares" or exacerbation of their symptoms when they are stressed out. Scheduling stress-free or stress-relieving activities such as meditation, yoga, walking, running, or any other type of activity that quiets your body is key to keeping your immune system calm, cool, and collected. It is surprising what a positive effect these activities can have on a flare-up.

Crohn's disease, a form of inflammatory bowel disease, is a chronic autoimmune disorder that results from the immune system attacking the cells lining the digestive tract. This assault causes the intestinal cell walls to thicken and form deep ulcers. Individuals with a family history of Crohn's and those of Jewish ancestry appear to be at the highest risk for developing the disease.

Lupus is another chronic autoimmune disorder that causes the body's immune system to attack its own cells and tissues such as the skin, joints, and kidneys. This attack can create inflammation throughout the body. Over time, arthritis, rashes, kidney disorders, and blood disorders can develop. Lupus is more common in woman than men, especially women of Asian or African descent.

The Bottom Line on Inflammation and Chronic Disease

The control of inflammation is absolutely essential if the prevalence of chronic diseases such as heart disease, cancer, Alzheimer's disease, diabetes, and autoimmune disorders is to be reversed. The first step is weight management, since obesity triggers chronic low-grade inflammation that sets the stage for numerous chronic diseases. The impact of obesity is clearly demonstrated by America's $147 billion obesity-related health care costs. All the anti-inflammatory dietary and lifestyle strategies that are essential for weight management will simultaneously keep a variety of chronic diseases in check. It's a win-win situation for all!

CHAPTER 3

The Inflaminators: Setting the Stage for Inflammation

Inflammation can operate in stealth mode for years, and certain conditions and lifestyle behaviors can act as allies to uncontrolled, silent inflammation. The location of body fat, excessive consumption of dietary sugars and unhealthy fats, stress, and smoking can all allow inflammation to get the upper hand. A comprehensive understanding of the inflammation-promoting factors encountered daily will allow individuals to make choices that beat inflammation before it takes hold.

Adipose Tissue: Friend or Foe?

Surplus body fat is linked to numerous negative health effects. An increased risk of heart disease and stroke top the list. Adipose tissue produces pro-inflammatory compounds that can increase the risk of cancer of the uterus, gallbladder, cervix, ovary, breast, and colon in women; cancer of the colon, rectum, and prostate in men; diabetes; sleep apnea; osteoarthritis; gallbladder disease; and fatty liver disease.

Body Mass Index

Government officials are currently using the body mass index (BMI) to determine healthy body weights in children and adults. BMI is based on an individual's weight and height. The healthiest BMI for an adult is between 18.5 and 24.9. This BMI range is associated with the lowest risk of disease and mortality. A BMI between 25.0 and 29.9 is classified as overweight. Approximately two-thirds of adults in the United States have a BMI greater than 25. Obesity-related diseases such as heart disease, diabetes, and high blood pressure are commonly found in people who have a BMI of 25 or higher. Once the BMI exceeds 30, which is categorized as obese, the risk of death for all causes increases by 50 to 150 percent.

QUESTION

How is body mass index calculated?
The following equation can be used to calculate the BMI:
BMI = [weight (lb)/height (in)2] × 704.5

BMI calculations and standards can also be applied to children. The BMI is calculated the same way for children as it is for adults, but the resultant numbers are evaluated differently for children and young adults aged two to twenty years. Charts have been developed so results can be compared to typical values for children of the same age and gender. Comparison of the BMI to the charts reveals a BMI percentile. A BMI that is less than the fifth percentile is classified as underweight, and above the ninety-fifth percentile is considered obese. BMIs between the eighty-fifth and ninety-fifth percentile are categorized as overweight. An ideal BMI for individuals ages two to twenty is somewhere between the fifth percentile and the eightieth percentile.

Pear Versus Apple Shapes

The amount of excess fat cells is clearly associated with inflammation, but it is even more important to consider where these fat cells reside. Premenopausal women tend to store their fat in and around their hips and thighs. This body fat distribution pattern is referred to as gynoid obesity, more commonly known as the "pear shape." Men, on the other hand, tend to assume the "apple shape," otherwise called android obesity. In this type of obesity, fat is distributed predominantly in the abdominal region.

ALERT

As a women goes through menopause, a greater proportion of body fat is stored in the abdominal region. This reallocation of body fat from the hips and thighs to a more central location increases a woman's risk of heart disease and breast cancer.

Abdominal fat encourages LDL cholesterol levels to rise. The rise in LDL cholesterol can lead to impairments in insulin function. Normally, when you eat a meal, the glucose (sugar) in your blood rises. In response to this rise, insulin is released to help transport the excess sugar from the blood into the body cells where it can be used for energy or stored for later use. Excess fat in the abdominal region disrupts normal processing of the sugars you eat. The impairment causes insulin to function ineffectively leading to chronically elevated blood glucose levels. As a result, the risk of heart disease and diabetes rises in the presence of android obesity.

Take This One Simple Measurement

To further reduce the risk of chronic inflammation, it is ideal for men to maintain a waist circumference of less than 40 inches and women less than 35 inches. This measurement can be completed by locating the upper portion of the hip bone. Then a tape measure is placed in a horizontal fashion around the abdomen approximately level with the hip bone and navel. The tape measure should be snug, but not cause compression or wrinkling of the skin. Generally, the higher the BMI and the waist circumference, the more pronounced the inflammation.

Sneaky Sugar Swellers

Often the major culprit blamed for increasing our BMI and body fat levels is sugar. Sugar has definitely taken a beating over the years, but surprisingly, research has only linked excessive sugar intake to dental caries, although this statement does need some clarification. First, the message needs to be spread that sugar is not fattening. It contains 4 calories per gram versus the 9 calories per gram found in fat. It is actually high fat intake, not excessive sugar intake, that is associated with the increasing incidence of obesity. But it is also important to note that many foods high in sugar are also high in fat, such as cookies, ice cream, and pastries. The bottom line is that whenever excess calories are consumed above and beyond your energy needs, whether they are from sugar, fat, or protein, weight gain will result. Even an extra leaf of lettuce will result in weight gain if its calories are not required by the body.

How Low Can You Go?

Low-glycemic-index (GI) weight loss diets have become popular over the past decade. These diets are based on a system of ranking carbohydrate foods based on their potential to raise blood glucose levels. Foods with a high GI trigger a sharp rise in blood sugar levels followed by a drastic drop in blood sugars frequently below pre-consumption levels. It is believed that high-GI foods lead to an insulin surge. Excess insulin leads to elevated levels of arachidonic acid in your blood. This acid promotes increased concentrations of pro-inflammatory chemicals in the body and subsequent inflammation. Hence, it would make sense to limit these types of foods as a means for lowering inflammation.

Conversely, foods with a low GI lead to slower, more moderate changes in blood sugar levels. Therefore, it would make sense that low-GI foods would have an anti-inflammatory effect.

The problem with the GI is that it is hard to definitively classify foods as having a high, moderate, or low GI since the type of carbohydrate; the cooking method; and the presence or absence of fat, protein, and dietary fiber can alter a food's GI. Because of the complexity and the questionable benefit of a low-GI diet, the American Diabetes Association and the advisory committee for the 2010 Dietary Guidelines for Americans do not endorse adoption of a low-GI diet. Until further research is completed, consumption of whole-grain, minimally refined carbohydrate-based foods such as breads, cereals, and crackers, and regular intake of fresh fruits and vegetables, will help minimize the pro-inflammatory effect that sugars may have in the body.

Have You Checked Your AGE lately?

Researchers have identified chemical reactions that occur in the body between sugar and protein or fats that lead to the production of pro-inflammatory substances called advanced glycation end (AGE) products. AGE products are synthesized both within the body and during food processing. Regardless of their source, all AGE products have been shown to exacerbate inflammation.

According to an article published in the *Journal of Food Science*, elevated AGE levels are associated with a variety of chronic diseases. For example, in individuals with diabetes, elevated AGE levels are linked to a reaction between chronically elevated sugar circulating in the blood and its reaction with proteins and fats in the body. In diabetic patients, a low-AGE diet followed for six weeks decreased C-reactive protein (CRP) levels by over 20 percent, indicating less silent inflammation. Diseases involving chronic inflammation, such as atherosclerosis, skin aging, rheumatoid arthritis, and Alzheimer's disease, are also linked to elevated AGE levels. These diseases and conditions tend to be common in adults and the elderly partly because AGEs accumulate in tissues over time.

QUESTION

What factors increase the production of AGE products in foods? AGE products do not exist in nature, but are easily produced during food processing. AGE production is most significant when a mixture of carbohydrates, fats, and proteins is exposed to prolonged thermal processing such as heating, sterilizing, or microwaving. Therefore, foods that have been fried, barbecued, broiled, or cooked in the microwave are most suspect to higher levels of AGEs.

In a nutshell, the foods high in AGE products are highly processed, refined foods such as:

- Frankfurters, bacon, and powdered egg whites
- Fast foods such as French fries, hamburgers, and fried chicken
- Prepackaged foods that have been preserved, pasteurized, homogenized, or refined, such as white flour, cake mixes, processed cereal, dried milk, dried eggs, pasteurized milk, and canned or frozen precooked meals
- Cream cheese, butter, margarine, mayonnaise, and dried fruits

In terms of lifestyle habits, smoking can also generate AGE products.

Reduce Your AGE

Although it is virtually impossible to avoid consumption of foods containing AGE products, eating fewer refined carbohydrate-based foods such as white bread, pastries, snack foods such as crackers and chips, and sweetened beverages such as soda and juice drinks will cause the body to produce fewer AGE products. It is also possible to reduce AGE exposure by steaming, boiling, poaching, stewing, stir-frying, and using a slow cooker. All of these cooking methods use lower temperatures but also retain moisture during the cooking process. Studies have shown that foods higher in water and moisture reduce AGE formation.

Overall, fresh foods contain the lowest concentrations of AGE products, and, as mentioned previously, promote minimal elevation in blood sugar levels. Fresh foods containing complex carbohydrates such as beans, whole grains, fruits, and vegetables possess low AGE concentrations. Garlic, mustard, cider vinegar, lemon juice, and dry wines also slow AGE formation. These foods also contain high levels of antioxidants such as vitamins A, C, and E and selenium, which can further delay AGE formation.

As with the glycemic index, more research is required to better understand the true significance of AGE products to chronic-disease risk reduction. If a low-AGE diet continues to reduce chronic-disease risk, ideally government food policies will evolve and require food industries to label AGE content on foods. This requirement would spur the development of food processing methods that produce fewer AGEs and subsequently lower the incidence of inflammation and chronic disease. Until this time, consume unprocessed carbohydrates that are as close to their original roots in nature as possible. If you focus on fresh, the foods will do the rest.

Frightful Fats and Deep-Fried Dangers

Nothing could be more inflammation-promoting than trans fatty acid–filled pastries, fast foods dripping with saturated fat, and cholesterol-ridden meat. These fats lead to the synthesis of pro-inflammatory prostaglandins. In our processed, refined, convenience-based culture, it's not so easy to keep away from these frightful fats.

Trans-ition Away from These Fats

Studies have linked high trans fat consumption with high blood levels of CRP, the protein linked to inflammation in the body. Foods that tend to be higher in trans fats include fried foods cooked in hydrogenated shortening, hydrogenated or partially hydrogenated margarine, nondairy creamers, many fast foods, shortening, commercial baked goods such as doughnuts, cakes, and cookies, and hydrogenated snack foods such as chips and crackers. The Nutrition Facts Food Labels can be used to help identify foods containing trans fats. Choose foods that have zero trans fat and no partially hydrogenated fats listed in the ingredients list.

FACT

Although chocolate is rich in saturated fat, it also contains numerous beneficial compounds. For example, chocolate is rich in antioxidants that fight free radicals as well as anti-platelet factors that reduce the risk of unnecessary blood clotting. Dark chocolate has the highest concentration of these healthy phytochemicals. Choose dark chocolate that offers at least 65 percent cocoa content to maximize the phytochemical infusion.

Out with Saturated Fats

Saturated fats are nonessential fats commonly found in meats, high-fat dairy products, and eggs. Although these foods provide important vitamins and minerals, saturated fats can promote inflammation, which is demonstrated by their ability to increase the inflammatory biomarkers in the blood known as fibrinogen and CRP. Additionally, once in the body, saturated fats compete with unsaturated fats to take up residence in cell membranes. Cell membranes containing unsaturated fats are more pliable and fluid. Those loaded with saturated fat become rigid, causing malfunctions such as insulin resistance, and the synthesis and release of pro-inflammatory chemicals. To make matters worse, diets high in saturated fats have been associated with higher levels of abdominal fat. Abdominal fat is a known risk factor for heart disease, high blood pressure, diabetes, and possibly even Alzheimer's disease.

Choose Your Omegas Carefully

Omega-6 fatty acids are a member of the polyunsaturated-fat family. Although they are unsaturated and considered essential in small quantities, excessive intake of omega-6 fatty acids promotes inflammation, encourages blood clotting, and can cause cells in the body to proliferate uncontrollably. While promotion of inflammation is key to a strong immune system, excessive inflammation is downright harmful. The same goes for blood clotting. Some is essential to prevent an individual from bleeding to death, while too much can result in a heart attack or stroke. When it comes to cell proliferation, some is vital for normal cell regeneration, but unhindered proliferation increases the risk of cancer. Moreover, omega-6 fatty acids, just like saturated fatty acids, are associated with increased release of pro-inflammatory chemicals throughout the body. These proteins trigger inflammation.

QUESTION

What foods are high in omega-6 fatty acids?
The modern diet is weighed down by omega-6 fatty acids because of overconsumption of meats and vegetable oils such as corn, safflower, soybean, and cottonseed commonly found in processed foods and fast foods.

Omega-3 fatty acids, polyunsaturated relatives of the omega-6 fatty acid family, have an anti-inflammatory effect in the body. To reduce inflammation, health authorities highly recommend that foods high in omega-6 polyunsaturated fatty acids be limited and replaced with omega-3 polyunsaturated fatty acids. Unfortunately, the typical American diet tends to contain fourteen to twenty-five times more omega-6 fatty acids than omega-3 fatty acids. Anti-inflammatory eating patterns will favorably reverse this potentially risky trend.

The Stress-Cortisol-Inflammation Connection

Numerous studies have been performed to better understand the effects of stress on the body. Since the beginning of time, stress exposure has initiated a fight-or-flight response that causes an increased heart rate and body temperature, elevated blood pressure, and a rise in the stress hormone referred to as cortisol. This response results in the delivery of oxygen and nutrients to the parts of the body that need them most in hopes of allowing the body to successfully deal with the stress. Once the stressor is gone, blood pressure, heart rate, and other factors modified by the stress should return to normal.

Factors that increase cortisol levels include:

- Caffeine
- Inadequate sleep
- Severe trauma and stress
- Intense or prolonged physical activity
- Stressful commuting

However, there are some factors that actually decrease cortisol levels:

- Omega-3 fatty acids
- Black tea
- Yoga and other relaxation techniques
- Massage therapy
- Laughing

The Stress-Cortisol Connection

Cortisol secretion in response to stress is completely normal and natural. Cortisol is responsible for increasing blood sugar levels, suppressing the immune system, and assisting in carbohydrate, fat, and protein metabolism. The problems with cortisol occur when it is secreted for prolonged periods of time.

ALERT

Smoking is a huge instigator of inflammation and has been linked to numerous chronic diseases such as cancer and heart disease. The major issue with smoking is that it sharply increases inflammatory biomarkers, including CRP, in the blood.

Day in and day out, humans are bombarded by "everyday" stressors related to jobs, relationships, finances, overloaded schedules, and major life changes. Unfortunately, your body cannot differentiate between "short-term" stressors and "chronic, everyday" stressors, so it continually secretes cortisol.

Over time, chronic stress can result in consistently elevated blood pressure levels that can lead to nicks and injuries within the blood vessels. These microscopic tears eventually trigger an inflammatory response in the body as it attempts to mend the tears. Ultimately, this inflammation can lead to a heart attack or stroke.

So although some stress is good and can motivate you to achieve your short- and long-term goals, too much stress will ultimately lead to numerous health problems. For example, studies have found that individuals who are angry and hostile have higher CRP levels than people who are more laid-back. These elevated CRP levels indicate that inflammation is loitering in the body.

CHAPTER 4

The Deflators: Quieting the Inflammatory Noise

You can extinguish the flames of chronic inflammation before they grow out of control. A combination of healthy fats, fruits and vegetables, lean proteins, and whole grains can help you nip inflammation in the bud and enjoy many disease-busting benefits.

Omega-3 Fatty Acids Rule the Roost

Research has confirmed how harmful trans fats and saturated fats can be in promoting inflammation, but where can you get taste without the flames? Introducing the omega-3 fatty acids. These fatty acids are converted into hormone-like substances called eicosanoids. The two most potent omega-3 eicosanoids are eicosapentaenoic acid (EPA) and docosahexaenoic acid (DHA). EPA and DHA have the overall effect of dilating blood vessels, minimizing blood clotting, and reducing inflammation. The physiological and psychological benefits of omega-3 fatty acids are endless. Here's a little taste of their goodness:

- Improvement in rheumatoid arthritis, psoriasis, asthma, and some skin conditions
- Reduced symptoms associated with ulcerative colitis and Crohn's disease
- Alleviation of the side effects connected to Alzheimer's disease, depression, and bipolar disorder
- Lowered triglycerides and increased HDL (healthy) cholesterol
- Improved circulation and blood vessel function
- Lowered blood pressure and reduced blood clotting
- Decreased insulin resistance
- Enhancement of neurodevelopment and brain function in the fetus, and in infants and children

Omega-3s are not newcomers to the food supply. They have been around since the beginning of time. The unfortunate trend over the past century has been away from omega-3 fats as a result of advances in agribusiness and modern food processing. These changes have led to a drastic increase in the appearance of omega-6 fatty acids and saturated and trans fats in the food supply. Currently, the typical American consumes fourteen to twenty-five times more omega-6 fatty acids than omega-3 fatty acids. Many health authorities believe it is this imbalance that plays a significant role in the rising rate of inflammatory disorders in the United States. Americans need to focus more on foods rich in omega-3 fatty acids with the goal of achieving an omega-3 to omega-6 ratio of 6:1. This ratio will promote anti-inflammatory mechanisms in the body.

Focus on Fatty Fish

The 6:1 ratio can easily be accomplished by consuming fatty fish two to three times per week. The top fish choices include cold-water fish such as albacore tuna, anchovies, Atlantic herring, halibut, lake trout, mackerel, sardines, stripped sea bass, and wild salmon. It only takes three ounces of salmon to obtain the daily recommendation of 1 gram of EPA and DHA.

The scientific evidence so significantly supports the numerous health benefits of omega-3 fatty acids that the Food and Drug Administration (FDA) has approved a health claim that links adequate omega-3 fatty acid consumption with a reduced risk of heart disease. This approval allows manufacturers of foods and supplements containing EPA and DHA to advertise that their product may reduce the risk of heart disease. Although the claim can be used on all foods containing EPA and DHA regardless of the quantity of each provided, the FDA highly advises that individuals limit themselves to no more than 3 grams of EPA and DHA daily with no more than 2 grams per day coming from supplements.

When choosing wild salmon, search for line-caught Alaskan fish. Studies have found that the healthiest populations of wild salmon exist in Alaska. Whenever possible, ask at the fish counter if their salmon have received the Marine Stewardship Council (MSC) label, which indicates that the particular salmon species has not been overharvested and was raised responsibly.

Farm-raised salmon are jam-packed into tiny bins with countless other salmon. Because of the confined space, farm-raised salmon do not get to move around much. As a result, they generally contain 52 percent more fat than wild salmon, and this fat consists of a higher proportion of inflammation-producing omega-6 fatty acids. The close quarters also require that the farm-raised fish are doused with antibiotics and pesticides. If this is not enough, farm-raised salmon are fed fish meal pellets that are believed to contain environmental contaminants and a salmon-colored dye to camouflage their unappealing gray color.

Not Wild about Fish?

Even though fish is your best option since it offers the most omega-3 bang for your buck, there are alternatives. The plant version of omega-3 fatty acids, alpha-linolenic acid (ALA), can be converted into the powerful anti-inflammatory substances EPA and DHA. ALA intake can be increased by using canola and flaxseed oils; adding ground flaxseeds to salads, cereal, and other dishes; snacking on walnuts; choosing eggs from chickens fed grains rich in omega-3s, and experimenting with food products rich in soy such as soybeans and tofu.

FACT

Studies have confirmed that monounsaturated fats are anti-inflammatory fats as well, and olive oil is at the top of the list. The polyphenols in olive oil protect the heart and blood vessels from inflammation. Other healthy foods high in monounsaturated fats include peanut and canola oil, avocados, and nuts such as peanuts, walnuts, almonds, and pistachios. These foods are a delicious and satisfying way to take the wind out of the sails of inflammation.

Unfortunately, the body is not very efficient at converting ALA into DHA and EPA. You need to consume three to four times as much ALA from plant-based foods to equal the amount of EPA and DHA found in a 3-ounce serving of fish. Therefore, individuals who avoid fish may want to consider taking a fish oil supplement that offers 500 to 1,000 mg of EPA and DHA to minimize internal inflammation.

Even though ALA is not the best way to get your DHA and EPA, it is a great addition to an anti-inflammatory diet. It can indirectly ease inflammation, and studies continually provide data that support the benefits of ALA-rich plant-based foods. For example, a study published in the *Journal of Nutrition* found that individuals who consumed at least 2.3 ounces—about a half-cup or 28 halves—of walnuts or flaxseeds daily experienced reduced levels of C-reactive protein (CRP) and other inflammatory markers.

Fruits and Vegetables Take Center Stage

Fruits and vegetables are major storehouses of phytochemicals and antioxidants, both of which have anti-inflammatory powers. Phytochemicals are chemicals found in plants, and although they are not essential for life, their benefits are far-reaching, with links to reduced risk of cancer, heart disease, and diabetes. Plants rely on phytochemicals for their own protection and survival. These potent chemicals help plants resist the attacks of bacteria and fungi, the potential havoc brought on by free radicals, and the constant exposure to ultraviolet light from the sun. Fortunately, when plants are consumed, their chemicals infuse into our body's tissues and provide ammunition against disease.

In a similar manner to phytochemicals, antioxidants halt and repair free radical damage throughout the body. The most potent antioxidants include vitamin A, vitamin C, vitamin E, and selenium. In addition to fruits and vegetables, these free radical squelchers inhabit whole grains, vegetable oils, nuts, and seeds.

Choosing Power-Packed Produce

To get the most bang for your buck in the produce section of your local grocery store, choose brightly colored fruits and veggies such as strawberries, blueberries, cantaloupe, spinach, and red, green, and yellow bell peppers. Aim to eat fruits and vegetables that represent each color of the rainbow. It's pretty simple: the more color, the more health benefits.

ESSENTIAL

Seek out five to nine servings of fruits and vegetables each day. Generally, the more, the better as long as you stay within your energy needs. For a 2,000-calorie diet, MyPyramid recommends two cups of fruit and two and a half cups of vegetables per day, with higher or lower amounts depending on calorie level.

According to MyPyramid (*www.mypyramid.gov*), it is ideal to vary your veggies by choosing from all five veggie subgroups (dark green, orange, legumes, starchy vegetables, and other vegetables) several times a week. When it comes to fruits, variety is important to ensure you are receiving all the beneficial phytochemicals, antioxidants, vitamins, and minerals while minimizing exposure to any single type of pesticide.

▼ SERVING SIZES FOR FRUITS AND VEGETABLES

Food Group	Food Item	Recommended Serving Size	Visual Representation of a Serving Size
Vegetables (3½ cups = suggested daily amount for a 2,000-calorie diet)			
	1 cup equivalents		
	Leafy vegetables (spinach, lettuce, etc.)	2 cups	2 large handfuls
	Broccoli, baby carrots, corn, cauliflower, green beans, mushrooms, tomatoes, zucchini	1 cup	1 large handful or woman's fist
	Sweet potato, baked	1 large	3 stacked oval sponges
	Baked potato	1 medium	Computer mouse
	Black, kidney, pinto beans, cooked	1 cup	1 large handful or woman's fist
	Vegetable juice, low-sodium	1 cup	Standard coffee cup filled three-quarters full
	Raw or cooked vegetables	½ cup	Ice cream scoop or half a baseball
Fruits (2½ cups = suggested daily amount for a 2,000-calorie diet)			
	1 cup equivalents		
	Banana	1 large (8 in. long)	Length of an ice cream scoop
	Apple, orange, mango, peach	1 medium; 1 large peach	Tennis ball
	Grapefruit	1 medium (4 in. diameter)	Softball
	Grapes	30	2 cupped hands
	Plums	2 large (2½ in. diameter)	2 pool balls
	Strawberries	1 cup	A woman's fist or cupped hands
	Fresh or canned chopped fruit, in light syrup	1 cup	A woman's fist or cupped hands
	Dried fruit	½ cup	Ice cream scoop or half a baseball
	Fruit juice, preferably 100% juice	1 cup	Standard coffee cup filled three quarters full

You can get antioxidants from dietary supplements, but the motto "foods first" is your best bet. Scientists currently feel there is not enough evidence to support the benefits of taking antioxidant supplements. Many studies have demonstrated that the benefits of antioxidants are more apparent when they come from foods rather than supplements. In a nutshell, the antioxidant actions of fruits and veggies are greater than their nutrients alone can explain. For example, most vitamin E supplements provide exclusively alpha-tocopherol, but foods provide vitamin E in a variety of different forms referred to as tocopherols, and also provide many other valuable nutrients that help fight the war on free radicals.

Organic or Conventional Produce?

Have you ever wondered if you really need to go the organic route? Good question, and the answer is—sometimes yes and sometimes no. The Environmental Working Group (EWG) generated a list called The Dirty Dozen, which identifies those fruits and vegetables that tend to have the highest level of pesticides and chemicals.

The list is as follows:

- Celery
- Peaches
- Strawberries
- Apples
- Blueberries
- Nectarines
- Bell peppers
- Spinach
- Cherries
- Kale and collard greens
- Potatoes
- Grapes (imported)

Government groups such as the U.S. Environmental Protection Agency (U.S. EPA) and Department of Agriculture (USDA) have agreed on the levels of pesticides that are considered safe in fruits and vegetables. All produce that made the Dirty Dozen list are within safe pesticide limits according to

U.S. EPA and USDA standards. Even the EWG has made it clear that The Dirty Dozen list was not meant to send the message that fruits and vegetables should be limited. This is far from their intention, but educating consumers on the fruits and veggies with more pesticides may encourage consumers to better wash their produce and go organic when the price is right.

FACT

Certain fruits contain enzymes that are believed to fight pain and inflammation. These fruits include papaya, pineapple, kiwi fruit, and figs. Make these part of your weekly fruit repertoire.

For example, blueberries are antioxidant powerhouses. They are high in phytonutrients that pack a mean anti-inflammatory punch against many chronic diseases. Strawberries, blackberries, raspberries, and cranberries all share the same health benefits as blueberries. So don't skimp on produce. And just to dissipate any remaining concerns consumers may have about pesticides, a 2008 report completed by the USDA found that 98 percent of the fruits and vegetables they sampled had no detectable pesticide residue and of those that did possess pesticides the levels were within an acceptable range.

The Clean Fifteen

Americans clearly need to make a conscious effort to increase their fruit and vegetable intake as a means for optimizing health. Fruits and veggies are dietary superstars and they should not be limited as a result of pesticide concerns. The EWG has also generated a list called the Clean Fifteen, which identifies produce that contains little to no pesticides.

- Onions
- Avocados
- Sweet corn
- Pineapples
- Mangoes
- Sweet peas

- Asparagus
- Kiwi fruit
- Cabbage
- Eggplant
- Cantaloupe
- Watermelon
- Grapefruit
- Sweet potatoes
- Honeydew melon

To ensure that your fruits and veggies are in tiptop shape, wash all fruit and vegetables under running water to remove dirt, bacteria, and possible pesticide residue. This includes the outside skin in fruits such as watermelons or oranges where the knife can transmit any remaining bacteria or pesticides into the edible portion of the food. And remember, purchasing organic produce can't hurt either.

Food for Thought

Although fruits and vegetables are extremely beneficial to your health, there are certain vegetables such as potatoes, tomatoes, and eggplant that are believed to exacerbate inflammation. These vegetables are members of the nightshade family of plants. They contain a chemical called solanine. Anecdotal evidence suggests that solanine may trigger pain and inflammation in some people, but currently there is no research to support the negative claims linked to nightshade vegetables. Individuals with inflammatory conditions can experiment with limiting nightshade vegetables to see if they get any relief from pain and inflammation. Other members of this plant family include sweet and hot peppers, including paprika, cayenne pepper, and Tabasco sauce; ground cherries; tomatillos; pepinos; and pimientos.

Lean on Your Protein

Dietary protein is responsible for the growth, maintenance, and repair of the body, but can also contribute to chronic disease development if not chosen properly and in the correct amounts. Fatty meats such as hot dogs, bologna, pork sausage, bacon, salami, and beef and pork ribs, and high-fat dairy items such as cheese and whole milk or whole yogurt need to be limited significantly in an anti-inflammatory eating style. These high-protein foods are high in inflammation-promoting saturated fats and cholesterol.

Lean meats, white-meat poultry, eggs, and low-fat milk, cheese, and yogurt, on the other hand, will give you clean protein without excessive amounts of pro-inflammatory fats. Cold-water fish offers plenty of quality protein with a kick of anti-inflammatory omega-3 fatty acids. Fish are also rich in arginine, a component of proteins. Arginine-rich foods, such as fish and nuts, have been shown to reduce the presence of inflammatory markers. Vegetable proteins, such as soy foods, beans, lentils, whole grains, seeds, and nuts, will further reduce the presence of pro-inflammatory agents in the body while giving you a blast of phytochemicals and antioxidants.

When portioning your plate, make sure you choose proper portions of even the leanest meats, beans, and dairy. Matching your total daily calorie intake with your energy requirements will prevent unnecessary weight gain and resultant inflammation.

▼ SERVING SIZES FOR PROTEIN

Food Group	Item	Recommended Serving Size	Visual Representation of a Serving Size
Meats and Beans (5–7 servings = suggested daily amount for a 2,000-calorie diet)			
	1 serving equivalents		
	Lean red meat, poultry or fish	1 ounce	Matchbox
	Lean deli meat, chicken, turkey, ham, roast beef	2 thin slices	Rolled-up looks like a highlighter
	Shrimp, cooked	3–4 medium	2 stacked Oreos
	Egg	1	1 egg
	Beans, cooked	¼ cup	Ping-Pong ball
	Hummus	2 tablespoons	2 tea bags
	Peanut butter	1 tablespoon	3 thumb tips or half a Ping-Pong ball

	Seeds	½ ounce or 2–3 tablespoons (pumpkin, sunflower, or squash seeds, hulled, roasted)	2–3 tea bags
	Nuts	½ ounce or 2–3 tablespoons (12 almonds, 24 pistachios, 7 walnut halves)	2–3 tea bags
Dairy Products (3 cups = suggested daily amount for a 2,000-calorie diet)			
	1 cup equivalents		
	Milk or yogurt	1 cup (8 ounces)	Standard yogurt container
	Frozen yogurt or ice cream, preferably low-fat	1 cup (8 ounces)	Standard yogurt container
	Cottage cheese	½ cup	Ice cream scoop or half a baseball
	Cheese, shredded	⅓ cup	Racquetball
	Cheese, slices	2	2 square deli slices
	Cheese, block	1½–2 ounces	6 to 8 dice

Managing the type and quantities of protein-rich foods will keep your waistline trim and your energy levels on an even keel. Try to include a lean protein source at each meal to help manage your appetite and prevent unnecessary cravings.

Grains: "The Staff of Life"

For some time now, people have questioned the healthfulness of carbohydrates. Numerous health authorities blame carbohydrates for the current obesity epidemic. This concern about carbohydrates has spurred the government to include specific recommendation for grains in the Dietary Guidelines. As part of these guidelines, whole grains are continually recommended and touted as a super food because of their high fiber content and significant contribution of vitamins, minerals, and phytochemicals. Currently, government recommendations advise that at least half of an individual's grain selections come from whole grains.

The Anatomy of a Whole Grain

To really understand the benefits of consuming whole grains, it is first essential to review the anatomy of a grain. Each kernel of a grain contains the husk, the bran, the germ, and the endosperm.

- **The husk** is the outermost coat of a grain. This portion is inedible and removed when processing all grains.
- **The bran** is the protective coating under the husk that surrounds the kernel. It is rich in niacin, riboflavin, iron, and zinc, and provides virtually all of the grain's dietary fiber. This part of the grain is always present in whole grains, but is stripped away during milling and is missing in refined grain products.
- **The germ** is the seed within the grain that can grow into the wheat plant if given the correct environmental conditions. Although this is the smallest part of the grain, it is a nutritional powerhouse. It is rich in many vitamins (B vitamins and vitamin E), minerals, and antioxidants, as well as polyunsaturated fats. This portion of the grain is often removed in refined grains to prevent rancidity of the final grain product so shelf life can be extended.
- **The endosperm** is the starchy portion of a grain that makes up a majority of the grain's weight. It is rich in starch and also contains some protein. White bread is mostly made up of endosperm. This portion of the grain has the least nutritional value.

Go for the Whole Grain

A whole grain consists of the bran, the germ, and the endosperm, in contrast to a refined grain, which contains only the endosperm. The bonus of keeping grains as close to their original form as possible is that in this form, the starch will be digested more slowly. Furthermore, the higher fiber content of whole grains reduces the speed at which nutrients empty from the stomach. Both of these processes prevent spikes in blood sugar levels, which subsequently helps in management of blood insulin levels. All of these adjustments can ultimately prevent numerous chronic diseases such as diabetes, heart disease, and cancer.

Refined grains are nutritionally inferior to whole grains because of their lack of the bran and germ. These grains are milled to produce flours. The flour is then used to make breads, but during the process of making commercial breads, a variety of unnatural chemicals are added. For example, dough conditioners are commonly added to bread dough so it stays fresher and softer longer. Frequently mono- and diglycerides are added to bread dough to further enhance its softness, and the flour is bleached for whiteness. Refined products must then be enriched with certain nutrients that were removed during the milling process such as the B vitamins niacin, thiamin, riboflavin, and folate, and the mineral iron. After all this work, you would think that enriched white bread would be a nutritional superstar, but the opposite is true.

Shopping for Whole Grains

When searching for whole grains, don't be deceived by the color of grain products. Bread can appear brown because of added molasses or other colorful ingredients, but this does not necessarily mean the product contains whole grains. You can be sure that whole grains are present by looking at the Nutrition Facts food labels. Look for the word "whole" on the label, and make sure it is listed as one of the first ingredients. Whole-grain products also generally possess higher amounts of fiber and protein than refined products.

Next time you visit the grocery store, try adding a new whole-grain product to your cart. Some grains to consider include:

- Amaranth
- Barley
- Brown rice
- Buckwheat
- Bulgur
- Couscous
- Flaxseed
- Millet
- Oats and oatmeal
- Popcorn
- Quinoa

- Rye
- Spelt
- Whole-wheat bread, pasta, crackers, and cereals
- Wild rice

Once you have the whole-grain products in your possession, it is time to manage your portions. As with all foods, the quantity of grains you choose to consume is very important to weight management. And weight management is essential for stifling inflammation.

▼ SERVING SIZES FOR GRAINS

Food Group	Item	Recommended Serving Size	Visual Representation of a Serving Size
Grains (6 servings = suggested daily amount for a 2,000-calorie diet)			
	1 serving equivalents		
	Pasta, rice, cooked cereal	½ cup	Cupcake wrapper or ice cream scoop
	Flaky cereal	1 cup (1 ounce)	1 large handful or woman's fist
	Bread, preferably whole-wheat	1 slice (1 ounce)	CD case
	Bagel, roll, biscuit, or English muffin	Half	6-ounce can of tuna, hockey puck, or a large to-go coffee lid
	Tortilla, preferably whole-grain corn	Half of an 8-in. diameter	half of a small salad plate
	Muffin	1 small or 2 mini muffins	Standard light bulb
	Chips or pretzels	1 cup (1 ounce)	1 large handful or woman's fist
	Crackers, preferably whole-grain	5–7 crackers	Length and width of a checkbook (not thickness)
	Popcorn, air-popped	3 cups	3 large handfuls

The benefits of whole grains are endless and are a very important part of anti-inflammatory eating. They can help manage blood sugar and insulin levels, offering protection against diabetes and heart disease. Their high fiber content makes the digestive tract happy, can alleviate constipation, and helps control cholesterol levels. These benefits will keep cancer away and offer additional benefits for your heart. All it takes is consumption of at least three whole-grain servings a day and you will be granted a 15 to 25 percent reduction in death from all causes.

Probiotic Power

All humans have millions and millions of naturally occurring bacteria in their bodies. Normally, bacteria get a bad rap, but the right types of bacteria, specifically lactobacilli and bifidobacteria, can keep you healthy and even prevent disease. More specifically, these bacteria support the immune system, keeping it strong and better able to fend off disease and illness. Other benefits include:

- Anti-inflammatory effects in the gut that can be helpful in treating constipation, diarrhea, inflammatory bowel disease, and irritable bowel syndrome
- Facilitation of nutrient absorption as food passes through the digestive tract
- Assistance in preventing invasion of pathogens and eradicating those that sneak into the body
- A reduction in the risk of developing allergies
- Possible reduction in the risk of colon cancer, infection with the *Helicobacter pylori* (H. pylori), a bacterium that causes most ulcers and many types of chronic stomach cancers, and urinary tract infections

Ideally, your bowels contain about 85 percent "good" bacteria and only about 15 percent "bad" bacteria, but modern life has thrown off this balance for many Americans. The processed food supply and overuse of antibiotics has reduced the colonies of good bacteria in the gut, but thankfully there is a solution.

Ways to Keep Your Gut Happy

You can help good bacteria flourish by consuming foods that contain high concentrations of healthy probiotics ("for life") such as *Lactobacillus acidophilus*. Fermented milk products such as yogurt, kefir, and some soy-based beverages will increase the probiotic bacteria within your body. Look on the label for the statement "live and active cultures" to ensure that you are increasing your consumption of probiotics. You can also search for the National Yogurt Association's seal, which identifies products that contain a minimum of 100 million live lactic acid bacteria per gram of yogurt. This is important to look for since not all brands of yogurt contain live, active cultures. Miso, a Japanese condiment consisting of fermented soybean paste, can also augment beneficial bacteria, but keep in mind that miso is also high in sodium.

Another option is to increase your intake of prebiotics. Prebiotics are the nondigestible nutrients, primarily soluble fibers, that are used as an energy source by the bacteria (probiotics) that live in your intestines. Food products such as whole grains, onions, bananas, garlic, artichokes, flaxseeds, and a variety of fortified foods, beverages, and dietary supplements naturally contain prebiotics. These foods can be fermented by bacteria in your intestines, which allows good bacteria to prosper. Implementing these dietary interventions will not only keep your digestive tract happy, but will affect all of your bodily systems in a positive manner.

Probiotics in a Pill?

The jury is still out on the potential benefits of dried probiotics administered via powders, capsules, or tablets. First, supplemental probiotics must contain significant levels of live bacteria to be useful, but standardized dosage levels that provide health benefits have not been identified. Second, there are numerous strains of probiotics, and helpful strains of "good" bacteria are still being identified. Finally, probiotic supplements must survive the high acid levels of the stomach and exposure to other digestive enzymes, which can lead to destruction of the probiotics found in pill form. On the other hand, foods such as yogurt can help buffer stomach acids, increasing the chance that the "good" bacteria will survive.

CHAPTER 5

Shrinking Supplements, Herbs, and Spices

Over the years, numerous dietary supplements, spices, and herbs have been found to have beneficial anti-inflammatory effects. Many of these substances can be incorporated into your diet without much effort and offer huge paybacks.

Fish in a Bottle

Omega-3 fatty acids, most notably eicosapentaenoic acid (EPA) and docosahexanoic acid (DHA), have received huge accolades for their ability to reduce the risk of numerous chronic diseases and conditions. Currently, the American Heart Association recommends 500 to 1,000 mg of EPA and DHA a day. Unfortunately, Americans just can't seem to get enough of this super nutrient by diet alone. The solution? Bring on the fish oil supplements—but not before you consider the following:

- Check with your physician prior to initiating fish oil supplementation, especially if you are currently taking any medications.
- Make sure the supplement you choose contains 1,000 mg of EPA and DHA, not just 1,000 mg of "fish oils."
- Choose fish oils that come from the flesh of the fish, not the fish liver, head, or tail. This one step will reduce the risk of exposure to unnecessary toxins and contaminants.
- Select enteric-coated fish oil supplements to avoid fishy burp-back.
- Fish oils can cause gastrointestinal upset such as diarrhea, nausea, and abdominal bloating in some individuals. These side effects can be minimized by consuming fish oil supplements with meals and slowly increasing the dose to desired levels.
- Vegetarians can choose supplements that come from algal oil.
- Since fish oils are vulnerable to rancidity, store them in the refrigerator to enhance their potency and effectiveness.
- If you have elevated triglycerides, consult with your physician to see if 2,000 to 4,000 milligrams of EPA and DHA may help undermine your triglycerides.

Overall, fish oils have the potential to help millions of Americans dodge chronic diseases and conditions that can negatively affect the quality of life. Consumption of two to three servings of fatty fish per week or popping a fish oil supplement is a very easy step toward disease prevention and management.

When consuming fish oil supplements, you don't have to worry about excessive amounts of mercury or polychlorinated biphenyls (PCBs) commonly found in fish, and whether they are present in fish oils. Mercury and other contaminates tend to accumulate in fish meat rather than in the oils of the fish. Studies have confirmed that fish oils are virtually mercury-free. Fish oil supplements are especially beneficial for pregnant women and children as a means for promoting healthy growth and development. Limit doses in children to between 200 and 500 mg EPA and DHA each day.

ALERT

Fish oil consumed in high doses may raise blood sugar levels, which can be a concern for diabetics. Additionally, since EPA and DHA thin the blood, they are contraindicated in individuals taking blood thinners or aspirin daily, or for individuals with blood clotting disorders or high blood pressure.

Vital Vitamin D

Recent research has found that 75 percent of Americans are not receiving the recommended amounts of vitamin D. The resulting deficiency can have a negative impact on the immune system, which can increase the risk of developing hypertension, heart disease, diabetes, cancer, and a variety of autoimmune conditions.

In 1997, the Food and Nutrition Board (FNB) of the Institute of Medicine recommended that American adults consume 200 IU of vitamin D each day. At the time, this recommendation seemed reasonable based on available research. The recommendations were actually aimed at preventing rickets, a vitamin D deficiency disease in children characterized by inadequate mineralization of bone. Vitamin D was praised exclusively for its ability to assist in absorption of in calcium and phosphorus.

But as the years have passed and vitamin D research has exploded, researchers are now recommending five to ten times more vitamin D for the average adult. In November 2010, the Institute of Medicine of the National Academies (IOM) changed the RDA for vitamin D from 200 IU to 600 IU for individuals aged one to seventy years. The recommendation is increased further from 600 to 800 IU for individuals aged seventy-one years and older due to reduced efficiency at making vitamin D via exposure to ultraviolet light, reduced outdoor activity, all-concealing clothing, and inadequate vitamin D intake. Finally, the tolerable upper intake level, the level below which vitamin D intake is considered safe, has been increased from 1,000 IU to 4,000 IU.

Because there are only a few natural food sources of vitamin D available, including fatty fish, fish oils, and fortified milk, alternate sources of vitamin D appear essential to satisfy current recommendations. Consuming fatty fish at least two times per week will not only boost your vitamin D intake but will provide your body with heart-healthy, inflammation-busting omega-3 fats as well. In addition to a variety of vitamin D–fortified foods, aim for two to three servings of low-fat, vitamin D–fortified milk, yogurt, or orange juice every day. If it is challenging for you to consume these foods day in and day out, then you may want to consider taking a vitamin D supplement daily.

The Versatile Sunshine Vitamin

Unlike any other nutrient, vitamin D can be made in the skin when the sun is shining. Individuals with fair skin should aim for ten to fifteen minutes, and those with dark skin thirty minutes, of unprotected sun exposure to the face, arms, and hands (25 percent of the skin's surface) two to three times a week between the hours of 10 A.M. and 3 P.M. To give you perspective, a fair-skinned person can manufacture 15,000 IU or more of vitamin D in as little as thirty minutes of optimal sun exposure. Not bad!

FACT

The skin can manufacture vitamin D when exposed to the ultraviolet rays offered by a tanning bed, but only at the risk of deadly skin cancer. Foods and supplements are a much safer bet to ensure you get your Ds.

Factors to Keep in Mind

As with all things in life, there are factors that must be considered when determining whether or not you receive enough vitamin D. First, if you use sunscreen with an SPF of eight or greater, your body's ability to synthesize vitamin D is drastically reduced. A good rule of thumb is to put your sunscreen on right before you head outside. Since it takes a good twenty minutes for sunscreen to become fully effective, you will get the rays necessary for some decent vitamin D production before your sun protection kicks in.

Second, for those living in northern areas of the country, your skin is unable to synthesize any vitamin D between the months of November and February. A supplement is highly advised during these "D"eficient months.

And third, the older you are, the less efficient your skin is at making vitamin D from the sun. For most healthy individuals, young and old, and especially vegetarians who avoid dairy products, a daily multivitamin-mineral supplement containing at least 400 IU to 600 IU of vitamin D is highly recommended. Choose supplements that provide the more absorbable vitamin D3, also known as cholecalciferol, versus vitamin D2, and take the supplement with meals to enhance its absorption.

ESSENTIAL

Zyflamend is a dietary supplement that contains a variety of substances such as ginger, turmeric, green tea, resveratrol and other herbs that are anecdotally believed to moderate inflammation in the body. The components of Zyflamend are said to inhibit the COX-2 enzymes. This allows for reduced production of pro-inflammatory hormones such as prostaglandins. The ingredients in Zyflamend have been used for years safely and effectively, but solid, clinical research is still lacking when it comes to the individual and combined effects of Zyflamend on chronic diseases and conditions.

Common Spices and Herbs That Ease Inflammation

Currently, there are many supplements and spices on the market that claim they can reduce inflammation and its associated pain in a natural manner, without side effects. Unfortunately, clinical research that supports these claims is very sparse and most claims are solely anecdotal. A few that have withstood the test of time are as follows:

- **Garlic** is no longer considered just a vampire repellant. It is now touted as a potent anti-inflammatory power food. Garlic contains chemicals that crush the inflammation-promoting substances in the body. As a result, regular garlic consumption can help minimize the side effects of asthma, and reduce the pain and inflammation associated with osteoarthritis and rheumatoid arthritis. Garlic can even reduce the production of cancer-causing chemicals that can result when protein-containing foods are subject to high temperatures through various cooking methods such as grilling. So flavor your foods with garlic to add a layer of protection with a little anti-inflammation mixed in.

- **Curcumin** is a substance found in the yellow curry spice, turmeric. Curcumin is touted as having antioxidant powers, anti-inflammatory qualities, and possibly even anticancer effects. This spice is popular in India, and some researchers believe there is a link between higher curcumin intake and a lower incidence of Alzheimer's disease. Preliminary findings from animal studies suggest that curcumin may actually possess anti-inflammatory and anticancer properties, but currently very little research exists that evaluates the actual effects of curcumin supplementation on disease risk in humans.

- **Ginger** is a tropical plant and a relative of turmeric. Certain constituents of ginger, referred to as gingerols, are touted to inhibit numerous biochemicals that promote inflammation, especially in cases of osteoarthritis and rheumatoid arthritis. Again, these claims are unsubstantiated, but one thing that ginger has been found to help with is pregnancy-induced nausea and vomiting. Fresh ginger adds a light spiciness and mellow sweetness to dishes and is a wonderful spice to incorporate into stir-fries and dipping sauces.

- **Cat's claw** comes from a woody vine that grows in many countries of Central and South America. Small studies in humans have shown a possible benefit of cat's claw in osteoarthritis and rheumatoid arthritis, but no large trials have been completed. In laboratory studies, cat's claw has been found to stimulate part of the immune system, but its effect on inflammation is still uncertain.

CHAPTER 6

Other Ways to Take a Vacation from Inflammation

There are a number of other simple dietary and lifestyle interventions that can keep inflammation from establishing a foothold over the body. Beating inflammation is not just about changing your diet. Your best defensive mode is to combine dietary and lifestyle interventions to ensure that your body is protected like a secured armored car.

The Anti-Inflammatory and Mediterranean Lifestyles Unite to Fight Inflammation

Observing the incidence of chronic disease in a variety of cultures and populations has allowed researchers to identify key dietary and lifestyle habits that translate to a lower incidence of inflammatory conditions and disease. The Mediterranean countries have gained the attention of researchers interested in the etiology of chronic disease since they have seem to have escaped the consequences of toxic modern living. *The Journal of the American Medical Association* reported recently that individuals following Mediterranean eating patterns possess fewer inflammatory biomarkers and lower occurrence of lifestyle-related diseases.

The Mediterranean diet emphasizes primarily plant-based foods such as fruits and vegetables, whole grains, legumes, and nuts. Olive oil replaces butter. Herbs and spices are used to flavor foods instead of salt. Red meat is limited to no more than a few times a month. Fatty fish and poultry are recommended at least twice a week. Red wine in moderation, as well as plenty of exercise, round out the dietary recommendations. You will find that the Mediterranean diet has many similarities to the anti-inflammatory dietary and lifestyle guidelines.

Hydrate for Health

Water is the most critical nutrient in our diet. It makes up over 60 percent of your body weight with the blood consisting of 85 percent water, and the muscles and brain encompassing 70 percent and 75 percent water, respectively. Bodily fluids are necessary for digestion, absorption and transportation of essential nutrients throughout the body. Adequate fluid intake can prevent headaches and fatigue, and enhance memory and circulation. Most importantly, adequate hydration has been shown to reduce bodily inflammation. Studies have shown that individuals with rheumatoid arthritis fare better when properly hydrated, due to the cushioning and nurturing effect of water on the joints.

Adequate hydration can also improve conditions such as diabetes and obesity, both of which foster inflammation if not properly managed. Furthermore, studies have found a significant reduction in breast and colon cancer risk in individuals who remain adequately hydrated. Conversely, if hydration is suboptimal, unnecessary wastes and toxins can buildup in the body and contribute to inflammation.

Since you cannot store water in the body to any great extent, it must be consumed at regular intervals throughout the day. Since the thirst alert mechanism in humans is a bit delayed, diligent and proactive consumption of fluids is a necessity. The key is to not wait until thirst occurs because at this point the early stages of dehydration are in play.

The Institute of Medicine recommends that men consume 125 ounces of fluids and women consume 90 ounces of fluids every day. These fluids can come from both foods and caffeinated and noncaffeinated beverages.

Foods high in water such as fruits and vegetables provide necessary hydration while enhancing the volume of the food consumed. A boost in food volume, especially when accompanied by dietary fiber and/or protein, can increase the feelings of fullness and subsequently decrease the quantity of food consumed. This scenario helps manage calorie intake and supports weight management efforts, both of which halt inflammatory processes in the body.

In terms of beverages, water, plain or sparkling, is ideal since you are talking high hydration accompanied by a low energy intake. It is ideal to limit beverages high in sugar to ensure weight and inflammation management. Small quantities of 100 percent juice are fine, but should still be limited since liquid calories are not as satisfying as solid food calories.

If you are worried about the cleanliness of your public water supply, purchase a countertop or faucet water purifier. These appliances are the cheapest, easiest, and most effective way to reduce potentially harmful chemicals in tap water. Make sure the water filter you choose reduces the following chemicals: trihalomethanes; haloacetic acids; heavy metals such as lead, mercury, copper, cadmium, benzene and chlorine; arasites such as *Giardia* and *cryptosporidium*; and agricultural pollutants such as herbicides and insecticides. The key to an effective water purifier is changing the water filters regularly. Manufacturer instructions may vary, but in general it is recommended that you change the filters for kitchen dispensers every 40 gallons of usage, every one to two months, and faucet filters every 100 gallons of usage, once every two to four months.

Tame Inflammation with Tea

After water, tea is the most commonly consumed beverage in the world. There are three main types of tea—green, black, and oolong. Green tea is made from unfermented leaves and contains the highest concentration of the potent antioxidants referred to as polyphenols. Oolong tea is prepared from partially fermented tea leaves, while black tea is fully fermented. Overall, the greater the degree of fermentation, the lower the polyphenol concentration and the higher the caffeine content. Hence, green tea appears to be the most potent of the teas. The polyphenols, better known as catechins, found in green tea help neutralize free radicals and combat inflammation. The result: reduced risk of certain cancers and heart disease. In general, two to three cups of green tea are recommended per day to provide the therapeutic dose of 240 to 320 mg of polyphenols.

The Dark Side of Chocolate

For years, chocolate was put on the "no-no" list because of its high concentrations of unhealthy fats, but things have changed. Recent research points to the health-promoting ingredients in chocolate, most notably the flavonoids and procyanidins found in the cocoa. These phytochemicals have been linked to a reduced risk of heart disease, cancer, and inflammation thanks to their powerful antioxidant effects. Studies have shown that when individuals consume these potent phytochemicals in chocolate and cocoa, the antioxidant status of their blood rises.

This is all promising data for fighting inflammation, but one must consider the following before gobbling up a large chunk of chocolate. Firstly, do not fret about the high levels of saturated fat, since the type found in chocolate does not raise cholesterol levels. Secondly, the flavonoid content of cocoa and chocolate varies considerably. Generally, the more cocoa a product contains, the higher the flavonoid content. There is a higher concentration of cocoa in dark chocolate than in milk chocolate, and white chocolate is completely devoid of cocoa. Choose chocolate that contains at least 65 percent cocoa to maximize your flavonoid intake. Also, be aware that cocoa drink mixes, most notably Dutch cocoa, generally contain cocoa treated with alkali, which drastically lowers the flavonoid content. Thirdly, limit the quantity of chocolate consumed. Moderation is key, seeing that 1½ ounces of chocolate (⅓ cup) contains 235 calories and 13 grams of fat. In comparison, ⅓ cup of fresh fruits or veggies contains a multitude of phytochemicals, antioxidants, and vitamins and minerals with only 15 to 50 calories and virtually no fat.

Red Wine, You Make Me Feel So Fine

Red wine has also continually been named as a top anti-inflammatory agent. Studies have shown that individuals who consume one to two glasses of red wine per day have lower levels of inflammatory substances in the blood, and higher levels of "good" HDL cholesterol. These benefits have been consistently in favor of red wine over white wine. This is believed to be due to the higher concentration of flavonoids and red anthocyanin pigments in red wine versus white. These flavonoids, most notably resveratrol, act as antioxidants and help to reduce inflammation. The wines that are thought to contain the highest levels of flavonoids include Cabernet Sauvignon and pinot noir. Remember, as with all foods and beverages, moderation is key with alcohol-containing beverages.

Bust a Move

Taming inflammation goes beyond dietary choices. Certain lifestyle habits and behaviors can contribute significantly to inflammation management. Lack of physical activity is the primary contributor to excessive weight gain and subsequent obesity. As you may recall, overweight and obesity are associated with chronic inflammation and increased disease risk. Unfortunately, only 22 percent of American adults satisfy the recommended levels of physical activity, 60 percent are not consistently active, and 25 percent are completely inactive.

The anti-inflammatory effects of regular, moderate exercise help to lower the risk of heart disease, diabetes, high blood pressure, osteoporosis, and obesity. Active individuals possess lower levels of C-reactive protein (CRP), indicating less inflammation. The anti-inflammatory effect of exercise may be related to the increase in antioxidant production that occurs as a body becomes more fit. The extra internal antioxidants destroy free radicals associated with chronic inflammation.

Individuals who exercise regularly are better equipped to deal with life's stressors and tend to experience a better sense of well-being, improved mood, and enhanced self-esteem.

There are three key components that you should include in your workout routine to ensure that your time is well spent.

Aerobic Exercise

Any exercise that gets your heart pumping and your glands sweating without taking your breath away is considered "aerobic" exercise. For maximum effectiveness, aerobic exercise should be performed three to five times a week for twenty to sixty minutes. To ensure that you are moving at the proper pace, you should be able to carry on a conversation while exercising. If you are huffing and puffing excessively, you're working too hard, which increases your risk of soreness and injury, reduces motivation, and causes you to burn more carbohydrates and less fat. On the other hand, if you can sing "Achy Breaky Heart" when you're exercising, you're not working hard enough and won't get the results you may expect. Great aerobic exercises include walking, jogging, cycling, aerobic dance, stair climbing, the elliptical trainer, and swimming.

Strengthening Exercise

After age twenty-five the "muscle robber" tries to attack the human body. If allowed access to your body, you will lose approximately a half pound of muscle each year to this thief. Muscle is very active tissue with high energy needs. Body fat, on the other hand, is a very lazy, sedentary tissue. Knowing this, your best bet is to gain muscle and lose fat in order to increase the number of calories your body burns, even at rest. The best way to do this is by strength training two to three times a week on nonconsecutive days. You should aim for eight to twelve repetitions for each of your major muscle groups, including the front and back of your legs, your abdominal and lower back muscles, your chest and upper back, and the front and back of your upper arms.

Flexibility Exercise

You don't have to bend your body like a pretzel to benefit from flexibility training, but stretching can make or break your workout routine. When you do not include stretching as part of your workout routine, your risk of injury increases significantly. If you become injured, you can't exercise. If you can't exercise, your weight loss or maintenance efforts will be hampered. Also, stretching makes your muscles longer, giving a leaner appearance to your body. Although stretching before exercise is certainly recommended, the best time to stretch is after exercise when your muscles are warm and pliable. Stretch the major muscle groups mentioned above in the strength-training section, especially the ones you will be using or used during exercise. Hold each stretch for fifteen to sixty seconds, stretch to the point of mild tension, and avoid bouncing.

Unwind with Yoga

When evaluating the benefits of different types of exercise, yoga ranks high on the anti-inflammatory spectrum. One recent study found that regularly practicing yoga can lower pro-inflammatory markers that rise as individuals age. Even after stressful experiences, the individuals who regularly practiced yoga showed smaller increases in inflammation in response to stress. Yoga helps individuals learn to manage everyday stressors more effectively. In a nutshell, yoga is clearly a simple and enjoyable activity that can combat inflammation and subsequent disease.

Cross-Training for Maximal Fat Burn

If you take an all-or-nothing approach to exercising, frequently dread working out, or just want to jolt your body into shape quickly and efficiently, cross-training may add an energizing spark to your fitness repertoire. Cross-training involves the inclusion of a variety of exercises instead of the same old routine over and over and over. This technique allows you to obtain multiple benefits from your exercise efforts that cannot be obtained from any one single exercise.

ALERT

Keep in mind that more exercise is not necessarily better. Severe exercise can cause a systemic inflammatory response which undermines the immune system and can even increase the risk of a heart attack. So keep it moderate and enjoyable to maximize the benefits of your exercise routine.

For example, aerobic exercises, such as brisk walking, improve heart health and the body's fat-burning ability, but do little for the development of the body's calorie-hungry muscle tissue. Weight training, on the other hand, increases muscle mass, but does not significantly improve flexibility or heart power.

The benefits of cross-training include the following:

- Cross-training is a great way to add variety to your workouts and reduces the boredom often associated with performing the same workout day after day and week after week. In other words, cross-training will make you much more likely to head to the gym for a workout instead of the couch. This technique makes working out fun!
- Cross-training allows you to work and develop your entire body, providing you with a more balanced, shapely appearance.
- Cross-training prevents you from reaching frustrating plateaus. Performing activities that use both the upper and lower body, such as swimming, rowing, and the elliptical trainer, will keep your metabolism supercharged and maximize your overall calorie burn.
- Cross-training minimizes overuse injuries and allows specific muscles to rest. By alternating high-impact activities such as running and aerobic dance with low-impact activities such as swimming and biking, you can prevent yourself from being sidelined by inconvenient injuries.

Get Some Shuteye

Sleep is essential for your immune system to function optimally. Inadequate sleep can lead to an increased release of pro-inflammatory chemicals. In one research study, acute sleep deprivation was found to cause a significant increase in the inflammatory marker interleukin-6 (IL-6), fibrinogen, and C-reactive protein. An increase in these markers indicates that there is some degree of systemic inflammation.

A more recent study analyzing the effects of chronic sleep deprivation found that sleep durations of 6 to 8.9 hours was linked to significantly lower levels of the inflammatory markers in the blood compared to sleep duration of less than 6 hours.

Both short and long sleep durations have also been associated with inflammation-producing processes such as high blood pressure, heart disease, diabetes, and stress. For individuals sleeping less than seven hours a night, the risk of overweight or obesity increases. Lack of sleep encourages excessive food consumption due to its effect on various appetite-regulating hormones. Subsequent weight gain can further foster inflammation.

While you sleep, your body focuses on restoring and repairing. After a good night's sleep, the brain and body is more alert, and better able to concentrate and focus. During sleep, the brain processes your day, making permanent memories that link to daily events and sensory input. With suboptimal sleep, memory formation is disturbed. Try the following steps to encourage good sleeping habits:

- Aim for seven to eight hours of sleep each night.
- Limit exposure to caffeine, large quantities of food, and stress within the two-hour period prior to sleep.
- Limit your screen time prior to sleep. These light-emitting devices can stimulate the brain and reduce the desire to snooze.
- Set a sleeping schedule and keep with it as best you can both during the weekdays and weekends.
- Exercise each day in the morning or afternoon. Limit exercise as bedtime arrives to reduce the risk of getting a second wind.

Baby Aspirin Gets an "A," but Beware

Aspirin belongs to a group of drugs called salicylates. These substances can reduce inflammatory substances in the body that lead to pain, fever and inflammation. Baby aspirin is often prescribed for individuals at risk for heart disease due to its beneficial anti-inflammatory effects and ability to inhibit the formation of blood clots. But beware, aspirin can also cause complications such as ulcers and bleeding. These side effects can cause the body to mount an immune response and exacerbate inflammation. Furthermore, it is highly advised that alcohol is not consumed with aspirin since this combination can increase the incidence of stomach bleeding. Use of enteric coated aspirin can reduce the risk of stomach discomfort and bleeding, but it is still highly advised that individuals consult with their physician prior to regular use of aspirin to see if low-dose aspirin therapy (81 to 162 milligrams) is advised.

CHAPTER 7

The Anti-Inflammatory Dietary and Lifestyle Guidelines

Now that the ins and outs and the ups and downs of the anti-inflammatory lifestyle have been investigated, it's time to bring together all the key recommendations so they can be used to purchase foods, create meal plans, and incorporate other essential anti-inflammatory lifestyle habits into your routine.

Portioning Your Plate

Most healthy adults should aim for 2,000 to 3,000 calories each day. Women and sedentary individuals generally require fewer calories than men. Aim to cover two-thirds of your plate with plant-based foods such as whole grains, fruits, and vegetables. The remaining one-third should consist of protein-rich foods such as lean animal proteins, beans, nuts and seeds, soy foods, and low-fat dairy. Use anti-inflammatory ginger and turmeric whenever possible to flavor your foods. For optimal meal satisfaction, it is ideal to include carbs, fats, and proteins at all meals and snacks.

Carbohydrates

You should obtain 45 to 65 percent of total daily calories from carbohydrates. This translates to about 225 to 325 grams of carbohydrate for a 2,000-calorie diet. Your fiber intake should be between 25 and 38 grams each day.

Aim to limit foods high in added sugar. Using Nutrition Facts food labels can help you easily identify those foods overflowing with sugar. Common names for sugar include brown sugar, confectioner's sugar, corn sweetener, corn syrup, dextrose, fructose, fruit juice concentrates, glucose, high-fructose corn syrup, honey, invert sugar, lactose, levulose, malt and maple syrup, maltodextrin, maltose, molasses, raw sugar, sucrose, and sugar syrup. Keep in mind that sugar is sugar to your body regardless of its source. Some sources of sugar such as honey and molasses provide additional vitamins and minerals, but in low, often insignificant amounts. Overall, whether the sugar you choose to consume is honey or high-fructose corn syrup, the ultimate goal is to limit added sugar intake to 25 percent of total calories.

At least 50 percent of your carbohydrate sources should come from whole grains to ensure optimal fiber intake and provision of a variety of powerful plant chemicals. Anti-inflammatory options include whole-grain breads, cereals, crackers, and pasta; brown and wild rice; bulgur wheat; flaxseeds; oats; quinoa; spelt; and wheat germ. Starchy veggies such as beans, colorful sweet potatoes, and any of the huge variety of winter squashes available in the produce section at your local grocery store will keep you feeling full, satisfied and inflammation free.

Fats

Adults should receive 20 to 35 percent of their total daily calories from fat, or 44 to 78 grams of fat a day for a 2,000-calorie diet. Aim to limit saturated fat to no more than 7 percent of your total calories, or 15 grams for a 2,000-calorie diet. Foods to limit include fatty cuts of beef (ribs, T-bone, regular ground beef, hot dogs, salami, bacon, and pepperoni), pork (hot dogs, Danish ham, and sausage), and lamb; unskinned chicken; butter; high-fat cheese; cream cheese; whole milk and yogurt; cream and half-and-half; coconut, palm, and palm kernel oil; and chocolate (exception: dark chocolate with a minimum cocoa content of 65 percent).

Check food labels to keep your trans fat intake as low as possible. Choose foods containing no trans fats and avoid all products made with partially hydrogenated oils. Aim to limit fried foods cooked in hydrogenated shortening; hydrogenated or partially hydrogenated margarine; nondairy creamers; fast foods made with unhealthy fats; shortening; commercial baked goods, including doughnuts, cakes, and cookies; and packaged hydrogenated snack foods, such as chips and crackers.

Limit cholesterol intake to no more than 300 mg per day with further reductions to 200 mg in persons with or at a high risk for heart disease or type 2 diabetes. This is best achieved by reducing the amount of fatty cuts of meats and poultry, eggs, and whole-milk dairy products in your diet. Also, limit fats high in polyunsaturated omega-6 fatty acids, such as corn, sunflower, safflower, soybean, and cottonseed oils. Although omega-6 polyunsaturated fats are a better option than saturated and trans fats.

Strive to consume foods high in monounsaturated fatty acids such as canola oil and olive oil; high-oleic, expeller-pressed safflower oil and sunflower oil; peanut oil and butter; nuts such as almonds and pecans; and avocados and olives. To boost your omega-3 fatty acid intake, you can enjoy plenty of fish, especially cold-water fish such as mackerel, salmon, bluefish, mullet, sablefish, anchovy, herring, lake trout, sardines, and albacore tuna. Make it a point to consume two to three servings of seafood a week, with each serving coming in at 4 ounces after being cooked. Other excellent sources of omega-3 fatty acids include omega-3-fortified eggs; flaxseed, canola, walnut, and soybean oils; walnuts; flaxseeds; and tofu and soy-based products.

Proteins

Obtain 10 to 25 percent of total daily calories from protein or about 50 to 175 grams of protein a day if consuming a 2,000-calorie diet. Aim for lean protein sources such as lean meats and low fat dairy, and try to choose more vegetable proteins such as beans, nuts, and seeds, and tofu and other soy products. Well-planned plant-based diets can easily meet protein requirements and offer other potential health benefits, such as enhanced fiber intake, and provision of a multitude of anti-inflammatory nutrients. Focus on spreading your protein throughout the day so that your appetite, energy levels and blood sugar levels remain on an even keel.

Water

Women should aim for 90 ounces and men 125 ounces of fluids daily. This recommendation includes beverages and fluid contained in foods. When it comes to beverages, water is your best bet, while 100 percent juice is fine in small quantities. Limit high-calorie drinks and juices since they provide minimal satisfaction, but a significant calorie punch. Use black and green teas to meet your fluid requirements and receive an anti-inflammatory bonus.

Planning Ahead for Anti-Inflammatory Success

The focus of an anti-inflammatory diet is to provide your body with foods that will help you create the right kind of eicosanoids, most notably the prostaglandins, that ward off inflammation and to limit foods known to promote inflammation. Choosing healthy, anti-inflammatory foods begins even before you walk into the grocery store. Prior to trekking to the store, plan your meals and make an anti-inflammatory grocery list.

▼ ANTI-INFLAMMATORY GROCERY SHOPPING LIST

GRAINS

Breads

- ☐ Whole-wheat bagels
- ☐ Whole-wheat bread
- ☐ Whole-wheat English muffins
- ☐ Whole-wheat buns or rolls

Cereals

- ☐ Whole-grain cereals
- ☐ Omega-3 fortified cereals
- ☐ Oatmeal

Other Grains

- ☐ Barley
- ☐ Brown or wild rice
- ☐ Bulgar wheat
- ☐ Cornmeal
- ☐ Flaxseed
- ☐ Oats
- ☐ Quinoa
- ☐ Spelt
- ☐ Wheat germ
- ☐ Whole-wheat pasta
- ☐ Whole-wheat pasta blends

Snacks

- ☐ Popcorn

MILK/DAIRY

- ☐ Low-fat or skim milk
- ☐ Low-fat yogurt with live active yogurt cultures
- ☐ Low-fat cottage cheese

VEGETABLES

Best to Buy Organic

- ☐ Celery
- ☐ Bell peppers
- ☐ Spinach
- ☐ Kale and collard greens
- ☐ Potatoes

Antioxidant-Rich Veggies

- ☐ Yellow, orange, and red vegetables
- ☐ Dark leafy greens
- ☐ Citrus fruits
- ☐ Artichokes

FISH, POULTRY, and MEATS

Fish

- ☐ Albacore tuna
- ☐ Anchovies
- ☐ Atlantic herring
- ☐ Halibut
- ☐ Lake trout
- ☐ Mackerel
- ☐ Sardines
- ☐ Stripped sea bass
- ☐ Wild salmon

Poultry

- ☐ White meat chicken and turkey
- ☐ Ground chicken or turkey breast

FRUITS

Best to Buy Organic

- ☐ Peaches
- ☐ Strawberries
- ☐ Apples
- ☐ Blueberries
- ☐ Nectarines
- ☐ Cherries
- ☐ Grapes (imported)

Antioxidant-Rich Fruits

- ☐ All berries
- ☐ 100% juice

MEAT ALTERNATIVES

- ☐ Dried or canned beans, peas, or lentils
- ☐ Peanut butter
- ☐ Hummus
- ☐ Tofu

Omega-3 Fatty Acid Rich Meat Alternatives

- ☐ Walnuts
- ☐ Flaxseed
- ☐ Soybeans
- ☐ Textured vegetable protein

OILS

- ❏ Falxseed oil
- ❏ Canola oil
- ❏ Walnut oil
- ❏ High oleic safflower and sunflower oils
- ❏ Olive oil
- ❏ Chocolate

DIETARY SUPPLEMENTS

- ❏ Vitamin D3: 500–1,000 IU
- ❏ Fish oils: 500–1,000 mg EPA and DHA

Meats

- ❏ Round steaks and roasts (round eye, top round, bottom round, round tip), top loin, top sirloin, and chuck shoulder and arm roasts
- ❏ Pork loin, tenderloin, center loin

CONDIMENTS

- ❏ Salsa
- ❏ Mustard

Spices and herbs

- ❏ Basil
- ❏ Black pepper
- ❏ Cayenne
- ❏ Chives
- ❏ Cinnamon
- ❏ Cilantro
- ❏ Cloves
- ❏ Garlic
- ❏ Ginger
- ❏ Nutmeg
- ❏ Oregano
- ❏ Parsley
- ❏ Rosemary
- ❏ Tumeric

BEVERAGES

- ❏ Black and green tea
- ❏ Red wine

While you are creating your shopping list, have a healthy snack. The worst thing you can do is go to the grocery store hungry. When your stomach is empty, the sugar swellers and frightful fats will beckon you from afar, persuading you to include them in your shopping cart.

Supermarket Savvy

Have you ever wondered why most grocery stores are set up in a similar manner? This is an attempt by the supermarket industry to maximize their sales without being too obvious. Profits are the store's priority. Choosing healthy foods is up to the consumer. Here are ways to maximize your healthy shopping trip:

- **Attractive Produce:** Think it's a coincidence that you almost always have to walk through the produce department when you enter the supermarket? The look of those shiny, neatly stacked fruits and vegetables is one of the most important influences on where people decide to shop. Invest a good portion of your grocery store time and money in the produce section.
- **The Meating Place:** Since the meat, poultry, and fish sections are the most profitable section of the store, they are always along the back of the supermarket. This is so you'll see them every time you emerge from an aisle. Keep it lean here and focus on fish.
- **On the Edge:** The more time you spend shopping along the sides and back of the supermarket, the more anti-inflammatory fresh foods you will find. On the edge of most stores you'll find fruits and veggies, milk and cheese, and meat, poultry, and fish. While shopping, always abide by the mantra "fresh foods first."
- **Prison Central:** Once you have entered the long, center aisles of a grocery store, you're a prisoner of marketing and placement trickery. This is where the least-fresh, most-processed items are located. This is the time and place to read the labels and not get tricked by sneaky advertisements. Remember, although these foods are convenient, it won't be too convenient if they contribute to the development of inflammation and ultimately chronic disease.

- **Space Eaters:** Some foods are so profitable that they are awarded their own aisles. For example, breakfast cereals bring in more dollars per foot of shelf space than any other product in the interior of the store. Soft drinks, on the other hand, aren't nearly as profitable as cereals on paper, but after cash rebates and free merchandise offers, carbonated soft drinks end up being one of the biggest money-makers in a typical store. That's why the aisles for these foods and beverages are quite extensive. Cereal can be expensive, but this cost can be offset by forgoing calorie and sugar-laden beverages. When choosing cereals, make sure the word "whole" occupies one of the top two items on the ingredients list.
- **Go the Distance:** Did you ever wonder why the dairy section is the farthest from the store entrance? Well, almost everybody buys milk when they shop, and to obtain it they've got to walk all the way through the store. Additionally, did you ever recognize that three other staples, bread, eggs, and butter, occupy the other four corners? This positioning strategy requires that consumers pass by multiple sections of the store, increasing the likelihood that the bottom line on their receipts will grow.

Attacking Inflammation Aisle by Aisle

As you meander throughout the grocery store, there are specific guidelines that you will want to consider when choosing certain foods. Keep in mind that some of your favorite foods may not meet the following guidelines, but this does not mean you should not enjoy them. Moderation is one of the most important guidelines to follow in an anti-inflammatory eating style.

BREADS, CEREALS, AND CRACKERS

- **Whole-grain breads:** These should have no more than 2 grams of fat and 200 milligrams of sodium, and 2 grams of fiber or more per slice, and one or more whole grain(s) should be listed at the beginning of the ingredients.
- **Whole-grain cereals:** Choose cereals made with all or mostly all whole grains, The ideal cereal bowl will provide less than 3 grams of fat and 8 grams of sugar, no more than 350 milligrams of sodium, and at least 4 grams of fiber per cup serving. Check the labels so you can

avoid products containing hydrogenated vegetable oils, whole eggs, egg yolks, or sugar amounting to more than 8 grams per cup. Remember, the lighter the box, the more empty the calories.

- **Whole-grain crackers:** These should have less than 3 grams of total fat, 1 gram of saturated fat per 100 calories, and no more than 200 milligrams of sodium. Also, look for at least 2 grams of fiber per serving and, preferably, whole-grain flour as the main ingredient.
- **Grains and pasta:** Choose brown rice, basmati, bulgur, couscous, barley, kasha, quinoa, corn tortillas, whole-wheat pastas, durum/semolina wheat pastas, and low-fat and low-sodium pasta/rice side dishes.

PASTA SAUCES

- Look for less than 500 milligrams of sodium and 3 grams of total fat per ½ cup serving. Good choices include meatless, mushroom, and vegetable sauces without added cream, cheese, or sugar.

SNACKS AND DESSERTS

- Try to choose snacks made without butter, hydrogenated oils, and/or saturated fat.
- **Popcorn, chips, and pretzels:** Choose unbuttered popcorn or popcorn cakes, baked potato and tortilla chips or pretzels (preferably low-sodium)
- **Frozen treats:** Fruity sherbets, nonfat and low-fat frozen yogurts, 100 percent frozen juice/fruit bars top the list in this department
- **Cookies/brownies:** Less than 15 grams of sugar, no hydrogenated oils, and less than or equal to 25 percent of calories from fat per serving
- **Granola/cereal bars:** Less than or equal to 15 grams of sugar per bar
- **Cakes:** Angel food cake

BAKING INGREDIENTS

- **Egg and sugar substitutes:** These substitutes generally consist of fruit, carbohydrate components, and/or egg whites. They come in various forms, including dried, liquid, and semi-gel. Look for those that are all-natural and have no added sugar.

SOUPS

- Go for soups with less than or equal to 3 grams of fat and 500 milligrams of sodium per serving.
- **Canned soups:** Choose broth- or stock-based soups, preferably low-fat and low-sodium.

PRODUCE SECTION

- **Fruits:** All fresh fruits; canned fruits packed in their own juices; dried fruits; unsweetened applesauce; 100 percent unsweetened fruit juices with no added sugar, avoiding those with pear, apple, or grape as the first ingredient since these are nutritionally poor juice choices.
- **Vegetables:** All fresh vegetables, especially dark-green leafy vegetables; frozen vegetables without butter or cheese sauces; 100 percent vegetable juice with less than or equal to 350 milligrams of sodium per 8-ounce serving.

SALAD DRESSINGS

- Preferably nonfat or low-fat dressings, balsamic vinegar, or lemon juice, with no more than 3 grams of fat and 200 milligrams of sodium per 2-tablespoon serving (1 ounce)

CONDIMENTS

- **Sandwich spreads:** Nonfat or low-fat mayonnaise, regular and flavored mustards (e.g., Dijon and honey mustard)
- **Salt and flavor substitutes:** Salt-free flavoring
- **Herbs and spices:** basil, black pepper, cayenne, chives, cilantro, cinnamon, cloves, garlic, ginger, nutmeg, oregano, parsley, rosemary, turmeric (Note: add herbs and spices during the last fifteen to twenty minutes of cooking for best results)

DAIRY CASE

- **Milk:** Skim or 1% milk
- **Cultured products:** Nonfat or low-fat buttermilk, (1%) cottage cheese, and sour cream
- **Other milks:** Skim or low-fat evaporated milk
- **Yogurt:** Nonfat or low-fat yogurt, preferably without artificial sweeteners and with less than or equal to 2 grams of fat per 6 ounce serving
- **Cheese:** Cheese products with less than 5 grams of fat per ounce or those made with part-skim milk, and nonfat or low-fat cream cheese.
- **Spreads (margarine, butter, etc.):** Whipped, diet, or light margarine or butter in tubs; fat-free butter-flavored sprays. Keep in mind that when it comes to margarine, the softer the better. Also, the healthiest ones list a liquid vegetable oil as the first ingredient rather than a partially hydrogenated oil.

MEAT, POULTRY, AND FISH

- The leanest meat cuts include round steaks and roasts (round eye, top round, bottom round, round tip), top loin, top sirloin, and chuck shoulder and arm roasts. "Select" grades are the leanest.
- Trim away all of the visible fat from meats and poultry before cooking. Choose meats with little marbling.
- Broil, grill, roast, poach, or boil meat, poultry, or fish instead of frying, and drain off any fat that appears during cooking.
- Skip or limit the breading on meat, poultry, or fish. Breading adds fat and calories. It will also cause the food to soak up more fat during frying.
- **Beef:** Choose top round, eye of round, round tip, or extra-lean ground beef. The label should say at least "90% lean." You may be able to find ground beef that is 93% or 95% lean. You can also have the butcher grind up some lean cuts of beef such as round or sirloin tip.
- **Pork:** Choose tenderloin, top loin, Canadian bacon, and very lean Danish ham.
- **Lamb:** Choose leg, loin chop, and shank cuts.

- **Veal:** All cuts of veal are acceptable, with the exception of the fatty breast
- **Chicken:** Choose white breast meat (remove skin before or after cooking).
- **Turkey:** Choose white breast meat (remove skin before or after cooking).
- **Fish and shellfish:** All fish except breaded or fried fish is fine. Fatty fish are high in omega-3 fatty acids. Choose water-packed tuna.
- **Ground meats:** Make sure the meat is ground white meat without dark meat or the skin.

THE DELI

- **Luncheon meats:** These should have no more than 3 grams of fat and less than 500 milligrams of sodium per 2-ounce serving.

VEGETARIAN FOOD PRODUCTS

- **Beans:** Choose fat-free refried beans, canned or dried beans, low-fat vegetarian baked beans.
- **Tofu and tofu-containing products:** Look for those processed with calcium sulfate, preferably the lower-fat versions.
- **Soy cheese, milk, and yogurt:** All types are fine, especially fat-free; also choose calcium-fortified soy products
- **Hummus:** Use as a sandwich spread or dip, but limit portions to 2 to 4 tablespoons per meal.
- **Peanut butter:** Make sure it's "natural" peanut butter and limit portions to 2 tablespoons per meal.
- **Meat substitutes:** Watch out for added oil, hydrogenated fats, and flavorings to mimic the taste of beef franks, salami, and turkey. Some products have 70 percent of their calories from fat and the hydrogenation process will add trans fatty acids.
- **Frozen vegetarian meals:** Aim for no more than 10 grams of total fat and 800 milligrams of sodium per entree.

Food Group	Total Daily Amounts	Breakfast	Snack	Lunch	Snack	Dinner
Grains	6+ servings	1 serving	1 serving	2 servings	1 serving	2 servings
Fruits	2–1/2 cups	1 cup	1 cup	1 cup	1 cup	
Vegetables	3½ cups			1–2 cups	1 cup	2 cups
Meat and Beans	5–7 servings	1 serving	1 serving	2 servings	1 serving	2 servings
Low-Fat Dairy	2–3 servings	1 serving		1 serving		1 serving
Fish Oils	250–500 mg EPA and DHA if you consume 2–3 servings of fatty fish per week					
	1,000 mg EPA and DHA if you do not consume fatty fish					
Vitamin D3	1,000 IU/day					
Exercise	5+ days per week including cardiovascular, strengthening, and flexibility exercise					

Other Anti-Inflammatory Essentials

The addition of a few lifestyle changes to the anti-inflammatory meal plan will make your body resilient to the ravages of inflammation. These lifestyle changes include:

- **Get some zzzz's.** Aim for at least seven to nine hours per night.
- **Exercise regularly.** Exercise at least five days per week, including the three essential components of an exercise program: cardiovascular, strengthening, and flexibility.
- **Manage stress:** Take time for yourself every day to chill out and smell the roses. Schedule regular breathing breaks. Research has shown that taking just one large, deep breath can help alleviate stress and its negative effects on the body.

- **Super supplements:** Supplement your diet every day with 1,000 IUs of vitamin D3 and 1,000 mg DHA and EPA from fish oils.

Following these anti-inflammatory guidelines coupled with bringing into play the anti-inflammatory recipes that follow will help you to progress through life one step ahead of inflammation and chronic disease.

CHAPTER 8

Anti-tizers

Roasted Garlic Served on Crostini

There are countless variations of this classic recipe. The garlic and olive oil will keep inflammation at bay and tantalize your taste buds. You can also try adding herbs such as thyme, sage, or rosemary to "wow" your guests.

INGREDIENTS | SERVES 6

1 bulb garlic
2 tablespoons virgin olive oil
½ bunch fresh parsley
½ loaf baguette

1. Preheat oven to 375°F.

2. Cut off the top quarter of the garlic bulb. Rub both cut sides of garlic with olive oil, then place the top back on the bulb and wrap in foil. Place in the oven and bake until the cloves are fork tender, about 5 to 10 minutes.

3. While the garlic cooks, chop the parsley. Slice the baguette thinly on the bias. Brush with the oil and place on a baking sheet. Toast until light brown.

4. Serve the bulb intact on a platter surrounded by crostini and sprinkled with parsley.

PER SERVING: Calories: 115 | Fat: 5 g | Protein: 2 g | Sodium: 127 mg | Fiber: 0 g | Carbohydrate: 16 g

Marinated Portobello Mushrooms

Portobello mushrooms have such a meaty flavor that they can be used in place of meat in many recipes. They will boost your fiber, protein, and B vitamin intake. They also give you a nice dose of the antioxidants vitamin C and selenium. Free radicals beware!

INGREDIENTS | SERVES 6

6 portobello mushrooms
1 teaspoon extra-virgin olive oil
2 teaspoons balsamic vinegar
Pinch of iodized salt
Freshly cracked black pepper, to taste
¼ bunch marjoram
¼ bunch oregano

1. Remove the stems from the caps of the mushrooms and scrape out the black membrane. Slice the stems in half.

2. Mix together the remaining ingredients. Combine the caps and stems with the marinade in a plastic container; marinate for at least 3 hours.

3. Preheat oven to 400°F.

4. Roast the mushrooms for 15 to 20 minutes on oven rack. Cut the caps into small wedges and serve.

PER SERVING: Calories: 25 | Fat: 1.5 g | Protein: 1 g | Sodium: 53 mg | Fiber: 1 g | Carbohydrate: 2 g

Vegetable Kebabs

Talk about a serious phytochemical concoction. Inflammation will shy away from this appetizer. Serve these kebabs as an appetizer at parties so your guests can easily handle the food without using cutlery.

INGREDIENTS | SERVES 6

Wooden skewers

12 scallions

1 large red pepper

1 large yellow pepper

1 large green pepper

12 large button mushrooms

1 tablespoon olive oil

Freshly cracked black pepper, to taste

Kosher salt, to taste

Soaking the Skewers

When using wooden skewers in cooking, always soak them in water for an hour before spearing the food items. Soaking the skewers allows you to place them on the grill for a time without them burning.

1. Cut standard wooden skewers in half for appetizer-size portions, then soak the skewers in water for a minimum of 1 hour.

2. Preheat grill or broiler.

3. Trim off the roots and dark green parts of the scallions. Dice the peppers into large pieces.

4. Thread the vegetables on to the skewers, and brush all sides of the vegetables with oil. Season with pepper and salt.

5. Place the skewers on the grill or under the broiler, paying close attention as they cook, as they can easily burn. Cook until the vegetables are fork tender.

PER SERVING: Calories: 38 | Fat: 2.5 g | Protein: 1 g | Sodium: 3.5 mg | Fiber: 2 g | Carbohydrate: 4 g

Haddock Fish Cakes

*This version of a familiar fish cake has the fresh flavor of haddock.
Serve this with a spicy sauce or a fresh spritz of lemon.*

INGREDIENTS | SERVES 6

1 pound haddock

2 leeks

1 red pepper

2 egg whites

Pinch of kosher salt

Freshly cracked black pepper, to taste

1 tablespoon olive oil

1. Finely shred the raw fish with a fork. Dice the leeks and red pepper. Combine all the ingredients except the oil in a medium-size bowl; mix well. Form the mixture into small oval patties.

2. Heat the oil in a medium-size sauté pan. Place the cakes in the pan and loosely cover with the lid; sauté the cakes for 4 to 6 minutes on each side. Drain on a rack covered with paper towels; serve immediately.

PER SERVING: Calories: 97 | Fat: 3 g | Protein: 13 g | Sodium: 67 mg | Fiber: 1 g | Carbohydrate: 5 g

Thai Peanut Sauce

This is a great sauce for grilled or broiled chicken and beef skewers. It will keep in the refrigerator, covered, for up to a week. Bring to room temperature before serving.

INGREDIENTS | SERVES 4

2 tablespoons water

¼ cup creamy peanut butter

2 tablespoons tamari

1 teaspoon red pepper flakes

2 teaspoons sesame oil

2 tablespoons chopped unsalted peanuts, for garnish (optional)

1. Place all the ingredients (except the peanuts) in the bowl of a food processor fitted with a metal blade or in a blender (or blend by hand with a sturdy whisk); cover and process until smooth. Add a little more water if necessary to adjust the consistency.

2. Place the sauce in a small serving bowl and garnish with the chopped peanuts.

PER SERVING: Calories: 146 | Fat: 13 g | Protein: 6 g | Sodium: 502 mg | Fiber: 1.5 g | Carbohydrate: 5 g

Island-Style Shrimp Cocktail

A nice twist on the traditional shrimp cocktail.
And it's easy to pack up to take to summer outdoor barbecues.

INGREDIENTS | SERVES 4

1 teaspoon minced garlic

¼ teaspoon salt

1 tablespoon minced fresh ginger

3 tablespoons finely chopped scallions

1 tablespoon finely chopped jalapeño
 pepper

¼ cup freshly squeezed lime juice

Sugar substitute equal to 2 tablespoons
 sugar

1 tablespoon canola oil

1 pound extra-large (21- to 25-count)
 shrimp, peeled, tails left on

¼ teaspoon salt

¼ teaspoon ground black pepper

Lemon and lime wedges

1. Combine the garlic, salt, ginger, scallions, jalapeño, lime juice, and sugar substitute in a small serving bowl and set aside.

2. Heat the oil in a medium-size, heavy-bottomed nonstick skillet over high heat until it starts to smoke. Season the shrimp with salt and pepper. Add the shrimp to the skillet and sauté until cooked through, about 2 minutes. Remove skillet from heat and immediately add 2 tablespoons of the jalapeño-lime sauce to the skillet; toss to coat the shrimp.

3. Transfer the shrimp to a baking sheet to cool for about 5 minutes. To serve, arrange the shrimp on a platter with the bowl of sauce. Garnish with lemon and lime wedges.

PER SERVING: Calories: 133 | Fat: 5 g | Protein: 17 g |
Sodium: 418 mg | Fiber: 0 g | Carbohydrate: 4 g

Is the Pan Hot Enough?

Hold your hand about 4 inches over the pan and count to 3. You shouldn't be able to keep your hand comfortably over the pan for more than 3 seconds. Avoid using extra-virgin olive oil for this dish. The high cooking temperature may give the oil an unusual flavor.

Turkey Meatballs with Fruit Sauce

This is a tasty change of pace. The fruit complements the turkey beautifully.
Use ground turkey breast, which contains white meat only.

INGREDIENTS | SERVES 6

Olive oil

2 slices toasted 100% whole-wheat bread

1 pound ground turkey breast

¼ cup dried cranberries

¼ cup chopped pecans

1 egg

¼ teaspoon cinnamon

¼ teaspoon curry powder

Pinch of kosher salt

Freshly cracked black pepper, to taste

½ cup Apple Chutney (see Chapter 17)

1. Preheat oven to 350°F. Brush a baking dish with oil.

2. Soak the bread in water until completely saturated and then squeeze out the excess liquid. Mix together the soaked bread and all the remaining ingredients in a bowl. Shape the mixture into small balls. Place the balls in the prepared baking dish. Cover with foil and bake for about 20 minutes. Serve with Apple Chutney (Chapter 17).

PER SERVING [WITHOUT APPLE CHUTNEY]: Calories: 140 | Fat: 7 g | Protein: 19 g | Sodium: 61 mg | Fiber: 1 g | Carbohydrate: 5 g

Artist at Work

Always keep a pastry brush or a small natural-bristle food-quality paintbrush handy as one of your basic kitchen tools. They are great for getting just the right amount of oil in a pan or for brushing food with a light layer of oil before cooking.

Asian Sesame Chicken Skewers

You can make the marinade and trim the chicken a day ahead.
Cook just before serving. This goes great with the Thai Peanut Sauce recipe earlier in this chapter.

INGREDIENTS | SERVES 8

24–30 (6-inch) wooden skewers

½ cup canned low-sodium chicken stock

¼ cup chopped fresh cilantro, plus extra for garnish

2 tablespoons tamari or low-sodium soy sauce

2 tablespoons sesame oil

2 garlic cloves, minced

4–5 drops (or to taste) hot sauce

1½ pounds boneless, skinless chicken breasts (about 6 halves)

Black sesame seeds, for garnish (about 2 tablespoons)

1. Place the wooden skewers in a tall glass of water to soak for at least 15 minutes while preparing the chicken. (This will help prevent them from burning under the broiler.)

2. To make the marinade, combine the stock, cilantro, tamari, sesame oil, garlic, and hot sauce in a medium-size bowl; whisk until blended.

3. Rinse the chicken under cold running water and pat dry with paper towels. Cut the chicken into ½-inch-wide strips the length of the breast. You should have about 18 to 24 strips. (The strips will vary somewhat in size.) Add the chicken strips to the marinade, cover, and refrigerate for 15 minutes.

4. Just before preparing to serve, lightly oil a broiler rack and position it about 4 inches from the heat source. Preheat oven broiler to medium.

5. Remove the chicken strips from the marinade and discard the marinade. Thread one strip on a presoaked wooden skewer. Thread the remaining chicken on the remaining skewers. (Threading the strips in the form of an S will help them stay on the skewer.)

6. Place the skewers on the broiler rack and broil for about 3 minutes. Turn the skewers over and broil for another 3 to 4 minutes, until the chicken is no longer pink. Remove from the oven and sprinkle with sesame seeds and chopped cilantro. Serve hot.

PER SERVING: Calories: 153 | Fat: 7 g | Protein: 21 g | Sodium: 340 mg | Fiber: 0.5 g | Carbohydrate: 1 g

Beef Tenderloin Bites with Creamy Horseradish Sauce

This is a delicious and impressive appetizer—well worth the cost.
The horseradish sauce can be made a day or two in advance and kept refrigerated.

INGREDIENTS | SERVES 6

¼ cup prepared horseradish

½ cup low-fat or fat-free sour cream or nonfat yogurt

2 (6-ounce) filet mignon steaks

1½ tablespoons olive oil

¼ teaspoon kosher salt

Freshly cracked black pepper, to taste

12 Asian soup spoons

12 toothpicks

Chopped fresh parsley, for garnish

How Do You Like It?

The beef tenderloin can be bought in 6-ounce steaks, already trimmed and ready to cook. If you like your beef rare, leave the steaks in the refrigerator until ready to cook. If you like your beef more well done, let the steaks come to room temperature before cooking. The internal temperature of the meat before cooking will help control the final outcome.

1. In a small bowl, mix together the horseradish and sour cream. Set aside.

2. Cut each steak into 6 cubes as evenly sized as possible. Transfer to a medium-size bowl and toss with 1 tablespoon of the olive oil, salt, and pepper until evenly coated.

3. Heat the remaining ½ tablespoon of olive oil in a nonstick sauté pan over medium-high heat. When very hot, but not smoking, add the beef cubes and sear on each side for about 1 minute per side for rare, about 1½ minutes per side for medium.

4. Transfer the meat to a plate and tent with tinfoil to keep warm. Let rest for about 7 minutes to allow the juices to reabsorb.

5. To serve, arrange the spoons on a serving platter. Use a toothpick to spear a piece of meat and place it on one of the spoons; continue with the remaining pieces. Drizzle any remaining beef juices over each piece. Add a dollop of the horseradish sauce just to the side of each piece of beef. Garnish with the chopped parsley and serve warm.

PER SERVING: Calories: 106 | Fat: 5.5 g | Protein: 9.5 g | Sodium: 177 mg | Fiber: 0.5 g | Carbohydrate: 4.5 g

Groovy Guacamole

A favorite party appetizer with a major healthy punch. Inflammation will stay away from any party serving this as an appetizer.

INGREDIENTS | SERVES 4

2 large ripe avocados, coarsely chopped

1 small white onion, diced

1 tomato, unpeeled and diced

1 jalapeño pepper, thinly sliced

Juice of 1 lime

Salt, to taste

Gently combine all the ingredients in a serving bowl and serve as a salad or dip for whole-grain tortilla chips.

PER SERVING: Calories: 136 | Fat: 11 g | Protein: 2 g | Sodium: 6.5 mg | Fiber: 5.5 g | Carbohydrate: 8 g

Avocados 101

Avocados are the main ingredient in guacamole. They may be high in fat, but it is the good anti-inflammatory, monounsaturated type. Avocados are also favorably high in fiber, potassium, many B vitamins, and vitamin E. Avocados darken easily when exposed to air, so it is best to save any leftovers with the pits and keep them in a tightly sealed container in the refrigerator. Use of lemon and lime juice in recipes will also keep discoloration at bay.

Fresh Pepper Salsa

Tomatoes are a great source of the antioxidant vitamin C, but are also classified as a nightshade vegetable. Try this salsa without worrying about inflammation. You can also get creative and make your salsa with other vegetables, fruits, and spices.

INGREDIENTS | YIELDS 1 PINT

1 yellow bell pepper
1 orange bell pepper
1 or 2 poblano chilies
2 Anaheim chilies
1 or 2 jalapeño peppers
2 cloves garlic
¼ of a red onion
Juice of ½ lime
Freshly crushed black pepper, to taste
Canola oil (enough to coat the pan)
Cilantro, chopped, to taste (optional)

1. Place all ingredients (except the oil) in a food processor and pulse until desired chunkiness results. Taste and adjust for saltiness and heat.

2. In a medium pot, heat oil until slightly smoking. Add blended pepper mixture. Cook on high for 8 to 10 minutes, stirring occasionally. Sprinkle some chopped cilantro on top, if desired. Serve hot, cold, or at room temperature with tortilla chips, as a garnish for fish or poultry, or in your favorite burrito.

PER SERVING: Calories: 104 | Fat: 1 g | Protein: 3 g | Sodium: 6 mg | Fiber: 6 g | Carbohydrate: 23 g

Traditional Hummus

Hummus is a popular dish throughout the Middle East and Mediterranean. It is a great source of iron and vitamin C, making it ideal for vegetarians, especially vegans. It also offers plenty of protein, fiber, and healthy monounsaturated fats.

INGREDIENTS | SERVES 6

1 lemon
¼ bunch fresh parsley
1 cup chickpeas (or other type of white bean), cooked
½ bulb roasted garlic
2 teaspoons extra-virgin olive oil
1 to 2 tablespoons tahini paste
Freshly cracked black pepper, to taste
Kosher salt or sea salt, to taste (optional)

1. Zest and juice the lemon. Chop the parsley.

2. In a blender, purée the cooked chickpeas, then add the garlic, lemon zest, and juice. Continue to purée until the mixture is thoroughly combined. Drizzle in the olive oil in a stream while continuing to purée until all the oil is incorporated and the mixture is smooth. Remove the mixture from the blender and season with salt and pepper. Adjust seasonings to taste. Before serving, sprinkle with chopped parsley.

PER SERVING: Calories: 143 | Fat: 3 g | Protein: 7 g | Sodium: 10 mg | Fiber: 6 g | Carbohydrate: 22 g

Fava Bean Hummus with Tahini and Pistachios

If you need extra liquid to help purée the fava beans, you may add olive oil or a splash of vegetable broth, but don't overdo it. The hummus should be thick, not runny. Serve this with toasted pita pieces or bagel chips or with fresh vegetables for dunking.

INGREDIENTS | SERVES 6

1 (15-ounce) can fava beans, drained and rinsed

3 cloves garlic, or to taste

Juice from 1 lemon, or more to taste

3 tablespoons olive oil, or more as needed to process

1 to 2 tablespoons tahini paste

Salt and freshly ground black pepper, to taste

½ cup minced parsley

¾ cup toasted pistachios

1. Put the beans, garlic, lemon juice, olive oil, tahini, salt, and pepper into a food processor or blender and purée.

2. Spoon the mixture into a bowl and stir in the parsley and pistachios. Chill until serving time.

PER SERVING: Calories: 217 | Fat: 15 g | Protein: 8 g | Sodium: 328 mg | Fiber: 4.5 g | Carbohydrate: 15 g

Avocado Cumin Dip

The unique flavor of cumin complements the avocado without being overbearing. This dip is perfect with a south-of-the-border menu or spread on warm tortilla chips.

INGREDIENTS | SERVES 4

2 medium-size ripe avocados

2 tablespoons fresh lemon juice

2 tablespoons extra-virgin olive oil

⅛ teaspoon garlic powder

1 tablespoon chives

1 teaspoon sea salt

1 teaspoon ground cumin

Dash of hot sauce

1. Peel and seed the avocados; in a medium-size bowl mash the meat until smooth.

2. Add remaining ingredients; mix to combine thoroughly.

3. Cover and keep in the refrigerator until ready to serve. Letting this dip sit for 15 minutes helps to blend the flavors.

PER SERVING: Calories: 184 | Fat: 18 g | Protein: 1.5 g | Sodium: 581 mg | Fiber: 5 g | Carbohydrate: 7.5 g

Curry-Cayenne Peanuts

The key to success for this recipe is a premium-quality curry powder and freshly shelled unsalted peanuts.

INGREDIENTS | SERVES 12

1 large egg white

2 tablespoons curry powder

1½ teaspoons kosher salt

Sugar substitute equal to 1 teaspoon
  granulated sugar

¼ teaspoon cayenne pepper

3 cups unsalted peanuts, shelled

Pea-nutty

Peanuts are actually not nuts at all. They are part of the legume "bean" family. They provide over 30 essential nutrients and phytochemicals. Even though peanuts are considered high in fat, they contain the good monounsaturated type of fat. Just keep an eye on your portions. Your waistline will thank you.

1. Preheat oven to 300°F.

2. Line 2 baking sheets with parchment paper and set aside.

3. In a medium-size bowl, whip the egg white until frothy. Add the curry powder, salt, sugar substitute, and cayenne pepper; whisk until evenly blended. Add the peanuts and stir until evenly coated.

4. Spread the nuts in a single layer on the prepared baking sheets. Roast, uncovered, for about 20 minutes until the nuts are dry and toasted. Stir and turn the nuts at least 2 times during the roasting process. (Be very watchful during the last half of baking, as the nuts can burn quickly.) Remove the nuts from the oven and transfer them to a sheet of parchment paper to cool.

PER SERVING: Calories: 219 | Fat: 18 g | Protein: 9 g | Sodium: 250 mg | Fiber: 3 g | Carbohydrate: 8.5 g

Hot Crabmeat Dip

Canned crabmeat works better than fresh crabmeat for this dish.
Serve as a dip with raw vegetables and whole-wheat crackers.

INGREDIENTS | SERVES 10

8 ounces low-fat or fat-free cream cheese, at room temperature

7½ ounces canned crabmeat

2 tablespoons finely chopped yellow onion

2 tablespoons low-fat milk

1 teaspoon prepared horseradish

1 teaspoon seasoned salt

Freshly cracked black pepper, to taste

⅓ cup sliced almonds

1. Preheat oven to 375°F.

2. Combine the cream cheese, crabmeat, onion, milk, horseradish, salt, and pepper in a medium-size bowl; mix until well blended.

3. Transfer the crabmeat mixture to a 9-inch pie plate or ovenproof dish and sprinkle with the sliced almonds. Bake uncovered for 15 minutes until hot and bubbly. Serve hot.

PER SERVING: Calories: 67 | Fat: 3 g | Protein: 7.5 g | Sodium: 210 mg | Fiber: 0.5 g | Carbohydrate: 2.5 g

Spicy Roasted Chickpeas

Spicy roasted chickpeas provide a nice dose of fiber and protein
without the fat and calories of regular nuts and seeds.

INGREDIENTS | SERVES 8

2 tablespoons olive oil

½ teaspoon each ground coriander, ground cumin, and red pepper flakes

¼ teaspoon seasoned salt

2 cups canned chickpeas, rinsed and drained

1. Preheat oven to 400°F. Spray a nonstick baking sheet with nonstick spray and set aside.

2. Combine the oil and seasonings together in a medium-size bowl. Add the chickpeas and toss until evenly coated. Spread out the beans in a single layer on the prepared baking sheet and place in the oven. Shake the pan every 10 minutes to make sure the beans are cooking evenly. Bake for 20 to 30 minutes, until crisp and golden. Let cool slightly before serving. Can be made the day before and kept in an airtight container.

PER SERVING: Calories: 101 | Fat: 4 g | Protein: 3 g | Sodium: 252 mg | Fiber: 2.6 g | Carbohydrate: 14 g

CHAPTER 9

Breathtaking Breakfasts

Fruit-Stuffed French Toast

The eggy flavor of challah creates the rich profile of this dish. If you never stray from whole grains, replace the challah with 100 percent whole-wheat bread.

INGREDIENTS | SERVES 6

½ teaspoon olive oil

3 small to medium loaves challah bread

1 pint seasonal fresh fruit

2 whole eggs or ½ cup egg substitute

4 egg whites

¼ cup skim milk

1 cup orange juice

¼ cup nonfat plain yogurt

¼ cup confectioners' sugar

1. Preheat oven to 375°F. Grease a baking sheet with the oil.

2. Slice the bread into thick (2½- to 3-inch) slices with a serrated knife at a severe angle to form long bias slices (a medium-large loaf of challah will yield 3 thick bias slices). Cut a slit into the bottom crust to form a pocket.

3. Peel the fruit if necessary, then dice into large pieces and fill the pockets in the bread. Press the pocket closed.

4. In a large mixing bowl, beat the eggs and egg whites, then add the milk. Dip the bread into the egg mixture, letting it fully absorb the mixture. Place the bread on the prepared baking sheet. Bake for 10 minutes on one side, flip, and bake 10 minutes more.

5. While the bread is baking, pour the orange juice in small saucepan; boil until reduced by half and the mixture becomes syrupy. Remove the French toast from the oven, and cut in half diagonally. Serve each with dollop of yogurt, a drizzle of juice, and a sprinkling of sugar.

PER SERVING: Calories: 202 | Fat: 2.5 g | Protein: 10 g | Sodium: 289 mg | Fiber: 2.5 g | Carbohydrate: 36 g

Blackberry Buckwheat Flapjacks

The seeds of blackberries are a good source of fiber, omega-3 fatty acids, and protein. These berries are available to enjoy fresh and frozen all year round.

INGREDIENTS | SERVES 4

½ cup all-purpose flour
½ cup 100% whole-wheat flour
½ cup buckwheat flour
3 tablespoons sugar
1½ teaspoons baking powder
1 teaspoon baking soda
½ teaspoon salt
2 eggs or ½ cup egg substitute
3 tablespoons melted butter
1½ cups buttermilk
1 cup blackberries

The Fruit of Knowledge

Although many people believe that buckwheat is a cereal grain, it is actually a fruit. It is ideal for individuals sensitive to wheat or other grains that contain protein glutens. Not only is this fruit being used in gluten-free foods, but it is now sneaking into energy bars and meatless entrees, and being used as a fat replacement.

1. Whisk together the three flours, sugar, baking powder, baking soda, and salt in a large bowl.

2. Whisk together eggs, melted butter, and buttermilk in another bowl.

3. Stir egg mixture into the flour mixture until combined. There will be lumps; be careful not to over-mix.

4. Pour about ⅓ cup batter for each pancake onto a hot oiled griddle or pan. Scatter several blackberries on top of batter. Flip pancake when bubbles have formed and started to pop through the batter. Cook on other side for a minute.

5. Serve hot with maple syrup.

PER SERVING: Calories: 352 | Fat: 12 | Protein: 13 g | Sodium: 448 mg | Fiber: 5.5 g | Carbohydrate: 56 g

Crepes with Blueberry Sauce

This crepe recipe can be used with roasted vegetables and Walnut-Parsley Pesto (Chapter 17), or with other cooked vegetables and topped with grated Romano cheese.

INGREDIENTS | SERVES 8

Crepes

4 eggs

1 cup soy or rice milk

½ cup water

½ teaspoon sea salt

1 cup spelt flour

3 tablespoons melted butter

Apple-Blueberry Filling

1 apple

1 pear

1 teaspoon stevia powder

1 cup water

2 cups blueberries

1 tablespoon cornstarch

Cinnamon, to taste (optional)

Herbal Sweetener

Stevia is an herbal sweetener used by diabetics and dieters. It can help balance blood sugar levels. It is 300 times sweeter than regular sugar, contains no calories, and is heat-stable. Finally, a great alternative to refined and artificial sweeteners!

Crepe

1. Combine all crepe ingredients in a blender; purée until smooth. Scrape sides and purée until everything is combined. Place in fridge for at least 2 hours, or overnight.

2. Heat a crepe pan; spray with oil. When hot, pour ¼ cup batter onto a 10-inch pan (2 tablespoons for a 7-inch pan); swirl around to cover the bottom. Cook until browned on bottom, about 1 minute.

3. Loosen the crepe with a spatula or knife; flip with your fingers. Cook the second side for about 30 seconds.

4. Stack the crepes to keep them warm; cover with a clean cloth towel.

Filling

1. Peel and core the apple and pear; slice and place in a heavy saucepan with sweetener and ½ cup water.

2. Add the blueberries; bring mixture to a simmer; cook until fruit is tender, about 10 minutes.

3. Dissolve the corn starch in the remaining water; add to the fruit while cooking. Stir until liquid thickens. Remove from heat and set aside.

4. Lay out a crepe on a plate; spoon some of the fruit mixture onto one half of the crepe. Fold the crepe over; sprinkle cinnamon on top, if desired.

PER SERVING: Calories: 185 | Fat: 8 g | Protein: 6.5 g | Sodium: 197 mg | Fiber: 3.5 g | Carbohydrate: 24 g

Banana–Oat Bran Waffles

Use either a standard nonstick waffle iron or a Belgian nonstick one that makes waffles with deep indentations to hold pools of rich maple syrup. This recipe yields 6 Belgian waffle squares, or 3 rectangles, but the yield may differ according to the size of your waffle iron.

INGREDIENTS | SERVES 4

2 large eggs or ½ cup egg substitute

1 cup buttermilk

2 very ripe bananas

4 tablespoons melted butter plus extra for serving

½ cup all-purpose flour

½ cup 100% whole-wheat flour

½ cup oat bran

2 teaspoons baking powder

½ teaspoon salt

½ cup crushed pecans

Maple syrup or other fruit syrup for serving

1. Preheat the waffle iron. Spray both surfaces with nonstick cooking spray.

2. Beat together the eggs, buttermilk, bananas, and butter until well blended and smooth. Fold in the flour, oat bran, baking powder, and salt, stirring until just combined and moistened; the batter should be stiff, not runny. Fold in the pecans.

3. Bake waffles according to the manufacturer's directions. Serve hot with extra butter and maple syrup.

PER SERVING: Calories: 487 | Fat: 25 g | Protein: 14 g | Sodium: 417 mg | Fiber: 9 g | Carbohydrate: 65 g

What's Oat Bran?

Because it is so high in fiber, oat bran has become one of the darlings of the health food world and is often touted as one of the soluble-fiber foods that help lower cholesterol levels in the blood. It's also a welcome ingredient in the kitchen for its cookability in cereals, baked goods, soups, and stews, adding some texture and a delicate nutty taste.

Edamame Omelet

The addition of cheese turns this into a fusion dish; to add more Asian flavors, you might want to stir in some shredded daikon and crushed chilies to taste into the mix.

INGREDIENTS | SERVES 2

3 tablespoons olive oil, divided

1 teaspoon minced garlic

1 bunch scallions, trimmed and cut into 1-inch pieces

½ cup shelled edamame

1 tablespoon low-sodium soy sauce, or to taste

3 large eggs or ¾ cup egg substitute

½ cup shredded regular or soy Cheddar cheese

Snips of fresh cilantro, for garnish

1. Heat 2 tablespoons oil in a small skillet over medium heat and sauté the garlic and scallion for about 2 minutes. Add the edamame and soy sauce and sauté 1 minute more. Remove from the skillet and set aside.

2. Heat the remaining 1 tablespoon oil in the same skillet. Beat the eggs until mixed and pour into the hot oil. Scatter the shredded cheese on top. Lift up the edges of the omelet, tipping the skillet back and forth to cook the uncooked eggs. When the top looks firm, sprinkle the scallion mixture over one half of the omelet and fold the other half over top.

3. Carefully lift the omelet out of the skillet. Divide it in half, sprinkle with the cilantro, and serve.

PER SERVING: Calories: 416 | Fat: 31 g | Protein: 27 g | Sodium: 640 g | Fiber: 3 g | Carbohydrate: 7.5 g

Almond Mascarpone Dumplings

Mascarpone is Italy's answer to cream cheese, with much more flavor.

INGREDIENTS | SERVES 6

1 cup whole-wheat flour

1 cup all-purpose unbleached flour

¼ cup ground almonds

4 egg whites

3 ounces mascarpone cheese

1 teaspoon extra-virgin olive oil

2 teaspoons apple juice

1 tablespoon butter

¼ cup honey

1. Sift together both types of flour in a large bowl. Mix in the almonds. In a separate bowl, cream together the egg whites, cheese, oil, and juice on medium speed with an electric mixer.

2. Combine the flour and egg white mixture with a dough hook on medium speed or by hand until a dough forms.

3. Boil 1 gallon water in a medium-size saucepot. Take a spoonful of the dough and use a second spoon to push it into the boiling water. Cook until the dumpling floats to the top, about 5 to 10 minutes. You can cook several dumplings at once—just take care not to crowd the pot. Remove with a slotted spoon and drain on paper towels.

4. Heat a medium-size sauté pan on medium-high heat. Add the butter, then place the dumplings in the pan and cook until light brown. Place on serving plates and drizzle with honey.

PER SERVING: Calories: 254 | Fat: 6.4 g | Protein: 7 g | Sodium: 20 mg | Fiber: 3.5 g | Carbohydrate: 44 g

Raisin Bran Muffins

A breakfast of a glass of orange juice (with pulp) and a bran muffin is a delicious way to start your day with fiber. The raisins add sweetness and fiber, and you can substitute whole-wheat flour for all-purpose flour to add even more fiber.

INGREDIENTS | MAKES 36 MUFFINS

1 cup boiling water

2½ cups All-Bran cereal

2½ cups all-purpose flour

2½ teaspoons baking soda

1 teaspoon salt

½ cup vegetable oil

1 cup sugar

2 eggs, beaten

2 cups buttermilk

1½ cups raisins

1 cup bran flakes

Quick Breads Versus Muffins

Most quick-bread recipes can be used for muffins. You will get a dozen standard muffins or 24 mini-muffins. Always prepare your muffin tins with nonstick spray, even those tins that are supposedly nonstick. Muffins bake in about 15–20 minutes and make nice equal portions. Never overfill the muffin cups or they will rise and lap over the pan.

1. Preheat oven to 400°F. Grease a muffin tin or line it with fluted paper cups. Pour the boiling water over 1 cup All-Bran, and let sit for 10 minutes.

2. Mix the flour, baking soda, and salt in a mixing bowl and set aside.

3. Mix the oil into the bran and water mixture, then add the remaining bran, sugar, eggs, and buttermilk.

4. Add the flour mixture to the bran mixture and mix to combine. Stir in the raisins and bran flakes and fill the muffin cups ¾ full with the batter.

5. Bake muffins for 20 minutes.

PER SERVING: Calories: 104 | Fat: 4 g | Protein: 2.5 g | Sodium: 187 mg | Fiber: 2 g | Carbohydrate: 17 g

Apple Bread

Moist and full of apples, this bread is a great snack with a piece of Cheddar cheese.
You give your family fiber with great flavor coming from the whole-wheat flour and apples.

INGREDIENTS | SERVES 8

1 packet yeast

3 tablespoons sugar

1⅓ cups warm water

3 tablespoons soft butter

1 teaspoon salt

¼ teaspoon baking powder

1¾ cups all-purpose flour

1¾ cups whole-wheat flour

1 cup peeled, chopped apples

1 tablespoon cinnamon mixed with 1 tablespoon sugar

100% Whole Wheat Takeover

If you want to boost the nutritional payoff of your recipes, you can replace white flour with whole-wheat flour by substituting one for one. However, products made with whole-wheat flour will be more dense. Try sifting the flour a few extra times to incorporate more air, resulting in a lighter, more tender final product.

1. Combine yeast, ½ teaspoon sugar, and ⅓ cup water in a bowl. Let sit for 5 minutes.

2. In a mixing bowl, combine remaining water, butter, remaining sugar, salt, and baking powder. Mix in the all-purpose flour and then the yeast mixture with an electric mixer. Add the whole-wheat flour. Knead with a dough hook for 10 minutes.

3. Turn dough into an oiled bowl. Cover and let rise in a warm place for 1 to 2 hours until doubled in bulk.

4. Punch down dough, then roll it into a rectangle. Scatter the apples over the dough and sprinkle them with the cinnamon sugar. Roll into a cylinder and place in an oiled loaf pan. Cover and let it rise in a warm place for 90 minutes until doubled in size.

5. Preheat oven to 350°F. Uncover bread and bake for 50 minutes.

PER SERVING: Calories: 258 | Fat: 5 g | Protein: 7 g | Sodium: 294 mg | Fiber: 4.5 g | Carbohydrate: 48 g

Zucchini Bread

This interesting zucchini bread has crunchy pecans and chewy raisins for added flavor and fiber.
When you add nuts to any recipe, you also add protein.

INGREDIENTS | SERVES 16

1½ cups all-purpose flour

1½ cups 100% whole-wheat flour

1 teaspoon salt

1 teaspoon baking soda

¼ teaspoon baking powder

1 tablespoon cinnamon

3 eggs, beaten, or ¾ cup of egg
   substitute

1 cup canola oil

2 cups sugar

2 cups grated zucchini

1 cup chopped pecans

1 cup raisins

1. Preheat oven to 350°F. Oil 2 loaf pans and set aside.

2. Combine the flour, salt, baking soda, baking powder, and cinnamon in a bowl.

3. Mix the eggs, oil, and sugar in another bowl.

4. Add the zucchini and dry ingredients alternately until fully incorporated into a smooth batter. Fold in the pecans and raisins and scrape the batter into the loaf pans.

5. Bake for 60 minutes, cool on a rack, and wrap when cool.

PER SERVING: Calories: 396 | Fat: 20 | Protein: 5 g | Sodium: 237 mg | Fiber: 3 g | Carbohydrate: 52 g

Zucchini and Carrot Bread

Adding vegetables to bread started during World War II when flour was rationed. Resourceful cooks substituted vegetables for flour. Today, this is done to add fiber and flavor to quick breads. Zucchini is a wonderful bread to make when you have a garden that is overproducing zucchini! Make extra loaves and freeze them for a nice treat in December.

Oatmeal-Raisin Scones

These luscious scones pack a whopping punch of fiber from oats, wheat germ, and raisins. Try using Irish oatmeal for these scones, but soak them first. Steel-cut oats will give you the most fiber while instant oats will have the least.

INGREDIENTS | SERVES 6

1½ cups rolled oats

½ cup all-purpose flour

2 tablespoons wheat germ

3 tablespoons sugar

½ teaspoon salt

1⅛ teaspoons baking powder

6 tablespoons cold, unsalted butter, cut in pieces

2 eggs or ½ cup egg substitute

⅔ cup buttermilk

½ teaspoon vanilla

1 cup raisins

1 egg white

2 tablespoons granulated sugar

Outrageous Oats

Oats are one of the best sources for soluble fiber, which is important in regulating cholesterol in the bloodstream. Also, oats lose only the outer husk during the milling process, so they are more nutritious than refined wheat.

1. Preheat oven to 400°F. Line a baking pan with parchment paper or spray lightly with oil. Grind half of the oats into flour in a food processor.

2. Combine remaining oats, oat flour, all-purpose flour, wheat germ, sugar, salt, baking powder, and butter in a food processor with a metal blade. Process until mixture resembles cornmeal.

3. In a large bowl, whisk together eggs, buttermilk, and vanilla. Stir in raisins with a spatula or wooden spoon.

4. Add dry ingredients and fold in with spatula. Drop scones into rounds onto prepared baking sheet.

5. Brush scones with egg white and sprinkle with granulated sugar. Bake for 15 minutes.

PER SERVING: Calories: 456 | Fat: 16 g | Protein: 13 g | Sodium: 277 mg | Fiber: 6 g | Carbohydrate: 70 g

Breakfast Fruit Bars

Deliciously portable, these nutrient-packed goodies taste like a cross between a granola bar and a blueberry muffin, and the cream cheese frosting brings it all together. Try using fresh or frozen cranberries in place of the blueberries.

INGREDIENTS | SERVES 6

1 stick of butter, softened

¾ cup firmly packed dark brown sugar

½ cup granulated sugar

2 large eggs or ½ cup egg substitute

1 teaspoon vanilla extract

2 cups old-fashioned rolled oats

1 cup 100% whole-wheat flour

1 teaspoon baking powder

1 teaspoon salt

2 cups blueberries, fresh or frozen

½ cup slivered almonds, optional

Whipped fat-free cream cheese for spreading, optional

1. Preheat the oven to 350°F. Butter and flour an 8" × 8" baking pan.

2. Beat the butter with the sugars until creamy. Add the eggs, one at a time, and beat well after each addition. Beat in the vanilla extract.

3. Stir or beat in the oats, flour, baking power, and salt until well combined. Fold in the blueberries and the almonds, if using. Spoon the mixture into the prepared pan.

4. Bake for about 40 minutes or until the center feels firm, the edges are brown, and a toothpick inserted in the center comes out clean. Remove and set aside to cool. Slice into squares and frost with fat-free cream cheese, if desired.

PER SERVING: Calories: 662 | Fat: 24 g | Protein: 16 g | Sodium: 594 mg | Fiber: 10 g | Carbohydrate: 101 g

Sweetened Brown Rice

This recipe is perfect for a cold winter day, providing a great alternative to cold cereal.

INGREDIENTS | SERVES 6

1½ cups soy milk

1½ cups water

1 cup brown rice

1 tablespoon honey

¼ teaspoon nutmeg

Fresh fruit (optional)

Place all the ingredients except the fresh fruit in a medium-size saucepan; bring the mixture to a slow simmer and cover with a tight fitting lid. Simmer for 45 to 60 minutes, until the rice is tender and done. Serve in bowls, topped with your favorite fresh fruit.

PER SERVING: Calories: 155 | Fat: 1.5 g | Protein: 3.5 g | Sodium: 35 mg | Fiber: 1.5 g | Carbohydrate: 13 g

Quinoa Breakfast Congee

Congee is a porridge traditionally made with rice, and is primarily eaten as a breakfast food. Congee takes a long time to cook, so it can be made in a rice cooker or slow cooker and cooked overnight.

INGREDIENTS | SERVES 4

¼ cup hijiki

½ onion

½ cup quinoa

½ cup brown rice

½ teaspoon sea salt

5 cups water

¼ cup toasted pumpkin seeds

1. Soak hijiki in hot water for 10 minutes. Drain and set aside.

2. Chop onion and set aside.

3. Before going to bed, plug in a 1.5-quart slow cooker and add quinoa, rice, hijiki, onion, sea salt, and water. Set the temperature on low and cook overnight.

4. In the morning, toast the pumpkin seeds in a dry skillet and set aside.

5. Stir the congee; spoon into individual serving bowls. Top with the pumpkin seeds and serve with cooked greens such as kale, spinach, or broccoli.

PER SERVING: Calories: 243 | Fat: 7.5 g | Protein: 8 g | Sodium: 299 mg | Fiber: 2.5 g | Carbohydrate: 22 g

Cornmeal Grits

This warm cereal is similar to oatmeal. It can be eaten in a variety of ways: as a breakfast cereal, as a side with lean ham and eggs, with cheese stirred in it and shrimp on top, or with gravy.

INGREDIENTS | SERVES 4

4 cups water
1 teaspoon salt
1 cup polenta meal
2 tablespoons butter

Polenta Power

Polenta is a dish made from boiled cornmeal. It is a great gluten-free alternative as long as wheat flour is not used in its preparation. Polenta is so versatile that it can be served as a meal or as a dessert. Just boil, bake, fry, grill, or microwave polenta at any time of day for a delicious grain alternative to wheat.

1. Put water and salt in a saucepan and bring to a boil.

2. Gradually add polenta and stir constantly over medium-low heat until it has thickened, about 15 minutes. Stir in butter.

3. Serve immediately for soft grits or pour into a greased loaf pan and let cool. When cool, grits can be sliced and fried or grilled.

PER SERVING: Calories: 177 | Fat: 6 g | Protein: 3 g | Sodium: 641 mg | Fiber: 2.5 g | Carbohydrate: 27 g

Granola

Serve this granola with fruit and yogurt or just eat it out of hand for an on-the-go breakfast. You can also turn this into trail mix by adding dried apples and/or raisins.

INGREDIENTS | SERVES 6

4 cups rolled oats
1 cup sliced almonds
½ teaspoon cinnamon
1 teaspoon vanilla
4 ounces orange blossom honey
⅛ cup canola oil
½ cup wheat germ
¼ cup sesame seeds
¼ cup millet
¼ cup flaxseeds

1. Preheat oven to 350°F.

2. Toss oats, almonds, cinnamon, vanilla, honey, and canola oil together in a big bowl. Spread the mixture on a baking pan and bake for 10 minutes.

3. Stir and add wheat germ, sesame seeds, and millet. Bake for 15 minutes.

4. Stir and add flaxseeds. Bake for 10 minutes.

5. Remove from oven. Cool and break up large chunks.

PER SERVING: Calories: 759 | Fat: 27 g | Protein: 26 g | Sodium: 7.5 g | Fiber: 18 g | Carbohydrate: 110 g

Grapefruit-Pomegranate Salad

Vegetable stock makes a refreshing alternative to dressings normally found with greens and fruit.

INGREDIENTS | SERVES 6

2 ruby red grapefruits

3 ounces Parmesan cheese

1 pomegranate

6 cups mesclun leaves

¼ cup Basic Vegetable Stock (see Chapter 10)

1. Peel the grapefruit with a knife, completely removing all the pith (the white layer under the skin). Cut out each section with the knife, again ensuring that no pith remains. Shave Parmesan with a vegetable peeler to form curls. Peel the pomegranate carefully with a paring knife; carefully remove berries/seeds.

2. Toss the mesclun greens in the stock.

3. To serve, mound the greens on plates and arrange the grapefruit sections, cheese, and pomegranate on top.

PER SERVING: Calories: 84 | Fat: 2 g | Protein: 4 g | Sodium: 102 mg | Fiber: 2 g | Carbohydrate: 14 g

Fresh Fruit Kebabs with Vanilla Yogurt Sauce

These are easy to prepare in advance. Use only the freshest, ripest fruits available.

INGREDIENTS | SERVES 4

4 skewers

1 cup diced cantaloupe (1-inch dice)

1 cup diced pineapple (1-inch dice)

1 cup strawberries

1 cup blueberries

¾ cup vanilla whole-milk yogurt

¼ cup heavy cream

Sugar substitute equal to 2–4 tablespoons granulated sugar

½ teaspoon vanilla extract

1. On each skewer, thread a piece of cantaloupe, a piece of pineapple, a strawberry, and 2 blueberries.

2. Whisk together the yogurt, heavy cream, sugar substitute, and vanilla extract in a small bowl. Pour into a serving dish. Serve the kebabs with the dipping sauce on the side.

PER SERVING: Calories: 163 | Fat: 6.5 g | Protein: 4.5 g | Sodium: 44 mg | Fiber: 3 g | Carbohydrate: 25 g

Yogurt Cheese and Fruit

This breakfast is worth the extra effort of making the yogurt cheese.
If you do not have the time or inclination, use farmer cheese instead.

INGREDIENTS | SERVES 6

3 cups plain nonfat yogurt
1 teaspoon fresh lemon juice
½ cup orange juice
½ cup water
1 fresh Golden Delicious apple
1 fresh pear
¼ cup honey
¼ cup dried cranberries or raisins

1. Prepare the yogurt cheese the day before by lining a colander or strainer with cheesecloth. Spoon the yogurt into the cheesecloth and place the strainer over a pot or bowl to catch the whey; refrigerate for at least 8 hours before serving.

2. In a large mixing bowl, mix together the juices and water. Cut the apple and pear into wedges, and place the wedges in the juice mixture; let sit for at least 5 minutes. Strain off the liquid.

3. When the yogurt is firm, remove from refrigerator, slice, and place on plates. Arrange the fruit wedges around the yogurt. Drizzle with honey and sprinkle with cranberries or raisins just before serving.

PER SERVING: Calories: 177 | Fat: 1 g | Protein: 6.5 g | Sodium: 87 mg | Fiber: 2 g | Carbohydrate: 35 g

Morning Sunshine Smoothie

You can vary the flavors by using any favorite fruit in the same quantity, but make sure you use only a vanilla-flavored soy protein powder.

INGREDIENTS | SERVES 1

1 cup low-fat vanilla yogurt

½ cup powdered skim milk

2 tablespoons flaxseed powder

2 tablespoons vanilla-flavored soy protein powder

2 tablespoons vanilla extract

1 cup chilled crushed pineapple

Combine all the ingredients in a food processor or blender and purée. Serve cold.

PER SERVING: Calories: 390 | Fat: 12 g | Protein: 26 g | Sodium: 716 mg | Fiber: 8 g | Carbohydrate: 74 g

Fruity Green Power Smoothie

Feel free to vary the fruit using frozen strawberries, blueberries, or banana. Add water to find the right consistency for your palate and adjust the sweetness to suit your taste.

INGREDIENTS | SERVES 1

1 cup vanilla-flavored hemp-seed milk

½ cup frozen blueberries

1 tablespoon microplant powder of choice such as hemp or spirulium

1 tablespoon flaxseed meal

1 tablespoon hemp-seed protein powder

Sweetener of choice, preferably stevia powder

1. Combine all ingredients in a blender and purée until smooth.

2. Serve immediately, while chilled and fresh, chewing well to better release the enzymes needed to digest the proteins, carbohydrates, and fats.

PER SERVING: Calories: 327 | Fat: 11 g | Protein: 26 g | Sodium: 149 mg | Fiber: 7 g | Carbohydrate: 24 g

Strawberry-Banana Smoothie

A classic combination, strawberries and bananas, forms the fiber-rich base of this breakfast beverage. If you are worried about not getting enough protein into your family, add a tablespoon of wheat germ.

INGREDIENTS | SERVES 2

1 banana
1 cup frozen strawberries, cut up
1 cup low-fat vanilla frozen yogurt
¼ cup orange juice
1 teaspoon honey

1. Place all ingredients in a blender and blend until smooth.

2. Pour into two glasses and serve as a quick breakfast.

PER SERVING: Calories: 282 | Fat: 4.5 g | Protein: 4 g | Sodium: 66 mg | Fiber: 5.5 g | Carbohydrate: 60 g

Bananas and Strawberries

Bananas are a very tasty source of soluble fiber. Strawberries have the added benefit of being high in both soluble and insoluble fiber in the form of pectin and seeds. Both are also higher in minerals than any other soft fruits.

Peach Yogurt Smoothie

*You may use frozen peaches in this for a sherbet-like texture.
The combination of yogurt and fruit will give your day a delicious boost.*

INGREDIENTS | SERVES 2

½ banana
1½ cups peaches, cubed
1 cup low-fat vanilla yogurt
¼ cup orange juice
1 teaspoon honey

1. Place all ingredients in a blender and blend until smooth.

2. Pour into two glasses and serve as a quick breakfast.

PER SERVING: Calories: 178 | Fat: 2 g | Protein: 7 g | Sodium: 81 mg | Fiber: 2 g | Carbohydrate: 36 g

Fiber Fact

If you use orange juice with pulp in it you increase your fiber consumption without even thinking about it, so don't pick up the pulp-free variety anymore. The same goes for grapefruit juice. For added color and fiber, eat a handful of fresh raspberries along with your juice.

CHAPTER 10

Shrinking Stocks, Soups, and Stews

Rich Poultry Stock

Use your favorite dry red wine. You may use a heavier white wine, if you would like a slightly more delicate flavor.

INGREDIENTS | YIELDS 1 GALLON; SERVING SIZE 1 CUP

1½ pounds yellow onions

2 leeks

½ pound carrots

1 pound parsnips

4 cloves garlic

1 pound celery

1 bunch fresh parsley stems

1 tablespoon olive oil

6 pounds any poultry (use meat, bones, and skin)

1 cup dry red wine

2 gallons water

6 sprigs fresh thyme

2 dried bay leaves

10–20 peppercorns

1. Peel and chop all the vegetables. Chop the parsley.

2. Heat the olive oil on medium in a stockpot; add the poultry and brown slightly. Remove the poultry and set it aside. Add the vegetables and sauté until brown. Return the poultry to the stockpot.

3. Add the wine and let it reduce by half, then add the water and simmer, uncovered, for 5½ hours.

4. Add the herbs and peppercorns; continue to simmer uncovered for 30 minutes.

5. Remove from heat, strain, and cool in an ice-water bath. Refrigerate overnight, then remove all fat that solidifies on surface before using or freezing.

PER SERVING: Calories: 86 | Fat: 3 g | Protein: 6 g | Sodium: 343 mg | Fiber: 0 g | Carbohydrate: 8 g

Take Out the Fat

This recipe is best prepared a day ahead of time so that you can thoroughly chill and remove all fat.

Basic Seafood Stock

Seafood shells such as those from lobster and shrimp are ideal for making a seafood stock. Also, be sure to thoroughly clean the leeks.

INGREDIENTS | YIELDS 1 GALLON

4 pounds seafood shells
3 large yellow onions
¼ pound shallots
1 white leek
½ pound parsnips
2 stalks celery
1 bunch fresh parsley stems
1 cup dry white wine
1½ gallons water
4 stems fresh thyme
2 dried bay leaves
10–20 peppercorns

Wine Choice

Use semidry to dry Mediterranean white wine. If you have a specific recipe in mind that would be complemented by a sweeter flavor, try experimenting with a sauterne or a late-harvest wine.

1. Thoroughly rinse the seafood shells in ice-cold water. Peel and roughly chop all the vegetables.

2. Place the shells, vegetables, wine, and water in a stockpot over medium heat; bring to a simmer and let cook, uncovered, for 2 hours.

3. Add the herbs and spices, and continue to simmer uncovered for 30 minutes.

4. Remove from heat, strain, and cool in an ice-water bath. Place in freezer-safe containers and store in the freezer until ready to use.

PER SERVING: Calories: 624 | Fat: 23 g | Protein: 78 g | Sodium: 7,748 mg | Fiber: 0 g | Carbohydrate: 16 g

Basic Vegetable Stock

Another great broth that is low on sodium and high on disease-fighting phytochemicals.
Try adding mushrooms for additional flavor.

INGREDIENTS | YIELDS 1 GALLON; SERVING SIZE 1 CUP

2 pounds yellow onions

1 pound carrots

1 pound celery

1 bunch fresh parley stems

1½ gallons water

4 stems fresh thyme

2 bay leaves (fresh or dried)

10–20 peppercorns

Homemade Stocks

Your homemade stocks give a special quality to all the dishes you add them to. Not only will the flavor of homemade stocks be better than that from purchased bases, but you will have added your own personal touch to the meal. Always cook them uncovered, as covering will cause them to become cloudy.

1. Peel and roughly chop the onions and carrots. Roughly chop the celery (stalks only; no leaves) and fresh parsley stems.

2. Put the vegetables and water in a stockpot over medium heat; bring to a simmer and cook, uncovered, for 1½ hours.

3. Add the herbs and peppercorns, and continue to simmer, uncovered, for 45 minutes. Adjust seasonings to taste as necessary.

4. Remove from heat and cool by submerging the pot in a bath of ice and water. Place in freezer-safe containers and store in the freezer until ready to use.

PER SERVING: Calories: 300 | Fat: 2 g | Protein: 0 g | Sodium: 691 mg | Fiber: 0 g | Carbohydrate: 67 g

Basic Chicken Soup

The major advantage of this soup is that it will be much lower in sodium than other canned chicken soups. The only limit is your imagination. Each time you make it, substitute different vegetables and seasonings to tantalize your taste buds.

INGREDIENTS | SERVES 6

5–6 pounds chicken (including giblets)

2 medium carrots

2 stalks celery

4 large yellow onions

¼ bunch parsley

12 cups water

Freshly cracked black pepper, to taste

Kosher salt, to taste

Don't Cry over Cut Onions

The sulfur in onions can cause the tears to flow. To avoid teary eyes, peel onions under cold water to wash away the volatile sulfur compounds. Onions are worth it, since they have anti-inflammatory effects on the joints.

1. Clean, trim, and quarter the chicken. Peel and chop all the vegetables. Chop parsley.

2. Place the chicken and giblets in a stockpot, add the water, and bring to a boil. Reduce heat to a simmer and skim off all foam.

3. Add all the remaining ingredients and simmer uncovered for about 3 hours.

4. Remove the chicken and giblets from the stockpot; discard giblets. Remove the meat from the bones, discard the bones, and return the meat to the broth; serve.

PER SERVING: Calories: 183 | Fat: 8 g | Protein: 16 g | Sodium: 84 mg | Fiber: 1.5 g | Carbohydrate: 5.5 g

Carrot-Lemon Soup

This is a great anytime soup and can be served either hot or cold.

INGREDIENTS | SERVES 6

2 pounds carrots

2 large yellow onions

2 cloves garlic

1 fresh lemon

3 tablespoons olive oil

6 cups Basic Vegetable Stock (Chapter 10) or low-sodium canned vegetable stock

1 teaspoon fresh minced ginger

Salt, to taste

Freshly cracked black pepper, to taste

3 fresh scallions, for garnish

Lemon Know-How

The thought of lemons may make your cheeks pucker, but it's well worth the powerful dose of cold-fighting vitamin C. The average lemon contains approximately 3 tablespoons of juice. Allow lemons to come to room temperature before squeezing to maximize the amount of juice extracted.

1. Peel and dice the carrots and onions. Mince the garlic. Juice and grate the lemon.

2. Heat the oil to medium in a large stockpot and lightly sauté the carrots, onions, and garlic.

3. Add the stock and simmer for approximately 1 hour. Add the ginger, lemon juice, and zest. Season with salt and pepper.

4. Chill and serve with finely chopped scallions as garnish.

PER SERVING: Calories: 153 | Fat: 7 g | Protein: 3 g | Sodium: 554 mg | Fiber: 5 g | Carbohydrate: 16 g

Coconut Curried Ban-Apple Soup

Bananas, apples, celery, potatoes, and onions all have plenty of fiber, and their flavors marry nicely with the coconut milk and a pinch of curry powder. Adding some roasted peanuts as a garnish ups the fiber too.

INGREDIENTS | SERVES 4

2 cups Basic Vegetable Stock (Chapter 10) or low-sodium canned vegetable stock

1 ripe banana

1 large potato

1 Granny Smith apple

1 celery heart

1 sweet onion

1 cup coconut milk

1 teaspoon curry powder

1 teaspoon salt

¼ cup toasted coconut, for garnish

2 tablespoons chopped fresh cilantro, for garnish

1. Put the vegetable stock in a soup pot.

2. Peel the banana and potato, chop them, and put them in the soup pot. Core the apple, chop it, and add it to the soup pot. Chop the celery heart and onion and add them to the soup pot.

3. Bring the soup to a boil, then lower the heat and simmer for 10 to 15 minutes. Add the coconut milk, curry powder, and salt.

4. Put the hot soup in a blender and purée.

5. Serve the soup hot. Garnish with toasted coconut and cilantro.

PER SERVING: Calories: 344 | Fat: 19 g | Protein: 6 g | Sodium: 886 mg | Fiber: 7 g | Carbohydrate: 40 g

Cut the Fat

Coconut milk adds a rich and exotic flavor to the soup. It has anticancer, antimicrobial, and antiviral characteristics. Although it is high in saturated fat, it contains lauric acids, which are also found in mother's milk. Lauric acid is key to proper brain development and bone health. To cut the fat in this recipe, substitute some other creamy liquid for the coconut milk. Try unsweetened soymilk, half-and-half, milk, or plain yogurt.

Roasted Root Vegetable Soup

This recipe can serve as either a hearty side dish or an entrée.

INGREDIENTS | SERVES 6

2 parsnips

3 carrots

2 medium sweet potatoes

3 stalks celery

3 yellow onions

1 tablespoon olive oil

1 fresh rosemary sprig

4 cups Basic Vegetable Stock (Chapter 10) or low-sodium canned vegetable stock

3 sprigs fresh thyme

¼ bunch fresh parsley

2 dried bay leaves

Freshly cracked black pepper, to taste

Kosher salt (optional)

Evergreen to the Rescue

Rosemary is the disease-fighting product of an evergreen tree. It has a wonderful pine-like fragrance and pungent flavor that can give chicken, pork, fish, and soups a major flavor boost. It also offers anti-inflammatory qualities that may reduce the severity of asthma attacks.

1. Preheat oven to 375°F.

2. Peel (as necessary) and chop all the vegetables.

3. Pour the oil into a large roasting pan. Place the vegetables and rosemary sprig in the pan and roast until al dente, probably 30–45 minutes. Remove from oven, discard rosemary sprig, and let cool slightly.

4. In a blender, purée the roasted vegetables thoroughly in small batches. Add vegetable stock to the blender as needed. Pour the mixture into a stockpot and bring to a simmer over medium heat.

5. Chop the thyme leaves (discard stems) and the parsley. Add the thyme, parsley, pepper, and salt (optional) to the pot and continue to simmer for 30 minutes to 1 hour.

PER SERVING: Calories: 153 | Fat: 2.5 g | Protein: 3 g | Sodium: 462 mg | Fiber: 6 g | Carbohydrate: 25 g

Wedding Soup

This Italian classic is served at weddings or on other special occasions.
Its ingredients will support a lifetime of health and happiness.

INGREDIENTS | SERVES 6

3 slices Italian bread, toasted

¾ pound lean ground beef

1 egg or ¼ cup egg substitute

1 yellow onion, chopped

3 cloves garlic, minced

¼ bunch fresh parsley, chopped

3 sprigs fresh oregano, chopped

2 sprigs fresh basil, chopped

Freshly cracked black pepper, to taste

4 ounces fresh grated Parmesan cheese

1 cup rough chopped fresh spinach with
  stems removed

2 quarts Rich Poultry Stock (Chapter 10)
  or low-sodium canned chicken stock

1. Preheat oven to 375°F.

2. Wet the toasted Italian bread with water, then squeeze out all the liquid.

3. In a large bowl, mix together the bread, beef, egg, onion, garlic, parsley, oregano, basil, pepper, and half of the Parmesan. Form the mixture into 1- to 2-inch balls; place in a baking dish and cook for 20 to 30 minutes. Remove from oven and drain on paper towels.

4. Steam the spinach al dente. In a large stockpot, combine the stock, spinach, and meatballs; simmer for 30 minutes.

5. Ladle the soup into serving bowls and sprinkle with remaining cheese.

PER SERVING: Calories: 245 | Fat: 10 g | Protein: 26 g | Sodium: 1,021 mg | Fiber: 0.5 g | Carbohydrate: 9 g

Pumpkin Soup

This is a perfect autumn soup to celebrate the harvest season. If you're short on time or pumpkins are out of season, substitute 1 (15-ounce) can of puréed pumpkin for the fresh pumpkin.

INGREDIENTS | SERVES 6

2 cups large-diced fresh sugar pumpkin, seeds reserved separately

3 leeks, sliced

1½ teaspoons minced fresh ginger

1 tablespoon olive oil

½ teaspoon grated fresh lemon zest

1 teaspoon fresh lemon juice

2 quarts Basic Vegetable Stock (Chapter 10) or low-sodium canned vegetable stock

Kosher salt, to taste

Freshly ground black pepper, to taste

1 tablespoon extra-virgin olive oil, for drizzling

Zesting

If you don't have a zester, you can still easily make lemon zest. Simply use your cheese grater, but be careful to grate only the rind and not the white pith, which tends to be bitter.

1. Preheat oven to 375°F.

2. Clean the pumpkin seeds thoroughly, place them on a baking sheet, and sprinkle with salt. Roast for approximately 5 to 8 minutes, until light golden.

3. Place the diced pumpkin in a baking dish with the leeks, ginger, and olive oil; roast for 45 minutes to 1 hour, until cooked al dente.

4. Transfer the cooked pumpkin mixture to a large stockpot and add the zest, juice, stock, salt, and pepper; let simmer for 30 to 45 minutes.

5. To serve, ladle into serving bowls. Drizzle with extra-virgin olive oil and sprinkle with toasted pumpkin seeds.

PER SERVING: Calories: 100 | Fat: 4 g | Protein: 3 g | Sodium: 748 mg | Fiber: 1.5 g | Carbohydrate: 10 g

Split Pea Soup

Legumes, such as peas, are a source of high fiber and a good source of protein in vegetarian diets. To make this meal completely vegetarian, omit the ham bone and use vegetable stock.

INGREDIENTS | SERVES 6

8 cups water
2 cups split peas
1 ham bone
½ cup diced carrot
¼ cup diced celery
1 cup diced onion
Salt, to taste
Pepper, to taste

1. In a large stockpot, simmer water, split peas, and ham bone for 60 minutes.

2. Add carrot, celery, and onion and simmer for another hour.

3. Remove the ham bone, season the soup with salt and pepper, and serve hot.

PER SERVING: Calories: 353 | Fat: 2 g | Protein: 25 g | Sodium: 255 mg | Fiber: 26 g | Carbohydrate: 61 g

Dandelion and White Bean Soup

If you like the taste of dandelion greens, try them in a salad!

INGREDIENTS | SERVES 6

1 teaspoon olive oil
2 yellow onions, chopped
3 carrots, diced
3 stalks celery, diced
4 cloves garlic, minced
2 quarts Basic Vegetable Stock (Chapter 10)
1 dried bay leaf
¼ bunch parsley, chopped
4 sprigs fresh thyme, leaves chopped (stems discarded)
Freshly cracked black pepper, to taste
2 cups fresh dandelion greens
1 cup cooked cannellini beans
2 ounces fresh Romano or Parmesan, grated

1. Heat the oil in a large stockpot over medium heat. Add the onions, carrots, celery, and garlic; sauté until light brown.

2. Add the stock and simmer for 1½ hours.

3. Add the herbs and spices; simmer for 30 minutes more.

4. Steam the dandelion greens until they are al dente. Add the beans and greens to the soup; simmer for 15 minutes. Ladle the soup into serving bowls and sprinkle with cheese.

PER SERVING: Calories: 155 | Fat: 2 g | Protein: 11 g | Sodium: 677 mg | Fiber: 6 g | Carbohydrate: 21 g

Minestrone

This soup is an ideal entrée for those cool, crisp fall days.

INGREDIENTS | SERVES 6

1 pound low-fat or fat-free Italian
sausage

1 bulb fennel

1 leek

1 medium yellow onion

1 shallot

4 cloves garlic

½ head Savoy cabbage

8 plum tomatoes

4 sprigs fresh marjoram

2 sprigs fresh oregano

¼ bunch fresh basil

1 teaspoon olive oil

1 cup dry red wine

2 quarts Basic Vegetable Stock (Chapter
10) or low-sodium canned vegetable
stock

1 cup cooked cannellini beans

1 cup pasta, cooked al dente

Freshly cracked black pepper, to taste

¼ cup toasted pine nuts

2 ounces fresh Romano, grated

2 ounces fresh Parmesan, grated

1. Slice the sausage into ½-inch coins. Cut the fennel
   bulb into wedges and roughly chop the top. Thinly
   slice the leek. Slice the onion and shallot. Mince the
   garlic. Shred the cabbage and chop the tomatoes.
   Chop the herbs.

2. Heat the oil to medium temperature in a large
   stockpot. Add the sausage, fennel, leek, onion, shallot,
   garlic, cabbage, and tomatoes; sauté for 5 to 10
   minutes.

3. Add the wine and let reduce by half. Add the stock
   and herbs; simmer for 3½ to 4 hours.

4. Add the beans and pasta; let cook for 5 to 10 minutes.

5. Serve with pepper, pine nuts, and cheese sprinkled
   over the top.

PER SERVING: Calories: 387 | Fat: 14 g | Protein: 26 g |
Sodium: 1,409 mg | Fiber: 7 g | Carbohydrate: 31 g

Pining for Nuts

Pine nuts are a wonderful addition to
soups, sauces, and other dishes. They offer
healthy fats, and numerous vitamins and
minerals with antioxidant benefits. Be
aware that raw pine nuts should be refrigerated to maintain freshness.

Gazpacho

This makes a great showcase for your summer garden!
Use only the freshest ingredients and remove the seeds from the vegetables.

INGREDIENTS | SERVES 6

2 large Vidalia or other yellow onions

3 medium cucumbers

1½ pounds plum tomatoes

3 cloves garlic

½ chipotle chili pepper (canned in adobo sauce)

½ bunch cilantro

Zest and juice of 1 lime

¼ teaspoon Tabasco sauce

Freshly cracked black pepper, to taste

1½ quarts Basic Vegetable Stock (Chapter 10) or low-sodium canned vegetable stock

The Scent of Garlic

To keep your hands from smelling like garlic after you've been working with it, wash them in cold water. Hot water will seal in the garlic smell.

1. Peel and chop all the vegetables into equal-size pieces. Chop the garlic and chili pepper. Reserve some cilantro sprigs for garnish, and chop the rest.

2. In a mixing bowl, mix together all the ingredients except the stock. Purée all but a quarter of this mixture in a blender. (The last quarter is reserved for garnish.)

3. Add the stock to the puréed mixture. Continue to purée until smooth. Adjust seasonings to taste. To serve, ladle into serving bowls. Garnish with reserved vegetable mixture and cilantro sprigs.

PER SERVING: Calories: 77 | Fat: 2 g | Protein: 3 g | Sodium: 22 mg | Fiber: 1.5 g | Carbohydrate: 14 g

Chickpea Stew

You'll need to start this dish one day in advance.
Serve on a bed of rice or pasta. Also, don't forget to serve bread for dipping!

INGREDIENTS | SERVES 6

1 cup dried chickpeas
1 large eggplant
Kosher salt
1 medium yellow onion
3 cloves garlic
4 medium tomatoes
1 large potato
1 large zucchini
1 teaspoon fennel seeds
3 tablespoons olive oil
1 cup Basic Vegetable Stock (Chapter 10) or low-sodium canned vegetable stock
Salt, to taste
Freshly cracked black pepper, to taste

1. Soak the peas overnight in water; rinse and drain.

2. Cube the eggplant and sprinkle it with salt. Place it in a colander and cover with a paper towel; let sit for about 30 minutes, then rinse and pat dry.

3. Meanwhile, chop the onion and mince the garlic. Peel and chop the tomatoes. Cube the potato and zucchini. Crush and chop the fennel seeds.

4. Heat the oil in a sauté pan over medium heat. Add the onion and garlic; sauté for 2 to 3 minutes or until the onion is translucent. Be sure not to let the garlic brown. Add the eggplant and sauté lightly until it becomes golden.

5. Add the tomatoes, potato, zucchini, fennel seeds, chickpeas, and stock. Season with salt and pepper to taste. Bring to a boil, cover, and simmer for 30 minutes or until the chickpeas are tender.

PER SERVING: Calories: 269 | Fat: 9 g | Protein: 9 g | Sodium: 109 mg | Fiber: 10 g | Carbohydrate: 39 g

Harvest Stew

Add fresh herbs from the garden to this soup to suit your taste, and throw in any extra vegetables you may have on hand. Maybe we should call this one "Phytochemical Powerhouse Stew."

INGREDIENTS | SERVES 6

1 pound stewing beef cubes

2 tablespoons olive oil

¼ cup flour

¾ cup diced onions

½ cup sliced carrots

½ cup diced celery

1 leek, cleaned and diced

6 garlic cloves, peeled

2 cups diced zucchini

1 potato, peeled and diced

3 turnips, diced

2 tomatoes, chopped

1 bay leaf

3 sprigs fresh thyme

4 cups low-sodium beef broth

2 tablespoons Worcestershire sauce

Salt and pepper, to taste

1. Brown the beef cubes in olive oil. Sprinkle the flour over the meat and stir to coat and distribute.

2. Add the onions, carrots, celery, leek, garlic, zucchini, potato, turnips, tomatoes, bay leaf, thyme sprigs, and beef broth. Bring to a boil, then lower the heat and simmer for 60 minutes.

3. Remove the bay leaf and thyme sprigs. Add the Worcestershire sauce, salt, and pepper. Serve hot.

PER SERVING: Calories: 254 | Fat: 9.5 g | Protein: 20 g | Sodium: 514 mg | Fiber: 3.5 g | Carbohydrate: 22 g

Mediterranean Stew

Serve this stew, redolent with the flavors of the sunny Mediterranean, with warmed pita bread.

INGREDIENTS | SERVES 4

3 tablespoons olive oil

3 cloves garlic, crushed and minced

1 (15½-ounce) can chickpeas, drained and rinsed

1 (19-ounce) can cannellini beans, drained and rinsed

2 cups roasted tomatoes

1½ cups artichoke hearts, quartered

1 cup Basic Vegetable Stock (Chapter 10) or low-sodium canned vegetable stock

4 tablespoons grated Parmesan cheese

1 teaspoon crushed red pepper, or to taste

1 teaspoon dried oregano

Salt and freshly ground black pepper, to taste

Chopped sun-dried tomatoes, for garnish

Chopped Italian parsley, for garnish

Garlic-seasoned croutons, for garnish

Crumbled feta cheese, for garnish

Fresh oregano leaves, for garnish

1. Heat the olive oil in a large saucepan over medium heat and sauté the garlic for 2 to 3 minutes or until golden.

2. Reduce the heat to medium-low. Stir in the chickpeas, cannellini beans, roasted tomatoes, artichoke hearts, stock, Parmesan cheese, crushed red pepper, oregano, salt, and pepper. Cook and stir for about 10 minutes. Serve in individual bowls, garnishing as desired.

PER SERVING: Calories: 445 | Fat: 16 g | Protein: 18 g | Sodium: 530 mg | Fiber: 12 g | Carbohydrate: 61 g

Spicy Seafood Stew

Use your favorite fish in this delicious spicy stew.
Pick a combination of firm-fleshed fish that won't easily fall apart or overcook.

INGREDIENTS | SERVES 6

2 tablespoons olive oil

½ cup chopped yellow onion

½ cup diced green pepper

1 tablespoon minced garlic

3 cups canned peeled, chopped tomatoes, undrained

½ cup coconut milk

1 teaspoon hot pepper sauce

¼ cup freshly squeezed lime juice

Seasoned salt, to taste

¾ pound skinless firm-fleshed fish fillets, such as cod, center-cut salmon, and/or halibut

¾ pound medium-size shrimp, shelled and deveined

½ cup thinly sliced scallions

½ cup chopped fresh cilantro

1. Heat the oil in a large nonstick skillet over medium-high heat. Add the onions, green pepper, garlic, and tomatoes. Bring to a simmer, stirring occasionally, and cook for 3 to 4 minutes.

2. Add the coconut milk, pepper sauce, lime juice, and seasoned salt. Bring to a simmer and cook for 2 minutes. Add the fish and stir, being careful not to break apart the fillets. Cook until the fish is cooked through, about 8 minutes. Add the shrimp and cook until opaque and cooked through, about 5 minutes.

3. To serve, use a slotted spoon to transfer equal amounts of the fish and shrimp to 4 shallow serving bowls. Pour the sauce over the seafood and garnish with scallions and cilantro. Serve hot.

PER SERVING: Calories: 219 | Fat: 11 g | Protein: 19g | Sodium: 375 mg | Fiber: 2 g | Carbohydrate: 10 g

Fish Storage Facts

If you're unable to cook fresh fish on the day it is purchased, store the fish on a bed of ice in the coldest part of the refrigerator. The same applies for shellfish.

Bean and Lentil Ragout

A hearty stew offering some serious inflammation-fighting ingredients with some veggie protein on top.

INGREDIENTS | YIELDS 1 QUART; SERVING SIZE 1 CUP

1 large yellow onion

1 stalk celery

½ leek

1 carrot

6 fresh tomatoes

3 cloves garlic

2 sprigs thyme, leaves only

¼ bunch parsley

2 tablespoons olive oil

½ cup cooked cannellini beans

¼ cup red lentils

¼ cup yellow lentils

2 dried bay leaves

½ teaspoon ground cinnamon

½ teaspoon turmeric or curry powder

½ teaspoon chili powder

½ teaspoon cumin

1 quart Basic Vegetable Stock (Chapter 10) or low-sodium canned vegetable stock

1. Finely dice the onion, celery, and leek. Peel and finely dice the carrot and tomatoes. Mince the garlic and chop the thyme and parsley.

2. Heat the oil in a large stockpot to medium temperature. Add the onion, celery, leek, carrot, and garlic; sweat for 2 minutes. Add the tomatoes, beans, and lentils; stir for 1 minute. Add the herbs and spices; stir for 1 minute, then add the stock. Reduce heat to medium-low, and simmer, uncovered, for 1 hour. Adjust seasoning to taste before serving.

PER SERVING: Calories: 293 | Fat: 8 g | Protein: 14 g | Sodium: 250 mg | Fiber: 12 g | Carbohydrate: 42 g

Benefits of Beans

Beans are an excellent source of 8 of the 9 essential amino acids necessary for the formation of a variety of proteins in the body. They also pack a powerful fiber punch with between 9 to 13 grams of fiber per cup. Their protein-fiber combination will keep hunger at bay for hours.

Black Bean Chili

This vegetarian dish can easily be transformed into something to satisfy a meat-lover with the addition of ground turkey breast, or lean beef or pork.

INGREDIENTS | SERVES 8

1½ cups dried black beans

2 tablespoons canola oil

2 large sweet onions, chopped

5 medium-size cloves garlic, minced

1 tablespoon ground cumin

1 tablespoon dried oregano

3 tablespoons salt-free chili powder

1 teaspoon freshly ground black pepper

1 teaspoon dried red pepper flakes

1 teaspoon dried lemon granules, crushed

3 jalapeño peppers, seeded and minced

2 (14½-ounce) cans no-salt-added diced tomatoes

1 cup chopped fresh pineapple

4 large carrots, peeled and sliced

1 cup uncooked long-grain brown rice

1 tablespoon apple cider or red wine vinegar

Tamari sauce (optional)

No-salt-added peanut butter or other nut butter (optional)

Fresh cilantro, for garnish

Chili Powders

Using a combination of chili powders such as ancho, chipotle, or specialty salt-free chili powder blends in the Black Bean Chili is an easy way to add layers of flavor. You can also substitute chunk pineapple canned in its own juice if fresh pineapple isn't available, or substitute 1 cup of fresh orange juice instead.

1. Rinse the beans and cover them with water in a large, heavy pot. Bring to a full boil over medium-high heat, drain, and rinse again. Return the beans to the pot over medium-high heat and add 7 cups of water, or a combination of water and mushroom broth. Once the water comes to a boil, reduce heat and simmer for 1 hour.

2. While the beans cook, place a large nonstick sauté pan over medium heat. Add the oil and onions; sauté for 4 minutes, stirring frequently. Lower the heat to medium-low. Add the garlic and sauté for 1 minute. Stir in the cumin, oregano, chili powder, black pepper, red pepper flakes, lemon granules, and jalapeños; sauté for an additional 4 minutes, then add the tomatoes. Simmer for 10 minutes, stirring frequently.

3. Stir the sautéed mixture into the pot of beans. Add the pineapple, carrots, and rice. Simmer partially covered for another hour, or until the beans are soft and the rice is done. Stir in the vinegar. Have tamari sauce or peanut or other nut butter, and freshly ground black pepper available at the table to flavor individual servings of the chili, if desired. Garnish with cilantro.

PER SERVING: Calories: 256 | Fat: 5 g | Protein: 7 g | Sodium: 76 mg | Fiber: 7.5 g | Carbohydrate: 32 g

Lentil and Walnut Chili

If you purchase already-shelled walnuts, be sure to spread them out on a flat surface and search for leftover shell fragments before using them.

INGREDIENTS | SERVES 6

2 cups red lentils

½ cup walnuts

2 shallots

4 cloves garlic

2 poblano chilies

1 tablespoon olive oil

1½ cups Basic Vegetable Stock (Chapter 10) or low-sodium canned vegetable stock

2½ cups canned low-sodium tomato sauce

1 teaspoon cumin

1½ tablespoons chili powder

1 tablespoon honey

½ cup plain nonfat yogurt (optional)

1. Lay out the lentils on a baking sheet and pick out any stones. Chop the walnuts and slice the shallots. Mince the garlic and dice the peppers.

2. Heat the oil to medium temperature in a saucepot. Add the shallots, garlic, and peppers; sauté for 1 to 2 minutes. Add all the remaining ingredients except the lentils and yogurt. Simmer for 1 hour, then add the lentils and cook for 30 minutes longer.

3. Ladle into bowls. Serve with a dollop of yogurt.

PER SERVING: Calories: 368 | Fat: 10 g | Protein: 20 g | Sodium: 154 mg | Fiber: 9.5 g | Carbohydrate: 52 g

It's Not Hot, It's Chili

Fruity, smoky, citrusy, woodsy . . . these are just a few words to describe the flavors of various chilies. Make dried chilies ready for use by toasting them in a 350°F oven for 5 minutes, until they soften, become fragrant, and smoke lightly. Then, soak them in enough water to cover for 1 hour, and purée in a blender with just enough soaking liquid to make a thick purée circulate in the blender vase. For less "heat," remove the seeds before soaking.

Fava Beans and Moroccan Couscous Chili

You'll need to soak the beans overnight. Use fresh fava beans when available. If you remove the outer casings prior to cooking, it will cut the cooking time by 3 hours.

INGREDIENTS | SERVES 6

1 cup dried fava beans

1 quart water

2 medium yellow onions

1 carrot

1 jalapeño or serrano pepper

3 cloves garlic

8 plum tomatoes

1 tablespoon olive oil

1 quart low-sodium canned chicken stock

1 cup brewed strong coffee (decaf or regular)

½ teaspoon red pepper flakes

1 tablespoon chili powder

1 teaspoon curry powder

Freshly cracked black pepper, to taste

1 teaspoon honey

1 cup couscous

1 cup Rich Poultry Stock (Chapter 10) or low-sodium canned chicken stock

¼ bunch cilantro

1. Soak the beans in the water overnight; rinse and drain.

2. Dice the onion. Peel and grate the carrot. Mince the chili pepper and garlic. Roughly chop the tomatoes.

3. Heat the oil to medium temperature in a large stockpot. Add the onions, carrots, chili pepper, and garlic; sauté for 5 minutes. Reduce heat to low and add the beans, tomatoes, the 1 quart chicken stock, coffee, red pepper flakes, chili and curry powder, black pepper, and honey; simmer slowly uncovered for 4 hours.

4. Fifteen minutes before the chili is done, cook the couscous by bringing the Rich Poultry Stock to a boil. Add the couscous and cook for 2 to 3 minutes. Cover, let sit for 1 minute, then fluff. Keep warm.

5. Adjust seasonings to taste. Chop the cilantro. Ladle the chili into serving bowls, top with the couscous, and sprinkle with the cilantro.

PER SERVING: Calories: 274 | Fat: 3g | Protein: 15 g | Sodium: 497 mg | Fiber: 10 g | Carbohydrate: 46 g

Turning Vegetarian

Almost all recipes that call for a meat or poultry stock can be transformed into a vegetarian meal. Simply substitute a vegetarian stock for the meat or poultry stock and enhance the seasonings!

Fish Chili with Beans

If you enjoy this dish, branch out and experiment with different types of fish and beans.

INGREDIENTS | SERVES 6

1¼ pounds fresh fish (Chilean sea bass, halibut, or red snapper)

1 leek

1 medium yellow onion

4 ounces firm tofu

12 fresh plum tomatoes

1 fresh jalapeño pepper

1 fresh serrano pepper

1 teaspoon curry powder

1 teaspoon chili powder

¼ teaspoon cayenne pepper

Freshly cracked black pepper, to taste

2 tablespoons olive oil

2 cups cooked beans (pintos, cannellini, or red kidney)

½ cup dry red wine

2 cups Basic Seafood Stock (Chapter 10) or low-sodium canned fish stock

½ cup brewed strong coffee

1 teaspoon brown sugar

1 tablespoon honey

1. Rinse the fish in ice water and pat dry. Slice the leek and medium-dice the onion. Dice the tomatoes. Cut the tofu into large dice. Mince the jalapeño and serrano. Mix together the curry and chili powders, the cayenne, and black pepper.

2. Heat 1½ teaspoons of the oil to medium temperature in a large saucepan. Add the leek, onion, tomatoes, and tofu; cook for 2 minutes. Sprinkle with some of the seasoning mixture, then add all the remaining ingredients except the fish. Stew for approximately 60 minutes.

3. Preheat grill to medium temperature.

4. Brush the fish with the remaining olive oil and seasoning mixture; grill on each side until cooked through (the cooking time will vary depending on the type of fish and thickness), about 5 to 15 minutes.

5. To serve, ladle the stew into bowls and top with grilled fish.

PER SERVING: Calories: 412 | Fat: 7 g | Protein: 30 g | Sodium: 428 mg | Fiber: 12 g | Carbohydrate: 54 g

CHAPTER 11

Perfect Animal Proteins

Fresh Tuna with Sweet Lemon Leek Salsa

*The tuna can be prepared the night before, refrigerated,
then either reheated or served at room temperature.*

INGREDIENTS | SERVES 6

Tuna

1½ pounds fresh tuna steaks (cut into
  4-ounce portions)
¼–½ teaspoon extra-virgin olive oil
Freshly cracked black pepper, to taste
Kosher salt, to taste

Salsa

1 teaspoon extra-virgin olive oil
3 fresh leeks (light green and white parts
  only), thinly sliced
1 tablespoon fresh lemon juice
1 tablespoon honey

Terrific Tuna

Tuna is truly a nutrient-dense food. This
omega-3 fatty acid–rich food has anti-
inflammation written all over it with heaps
of other valuable disease-fighting nutrients
as well. Health authorities are urging consumers to gobble up fish two times per
week to reap the significant health
benefits.

1. Preheat grill to medium-high temperature.

2. Brush each portion of the tuna with the oil and drain
   on a rack. Season the tuna with pepper and salt, then
   place the tuna on the grill; cook for 3 minutes. Shift
   the tuna steaks on the grill to form an X grill pattern;
   cook 3 more minutes.

3. Turn the steaks over and grill 3 more minutes, then
   change position again to create an X grill pattern.
   Cook to desired doneness.

4. For the salsa: Heat the oil in a medium-size sauté pan
   on medium heat, then add the leeks. When the leeks
   are wilted, add the lemon juice and honey. Plate each
   tuna portion with a spoonful of salsa.

PER SERVING: Calories: 171 | Fat: 5.5 g | Protein: 21 g |
Sodium: 43 mg | Fiber: 1 g | Carbohydrate: 9.5 g

Tuna Casserole

To add a little excitement to the dinner table, try this recipe with shark or swordfish, too!

INGREDIENTS | SERVES 6

2 pounds fresh tuna steak

2 red onions

3 cloves garlic

3 pimientos

5 fresh plum tomatoes

4 medium potatoes

6 tablespoons olive oil

½ teaspoon cayenne pepper

2 tablespoons chopped parsley

2 bay leaves

½ cup dry white wine

1 cup Basic Seafood Stock (Chapter 10) or low-sodium canned fish stock

Freshly cracked black pepper, to taste

Salt, to taste

1. Preheat oven to 350°F.

2. Cut the tuna into cubes. Chop the onions and mince the garlic. Peel and chop the tomatoes. Cut the pimientos into strips. Cube the potatoes.

3. Heat the oil in a medium-size sauté pan; sauté the onions and garlic until tender.

4. Add the tuna, and lightly brown. Add the tomatoes, pimientos, cayenne, parsley, and bay leaves. Then immediately add the wine, stock, and potatoes. Transfer to a casserole dish and bake, covered, for approximately 1 hour. Remove the bay leaves and season with salt and pepper before serving.

PER SERVING: Calories: 423 | Fat: 20 g | Protein: 30 g | Sodium: 285 mg | Fiber: 2.5 g | Carbohydrate: 28 g

Baked Haddock

Marinating the fish in milk lightens the flavor and adds a touch of sweetness.

INGREDIENTS | SERVES 6

1 cup skim milk

Freshly cracked black pepper, to taste

3 sprigs rosemary, needles only

1½ pounds haddock fillet

1 teaspoon virgin olive oil

Superior Fish Storage

To optimize the freshness of your fish, wrap tightly in plastic wrap and lay it on ice in a baking dish. Place the dish at the bottom of the refrigerator. Refresh the ice once or twice a day. Very fresh fish can be stored like this for up to four days while fish that is up to a week old should be eaten immediately.

1. Mix together the milk, pepper, and half of the rosemary in a shallow bowl or pan. Place the haddock fillet into the milk mixture and let marinate for 8 hours.

2. Preheat oven to 375°F.

3. Grease a baking pan with half of the oil. Gently remove the fish from the marinade, drain, and place in the greased baking pan. Cover with aluminum foil and bake for 15 to 20 minutes, until the fish is flaky.

4. Remove the fish from the oven and let it rest 5 minutes. Cut the fish into 6 portions. Drizzle with the remaining oil and sprinkle with the remaining rosemary.

PER SERVING: Calories: 95 | Fat: 1.5 g | Protein: 18 g | Sodium: 79 mg | Fiber: 0 g | Carbohydrate: 2 g

Salmon in Anchovy-Caper Sauce

Grab some specialty tomatoes such as golden, purple, or heirloom to give this dish a unique flair.

INGREDIENTS | SERVES 6

1 tablespoon olive oil

6 portions salmon (sushi grade)

6 anchovy fillets

1 beefsteak tomato, thinly sliced

½ cup Yogurt Cheese (Chapter 17)

¼ cup capers

¼ bunch chives, finely chopped

1. Preheat oven to 375°F.

2. Pour the oil into a rack pan, then place the salmon in the pan. Place the anchovies on top, and roast for 10 minutes.

3. Remove from oven. Slice the salmon and place on plates. Top with tomato slices. Dollop yogurt cheese on top of the tomato, then sprinkle with capers and finely chopped chives.

PER SERVING: Calories: 265 | Fat: 12 g | Protein: 38 g | Sodium: 796 mg | Fiber: 2 g | Carbohydrate: 1 g

Grilled Red Snapper with Polenta

Try out different types of fish with this recipe.
You can also substitute Romano or Parmesan for the Manchego.

INGREDIENTS | SERVES 6

½ serrano pepper

2 teaspoons olive oil

1 quart Basic Seafood Stock (Chapter 10) or low-sodium canned fish stock

1½ cups cornmeal

1 teaspoon extra-virgin olive oil

1½ pounds red snapper

Pinch of coarse sea salt

Freshly cracked black pepper, to taste

3 ounces Manchego cheese

1 tablespoon cider vinegar

Snapper Is Super for Supper

Snapper is high in protein and low in saturated fat while providing 15 percent of the daily value for omega-3 fatty acids in a 4-ounce serving. Manchego cheese, derived from sheep's milk, gives this recipe a protein and calcium boost, but it is high in saturated fat. If you cannot locate Manchego cheese, you can substitute Monterey jack, mozzarella, or Cheddar cheese.

1. Preheat grill to medium heat. Stem, seed, and dice the serrano pepper.

2. Heat the 2 teaspoons of olive oil in a stockpot on medium. Lightly sauté the chili, then add the stock and bring to a boil.

3. Whisk in the cornmeal slowly; cook for approximately 20 to 30 minutes, stirring frequently (add more stock if necessary).

4. While the polenta cooks, lightly dip the fish in the 1 teaspoon of extra-virgin olive oil and place on a rack to drain. Season with salt and pepper.

5. When the polenta is done cooking, remove it from the heat and add the Manchego; keep warm.

6. Grill the fish for 3 to 5 minutes on each side, depending on the thickness of the fish.

7. To serve, spoon out a generous dollop of polenta on each serving plate and arrange the fish on top. Drizzle with the vinegar.

PER SERVING: Calories: 308 | Fat: 7.5 g | Protein: 31 g | Sodium: 673 mg | Fiber: 3 g | Carbohydrate: 28 g

Almond-Encrusted Salmon on Toast Points

Serrano peppers have such a thin skin that you don't need to bother removing it.

INGREDIENTS | SERVES 6

6 100% whole-wheat flour or corn
  tortillas

1 serrano pepper

¼ cup almonds

1 teaspoon chili powder

1 pound salmon fillet

¼ cup low-fat milk

1 tablespoon olive oil

1 tablespoon extra-virgin olive oil, plus
  extra for drizzling

Honey, for drizzling

1. Toast the tortillas under the broiler.

2. Mince the serrano and finely chop the almonds; mix together the serrano, almonds, and chili powder.

3. Clean the salmon in ice water, cut it into 6 portions, then dip it into the milk. Dredge in the almond mix.

4. Heat the olive oil to medium temperature and cook the salmon on each side for approximately 5 minutes, until thoroughly cooked.

5. Serve on tortillas, drizzled with extra-virgin olive oil and honey.

PER SERVING: Calories: 240 | Fat: 11 g | Protein: 23 g | Sodium: 498 mg | Fiber: 2.5 g | Carbohydrate: 13 g

Asian Salmon Patties

Serve this with Asian Chili Aioli (Chapter 17) for a great Asian treat.

INGREDIENTS | SERVES 1

1 egg, beaten or ¼ cup of egg substitute

1 tablespoon chopped cilantro

1 teaspoon hoisin sauce

½ tablespoon low-fat mayonnaise

½ tablespoon chopped scallion

Pinch minced fresh ginger

1 garlic clove, minced

1 teaspoon seasoned salt

Freshly cracked black pepper, to taste

¼ pound skinless salmon fillet, cut into
  ⅓-inch pieces

3 tablespoons fresh bread crumbs

Lime wedges, for garnish

1. In a medium-size bowl, mix together all the ingredients except the salmon, bread crumbs, and lime wedges. Add the salmon and bread crumbs and lightly toss until blended.

2. Heat a small nonstick skillet over medium-high heat. Halve the salmon mixture; place the 2 portions in the skillet, 1 inch apart. Cook the cakes until the underside is golden, about 1½ minutes. Carefully flip and cook for about 1 to 2 minutes more. Transfer the cakes to a plate and let rest for several minutes. Serve at room temperature.

PER SERVING: Calories: 314 | Fat: 10 g | Protein: 36 | Sodium: 1,106 mg | Fiber: 2.5 g | Carbohydrate: 19 g

Scallops Madras

Check out www.thespicehouse.com to find specialty spices that will excite your taste buds with new tastes and aromas.

INGREDIENTS | SERVES 4

1 teaspoon curry powder

1 teaspoon garam masala

1 teaspoon minced fresh garlic

2 tablespoons olive oil

1½ pounds diver sea scallops, abductor muscle removed

1 tablespoon ketchup

¼ cup low-fat coconut milk

¼ teaspoon kosher salt

⅛ teaspoon cayenne pepper

1 tablespoon freshly squeezed lemon juice

1. Combine the curry powder, garam masala, garlic, and olive oil in a medium-size mixing bowl. Add the scallops and toss to coat.

2. Heat a medium-size nonstick skillet over medium-high heat. Add the scallops and sear until almost cooked through, about 2½ to 3 minutes, turning and tossing throughout. Whisk in the ketchup, coconut milk, salt, and pepper. Continue to cook until the sauce is reduced and the scallops are opaque in the center and cooked through, about 4 to 5 minutes. Stir in the lemon juice. Taste and adjust seasoning as desired. Serve hot.

PER SERVING: Calories: 288 | Fat: 13 g | Protein: 40 g | Sodium: 640 mg | Fiber: 0.5 g | Carbohydrate: 2 g

Getting to Know Your Anti-Inflammatory Spices

Garam masala and cumin are both spice blends common in South Asian cuisines. Together they contain a number of inflammation-fighting spices such as turmeric, fenugreek, black peppercorns, cloves, cinnamon, and cardamom. Together these spices are pungent, but not "hot."

Grilled Mahi-Mahi with Pineapple Salsa

This salsa is also good on pork tenderloin.
The fruit and vegetables add fiber, texture, and piquancy to simple foods.

INGREDIENTS | SERVES 8

1 cup diced pineapple

½ cup diced red onion

¼ cup minced green bell pepper

¼ cup minced red bell pepper

¼ bunch cilantro

1 tablespoon white wine vinegar

¼ teaspoon hot pepper sauce

Salt, to taste

2 pounds cod or other firm-fleshed white fish

2 tablespoons olive oil

Pepper, to taste

1. Combine the pineapple, red onion, green bell pepper, and red bell pepper in a large bowl.

2. Chop the cilantro and add it to the bowl.

3. Add the vinegar, hot sauce, and a pinch of salt. Stir well, taste, and add more salt if needed.

4. Prepare your grill. Coat the fish with olive oil and season with pepper. Place on hot grill. Let cook for 3 to 4 minutes per side or until fish is opaque. Top with pineapple salsa and serve.

PER SERVING: Calories: 118 | Fat: 4 g | Protein: 15 g | Sodium: 46 mg | Fiber: 0.5 g | Carbohydrate: 3.5 g

Anti-Inflammatory Fruits

Pineapple contains an enzyme called bromelain. This enzyme may block pro-inflammatory substances that can speed up and worsen the inflammatory process. Extracts of bromelain may be as effective as non-steroidal anti-inflammatory drugs. Hence, this wonder enzyme may be a useful tool for fighting arthritis, but don't get too excited. It does not currently carry a health claim indicating its approval by the Food and Drug Administration. Still, until further research is completed, eat your pineapple!

Broiled Swordfish Kebab

Buy the freshest swordfish fillet possible—you can substitute tuna or halibut if you like.

INGREDIENTS | SERVES 1

1 teaspoon freshly squeezed lime juice

1 tablespoon olive oil

1 teaspoon Dijon mustard

1 teaspoon snipped chives

Salt, to taste

Freshly cracked black pepper, to taste

1 (5-ounce) swordfish fillet, about 1 inch thick

¼ red onion

¼ red pepper

¼ green pepper

2 cherry tomatoes

1 (10-inch) skewer

Sensitive Vitamins

Certain vitamins are sensitive to the elements. For example, vitamin C is sensitive to heat, air, and water. Vitamin D is sensitive to fat. What does it mean? Broil fish that is rich in vitamin D instead of pan-frying to retain the rich nutrients.

1. Combine the lime juice, olive oil, Dijon, chives, and salt and pepper (to taste) in a small, nonmetal bowl. Cut the swordfish fillet into 4 even-sized pieces and add to the marinade, stirring once or twice to coat evenly. Refrigerate for 5 minutes.

2. Prepare the onion and peppers by cutting them into 1-inch squares. Oil broiler rack and place it about 4 inches from the heat source. Preheat broiler to medium-high.

3. Remove the fish from the marinade, reserving the marinade. Thread the vegetables and fish cubes onto the skewer, alternating the fish cubes with the vegetables. Brush the kebab with the reserved marinade.

4. Place the kebab on the oiled rack and cook for about 2 minutes per side, brushing with the marinade after each turn. Discard any remaining marinade. Cook about 10 to 12 minutes total, until the fish is cooked through and the vegetables are browned at the edges. Serve hot.

PER SERVING: Calories: 295 | Fat: 18 g | Protein: 21 g | Sodium: 101 mg | Fiber: 1 g | Carbohydrate: 2 g

Curried Shrimp Salad in a Papaya

Chilled shrimp and toasted almonds complement the fruits and vegetables in this knockout luncheon salad. You can add some toasted sesame seeds to increase the nutrition and fiber value.

INGREDIENTS | SERVES 4

¼ cup olive oil
½ cup plain low-fat yogurt
2 tablespoons lemon juice
2 teaspoons grated lemon zest
1 teaspoon curry powder
Salt and pepper, to taste
2 cups cooked peeled shrimp, chilled
½ cup diced celery
½ cup diced cucumber
½ cup seedless green grapes, halved
2 medium papayas
½ cup toasted sliced almonds

Fruit of the Angels

Papaya is a deliciously sweet fruit with musky undertones. Papaya contains several unique protein-digesting enzymes such as papain. This enzyme has been shown to help lower inflammation. Additionally, papaya is rich in antioxidant nutrients such as vitamin C, vitamin E, and beta carotene, which have been shown to lower free radical damage and subsequent inflammation.

1. Whisk together olive oil, yogurt, lemon juice, lemon zest, curry powder, salt, and pepper in a mixing bowl.

2. Add the shrimp, celery, cucumber, and grapes and toss to coat with the dressing. Chill salad until ready to serve.

3. Cut the papaya in half lengthwise through the stem area and scoop out the seeds.

4. Fill the papaya with the shrimp salad, mounding it up on top.

5. Sprinkle the almonds on top of the shrimp salad. Serve with a fork and spoon so the papaya flesh can be scooped and eaten after the salad is gone.

PER SERVING: Calories: 339 | Fat: 21 g | Protein: 22 g | Sodium: 163 mg | Fiber: 3.5 g | Carbohydrate: 18 g

Seafood in Thai-Curry Bean Sauce

This recipe tastes as if it should have lots of sodium, but it doesn't. The beans are a prime source of fiber.

INGREDIENTS | SERVES 4

2 teaspoons sesame or canola oil

1 teaspoon curry powder

¼ teaspoon freshly ground black pepper

⅛ teaspoon ground cumin

⅛ teaspoon ground coriander

Pinch dried red pepper flakes

Pinch ground fennel seeds

Pinch ground cloves

Pinch ground mace

1 tablespoon water

1 small sweet onion, finely chopped

2 cloves garlic, minced

1 tablespoon no-salt-added, unsweetened applesauce

¼ cup dry white wine

¼ teaspoon low-sodium chicken bouillon

¼ cup water

1 tablespoon lime juice

⅛ teaspoon dried ground lemongrass

¼ packed cup fresh parsley leaves

¼ packed cup fresh basil leaves

1 tablespoon freeze-dried shallots

1⅓ cups canned no-salt-added cannellini beans, drained and rinsed

½ pound shelled and deveined shrimp

½ pound scallops

1. Heat the oil in a large, deep, nonstick sauté pan over medium heat. Add the curry powder, pepper, cumin, coriander, red pepper flakes, fennel seeds, cloves, and mace; sauté for 1 minute. Remove 1 teaspoon of the seasoned oil from the pan and set aside. Heat 1 tablespoon water, stirring to mix it with the seasoned oil in the pan. Add the onion and sauté over low heat until the onion is soft. Add the garlic and sauté for 1 minute.

2. Add the applesauce and wine and simmer until the wine is reduced by half. Add the chicken base and stir into the onion mixture. Add the ¼ cup water and bring to a boil. Add the lime juice granules, lemongrass, parsley, basil, shallots, and ⅓ cup of the beans. Reduce heat and simmer, stirring, for 1 minute.

3. Transfer the wine-bean mixture to a blender; purée. Pour the wine-bean purée back into the saucepan and add the remaining beans. Simmer briefly, then keep warm.

4. Wash the shrimp and scallops under cold water. Blot dry between paper towels. Warm a nonstick skillet or sauté pan over moderately high heat. Add the seasoned oil. When the oil is hot (but not smoking), add the shrimp and sauté for 2 minutes on each side or until cooked through. Using a slotted spoon, transfer the shrimp to a plate and keep warm.

5. Add the scallops to the skillet and sauté for 1 minute on each side or until cooked through. Divide the bean sauce among 4 shallow bowls and arrange the shellfish on top.

PER SERVING: Calories: 143 | Fat: 4 g | Protein: 22 g | Sodium: 214 mg | Fiber: 0 g | Carbohydrate: 1.5 g

Zesty Pecan Chicken and Grapes

Coating your chicken with nuts adds a crispy skin to keep the breast inside moist and tender.

INGREDIENTS | SERVES 6

¼ cup chopped pecans

1 teaspoon chili powder

¼ cup olive oil

1½ pounds boneless, skinless chicken breasts

12 ounces white grapes

6 cups salad greens

Toasting Nuts for Fresher Flavor and Crispness

To wake up the natural flavor of nuts, and to ensure that they're crisp and delicious, heat them on the stovetop or in the oven for a few minutes. It improves the quality of very fresh nuts, and livens up nuts that may not be completely fresh. For the stovetop, spread the nuts in a dry skillet and heat over a medium flame until their natural oils come to the surface, giving them a sheen. For the oven, spread the nuts in a single layer on a baking sheet and toast for 5 to 10 minutes at 350°F, until the oils are visible. Cool nuts to just above room temperature before serving.

1. Preheat oven to 400°F.

2. In a blender, mix the chopped nuts and chili powder. Pour in the oil while the blender is running. When the mixture is thoroughly combined, pour it into a shallow bowl.

3. Coat the chicken with the pecan mixture and place on racked baking dish; roast for 40 to 50 minutes, until the chicken is thoroughly cooked. Remove from oven and thinly slice. Slice the grapes and tear the greens into bite-size pieces. To serve, fan the chicken over the greens and sprinkle with sliced grapes.

PER SERVING: Calories: 299 | Fat: 16 g | Protein: 28 g | Sodium: 69 mg | Fiber: 2 g | Carbohydrate: 12 g

Ginger-Orange Chicken Breast

This recipe is great chilled, sliced, and served on a crispy green salad.

INGREDIENTS | SERVES 4

4 (5-ounce) skinless, boneless chicken
  breasts
2 tablespoons butter
½ teaspoon seasoned salt
Freshly cracked black pepper, to taste
2 cloves garlic, minced
2 tablespoons grated ginger
2 teaspoon orange zest
½ cup 100% orange juice

Working with Chicken

Quick and easy cooking means using pre-processed products, especially chicken. Boneless, skinless chicken breasts are available in many forms: fresh, frozen, marinated, seasoned, and even precooked. Use fresh boneless, skinless breasts available in the meat section of your grocer. Use a good reputable brand and check the freshness date. Prior to cooking or preparing, always rinse the meat under cold running water and pat dry with paper towels.

1. Rinse the chicken under cold running water and pat dry with paper towels. Melt the butter in a small nonstick skillet over medium-high heat. Season the chicken with salt and pepper. Brown the chicken, turning it once, about 8 minutes per side. Transfer the chicken to a plate and keep warm.

2. Add the garlic to the pan and cook for about 1 minute, stirring frequently to prevent burning. Add the ginger, orange zest, and juice, and bring to a simmer. Add the chicken and any reserved juices and heat through, about 4 to 5 minutes. Cut through the bottom of the chicken to make sure it is cooked. Adjust seasoning to taste. Serve hot with the sauce.

PER SERVING: Calories: 240 | Fat: 9.5 g | Protein: 34 g | Sodium: 138 mg | Fiber: 0g | Carbohydrate: 3 g

Spicy Chicken Burgers

You can substitute ground turkey or pork for the chicken. Adjust the quantity of pepper sauce to control the spiciness.

INGREDIENTS | SERVES 4

1 pound ground chicken breast
¼ cup finely chopped yellow onion
¼ cup finely chopped red bell pepper
1 teaspoon minced garlic
¼ cup thinly sliced scallions
½ teaspoon hot pepper sauce
1 teaspoon Worcestershire sauce
Salt, to taste
Freshly cracked black pepper, to taste

1. Clean and oil broiler rack. Preheat broiler to medium.

2. Combine all the ingredients in a medium-size bowl, mixing lightly. Broil the burgers for 4 to 5 minutes per side until firm through the center and the juices run clear. Transfer to a plate and tent with tinfoil to keep warm. Allow to rest 1 or 2 minutes before serving.

PER SERVING: Calories: 145 | Fat: 3 g | Protein: 27 g | Sodium: 78 mg | Fiber: 0 g | Carbohydrate: 1 g

Chicken à la King

This classic recipe can also be made with turkey in the title role.

INGREDIENTS | SERVES 4

1 can low-fat condensed cream of chicken soup
¼ cup skim milk
½ teaspoon Worcestershire sauce
1 tablespoon low-fat mayonnaise
¼ teaspoon ground black pepper
2 cups frozen mix of peas and pearl onions, thawed
1 cup sliced mushrooms, stemmed
½ pound cooked, chopped chicken
4 slices whole-wheat bread, toasted

1. Combine the soup, milk, Worcestershire, mayonnaise, and pepper in a saucepan and bring to a boil.

2. Reduce heat and add the peas and pearl onions, mushrooms, and chicken. Simmer until the vegetables and chicken are heated through.

3. Serve over toast.

PER SERVING: Calories: 284 | Fat: 5.5 g | Protein: 22 g | Sodium: 373 mg | Fiber: 5.5 g | Carbohydrate: 38 g

Chicken with Curry and Apricot Sauce

This dish has a sweet taste and the apricot preserves add a nice texture to the sauce.

INGREDIENTS | SERVES 4

4 (5-ounce) skinless, boneless chicken breasts

½ teaspoon seasoned salt

Lemon pepper, to taste

¼ cup vegetable oil

1 cup sliced red onion

3 cloves garlic, minced

1 cup chicken broth

2 teaspoons curry powder

1 cup apricot preserves

1 cup plain low-fat yogurt, at room temperature

1. Rinse the chicken under cold running water and pat dry with paper towels. Season the chicken with salt and lemon pepper. Heat the oil in a small nonstick skillet over medium-high heat. Cook the chicken until lightly browned, about 4 to 5 minutes per side. Transfer the chicken to a plate and tent with tinfoil to keep warm.

2. Reduce heat to medium-low and add the red onion. Cook until soft, about 2 minutes, stirring occasionally. Add the garlic and stir to combine. Add the broth, curry powder, and apricot preserves; bring to a simmer and cook until thickened, about 5 minutes.

3. Return the chicken and any accumulated juices to the pan and cook until the chicken is cooked through, about 5 minutes. Transfer the chicken to a serving plate and keep warm. Add the yogurt to the pan and stir to combine. Ladle sauce over the chicken and serve.

PER SERVING: Calories: 532 | Fat: 18 g | Protein: 39 g | Sodium: 587 mg | Fiber: 0 g | Carbohydrate: 56 g

Chicken and Green Bean Stovetop Casserole

This is a dressed-up variation of a popular Thanksgiving favorite.
It's meant to have a hint of the flavor of a green bean casserole, but it can stand on its own as a meal.

INGREDIENTS | SERVES 4

1 can low-fat condensed cream of chicken soup

¼ cup skim milk

2 teaspoons Worcestershire sauce

1 teaspoon low-fat mayonnaise

½ teaspoon onion powder

¼ teaspoon garlic powder

¼ teaspoon ground black pepper

4-ounce can sliced water chestnuts, drained

2½ cups frozen green beans, thawed

1 cup sliced mushrooms, steamed

½ pound cooked, chopped chicken

1⅓ cups cooked brown long-grain rice

1. Combine the soup, milk, Worcestershire, mayonnaise, onion powder, garlic powder, and pepper in a saucepan and bring to a boil.

2. Reduce heat and add the water chestnuts, green beans, mushrooms, and chicken.

3. Simmer until vegetables and chicken are heated through.

4. Serve over rice.

PER SERVING: Calories: 304 | Fat: 3.5 g | Protein: 20 g | Sodium: 202 mg | Fiber: 4 g | Carbohydrate: 48 g

Marinated London Broil

To maintain the tender texture of the London broil, marinate the meat prior to grilling,
cook until medium rare, and cut across the grain into small strips.

INGREDIENTS | SERVES 6

1 cup dry red wine

1 tablespoon olive oil

1 teaspoon ground cinnamon

½ teaspoon ground cloves

1 teaspoon ground cumin

Freshly cracked black pepper, to taste

Kosher salt, to taste

1½-pound London broil

Preheat grill. Mix together the wine, oil, and seasonings. Coat the broil in the mixture, then grill to desired doneness. Slice on a bias and serve.

PER SERVING: Calories: 248 | Fat: 10 g | Protein: 35 g | Sodium: 75 mg | Fiber: 0 g | Carbohydrate: 0.5 g

Spicy Turkey Breast with Fruit Chutney

*There are several types of pears to choose from,
but first try either Bosc or Anjou (if available) in this recipe.*

INGREDIENTS | SERVES 6

2 jalapeño peppers
2 cloves garlic
1 tablespoon olive oil
2 teaspoons whole-wheat flour
Freshly cracked black pepper, to taste
Cooking spray
1½ pounds whole boneless turkey breast
1 shallot
2 pears
1 lemon
1 tablespoon honey

1. Preheat oven to 350°F.

2. Stem, seed, and mince the peppers. Mince the garlic. In a blender, purée the chili peppers, garlic, and oil. Mix together the flour and black pepper.

3. Spray a rack with cooking spray. Dredge the turkey in the flour mixture, then dip it in the pepper mixture and place on rack. Cover loosely with foil and roast for 1 hour. Remove foil and brown for 10 minutes.

4. While the turkey cooks, prepare the chutney: Finely dice the shallot. Juice the lemon and grate the rind for zest. Dice the pears. Mix together the pears, shallots, lemon juice, zest, and honey.

5. Thinly slice the turkey, and serve with chutney.

PER SERVING: Calories: 171 | Fat: 3.5 g | Protein: 17 g | Sodium: 353 mg | Fiber: 2 g | Carbohydrate: 20 g

Turkey Breast Piccata

If you prefer, chicken or veal may be substituted for the turkey.

INGREDIENTS | SERVES 6

1½ pounds whole boneless turkey breast

¼ cup flour

1 lemon

¼ bunch parsley

1 tablespoon olive oil

¼ cup dry white wine

½ cup Rich Poultry Stock (Chapter 10)

½ tablespoon capers

Lemon Supremes

Lemon Supremes can be used as a garnish. They are made by completely removing all peels and pith from the lemon and cutting out each section. Then simply arrange them on a plate to suit your artistic style.

1. Slice the turkey breast into thin scalloping-size portions and dredge in the flour. Grate the lemon rind for zest and juice the lemon. Chop the parsley.

2. Heat the oil to medium-high temperature in a large sauté pan. Sauté the turkey until light golden brown, approximately 2 minutes on each side.

3. Add the wine and lemon juice, and let reduce by half. Add the stock and simmer on high temperature for 1 minute. Remove the turkey from the pan and keep warm. Allow the liquid to reduce by half.

4. To serve, sprinkle with capers and parsley, and drizzle with sauce.

PER SERVING: Calories: 160 | Fat: 4.5 g | Protein: 20 g | Sodium: 1,018 mg | Fiber: 1.5 g | Carbohydrate: 8.5 g

Filet Mignon with Horseradish Cream

The extra dollop of horseradish is for those who like a little more zest with their steaks.
Prepare the sauce in advance to save time.

INGREDIENTS | SERVES 4

½ cup low-fat sour cream

¼ cup low-fat mayonnaise

2 teaspoons freshly squeezed lemon juice

2 tablespoons bottled horseradish, slightly drained

Dash hot pepper sauce

2 teaspoons chopped parsley

Pinch seasoned salt

Freshly cracked black pepper, to taste

3 tablespoons olive oil

4 (6-ounce) filet mignons

Additional horseradish, for garnish

Cut to the Chase

Always put a damp cloth or nonskid plastic mat under your cutting board. Sliding cutting boards are one of the main causes of accidental knife cuts.

1. Mix together the sour cream, mayonnaise, lemon juice, horseradish, pepper sauce, parsley, salt, and pepper. Set aside.

2. Heat the oil in a small nonstick skillet over high heat. Season the filets with salt and pepper. Cook, searing quickly over high, until the underside is browned, about 4 to 5 minutes for medium-rare. Flip the filets and cook for another 4 to 5 minutes.

3. Transfer the filets to a plate and tent with tinfoil to keep warm. Let rest for 4 to 5 minutes to allow the juices to reabsorb.

4. To serve, place the steaks on serving plates and dollop the sauce on top. Garnish with additional horseradish, if desired.

PER SERVING: Calories: 509 | Fat: 29 g | Protein: 54 g | Sodium: 156 mg | Fiber: 0 g | Carbohydrate: 4.5 g

Apricot-Stuffed Pork Tenderloin

You can use dried apricots instead of fresh.
However, you'll probably want to rehydrate them slightly in red wine.

INGREDIENTS | SERVES 6

1½-pound pork tenderloin
1 shallot
3 cloves garlic
6 apricots
½ cup pecans
3 fresh sage leaves
Freshly cracked black pepper, to taste
Kosher salt, to taste
Cooking spray

Be Food Safe

Make sure you cook your pork until its internal temperature reaches 160°F to avoid exposure to potentially harmful microorganisms such as E. coli, Salmonella, and Staphylococcus aureus.

1. Preheat oven to 375°F.

2. Butterfly the tenderloin by making a lengthwise slice down the middle, making certain not to cut completely through.

3. Mince the shallot and garlic. Remove pits and slice apricots. Chop the pecans and sage.

4. Lay out the tenderloin. Layer all ingredients over the tenderloin and season with pepper and salt. Carefully roll up the loin and tie securely.

5. Spray a rack with cooking spray, then place the tenderloin on the rack and roast for 1 to 1½ hours. Let cool slightly, then slice.

PER SERVING: Calories: 325 | Fat: 21 g | Protein: 24 g | Sodium: 36 mg | Fiber: 2.5 g | Carbohydrate: 11 g

Pork Medallions with Jalapeño Mustard

Adjust the amount of jalapeños in this recipe to control the heat,
and wear rubber gloves while working with them.

INGREDIENTS | SERVES 4

¼ cup Dijon mustard

1 tablespoon honey

2 teaspoons minced garlic

2 tablespoons freshly squeezed lemon juice

2 tablespoons finely minced jalapeño pepper, seeded, optional

Garlic salt, to taste

1½ pounds pork tenderloin, trimmed of excess fat

Salt, to taste

Freshly cracked black pepper, to taste

6 tablespoons all-purpose flour

¼ to ½ cup olive oil

Put Down That Fork!

Never use a fork to turn meats. It pierces the meat and allows the flavorful juices to escape. Use a spatula or tongs to gently turn or flip meats.

1. Combine the Dijon, honey, garlic, lemon juice, jalapeño, and garlic salt in a small nonreactive bowl and mix to combine.

2. Cut the pork tenderloin into 1-inch-thick slices and lightly season with salt and pepper. Place the flour in a shallow bowl. Dredge the pork medallions in the flour, shaking off excess.

3. Heat 3 tablespoons of the oil in a medium-size nonstick skillet over medium-high heat. Add the pork medallions and cook until both sides are golden brown, about 6 to 7 minutes per side. Add more oil if needed.

4. Add the jalapeño glaze to the pork and stir to coat the medallions. Cook until the pork is firm to the touch and no pink shows in the center, about 2 to 3 minutes. Remove the pan from heat, tent with tinfoil, and let rest for 4 to 5 minutes. Stir to blend the juices, and adjust seasoning to taste. Serve hot.

PER SERVING: Calories: 521 | Fat: 34 g | Protein: 35 g | Sodium: 67 mg | Fiber: 0.5 g | Carbohydrate: 13 g

CHAPTER 12

Green Protein and Beneficial Beans

Lentil-Stuffed Peppers

Use both red and yellow bell peppers for variety in color and flavor.

INGREDIENTS | SERVES 6

2 medium yellow onions

2 stalks celery

2 carrots

6 sprigs oregano

1 tablespoon olive oil

4 cups Basic Vegetable Stock (Chapter 10) or low-sodium canned vegetable stock, divided

3 cups red lentils

6 bell peppers

3 ounces feta cheese

Freshly cracked black pepper, to taste

1. Finely dice the onions and celery. Peel and finely dice the carrots. Reserve the top parts of the oregano sprigs and chop the remaining leaves.

2. Heat the oil to medium temperature in a large saucepot. Add the onions, celery, and carrots; sauté for 5 minutes, then add 1 cup Basic Vegetable Stock and the lentils. Simmer for 15 to 20 minutes, until the lentils are fully cooked.

3. Cut off the tops of the peppers, leaving the stems attached, and remove the seeds. Place the peppers in a shallow pot with 3 cups vegetable stock. Cover and simmer for 10 minutes, then remove from heat.

4. In a bowl, mix together the lentil mixture, the chopped oregano, feta, and black pepper; spoon the mixture into the peppers. Serve the peppers with the stem tops ajar. Garnish with reserved oregano tops.

PER SERVING: Calories: 450 | Fat: 6 g | Protein: 29 g | Sodium: 513 mg | Fiber: 14 g | Carbohydrate: 71 g

Succotash

If you use dried beans, be sure to soak them overnight and then cook them in water until they are al dente.

INGREDIENTS | SERVES 6

½ pound fresh lima beans

2 ears fresh corn

1 large yellow onion

1 red pepper

1 teaspoon olive oil

Freshly cracked black pepper, to taste

1 tablespoon flour

½ cup skim milk

½ cup Basic Vegetable Stock (Chapter 10) or low-sodium canned vegetable stock

1. Cook the beans and corn separately in boiling water until just tender (not quite done). Remove the corn kernels from the cobs. Small-dice the onion and red pepper.

2. In a large saucepan, heat the oil to medium temperature, add the onion, and sauté until light golden in color. Add the red pepper and cook for 1 minute. Season with black pepper.

3. Add the beans and corn, sprinkle with flour, and stir. Whisk in the milk and stock; simmer at low heat for approximately 30 to 45 minutes, until the beans and corn are thoroughly cooked.

PER SERVING: Calories: 194 | Fat: 1.5 g | Protein: 10 g | Sodium: 19 mg | Fiber: 8.5 g | Carbohydrate: 36 g

Edamame

Edamame are fresh soybeans. You can eat them as a snack before sushi or as part of a crudités platter. Edamame are also an excellent addition to salads, soups, and rice dishes.

INGREDIENTS | SERVES 6

6 cups of water
½ teaspoon salt
1 pound frozen edamame in pods

1. Bring the water and the salt to a boil in a saucepan.

2. Add the edamame and let the water come back to a boil.

3. Cook on medium-high for 5 minutes.

4. Drain the edamame and rinse with cold water.

5. Drain again and serve either warm or cool.

PER SERVING: Calories: 107 | Fat: 5 g | Protein: 9 g | Sodium: 204 mg | Fiber: 3 g | Carbohydrate: 8.5 g

Baked Beans

Baked beans are an example of picnic food being a sort of "health" food and not a junk food like the fried chips, French fries, and sugary snacks they often accompany.

INGREDIENTS | SERVES 6

4 cups cooked white beans
1 cup sliced onion
4 slices turkey bacon, chopped
1 teaspoon dry mustard
½ cup brown sugar
½ cup maple syrup
2 tablespoons ketchup
½ teaspoon salt
1 teaspoon pepper
1½ cups water

1. Preheat oven to 350°F.

2. Drain the beans and layer them with the onions and bacon in a casserole dish.

3. Combine the dry mustard, brown sugar, maple syrup, ketchup, salt, pepper, and water, and pour the mixture over the beans.

4. Cover and bake the beans for 2 hours.

5. Uncover and bake for 15 minutes more.

PER SERVING: Calories: 551 | Fat: 3 g | Protein: 33 g | Sodium: 437 mg | Fiber: 20 g | Carbohydrate: 99 g

Refried Pinto Beans

You can give refried beans added crunch and flavor by sprinkling a mixture of minced carrots, celery, chives, peanuts, or pumpkin seeds over the top. Either cilantro or parsley will add a bright green note.

INGREDIENTS | SERVES 4

½ cup diced onion

1 clove minced garlic

2 tablespoons olive oil

2 cups cooked pinto beans, with liquid

1 cup water

1 teaspoon salt

1. Sauté onion and garlic in olive oil until translucent.

2. Mash beans and stir half of them into the onion mixture over medium heat.

3. Stir in half the water and then the remaining beans.

4. Stir in the rest of the water and the salt and cook for 10 minutes, stirring often.

PER SERVING: Calories: 399 | Fat: 8 g | Protein: 20 g | Sodium: 593 mg | Fiber: 15 g | Carbohydrate: 61 g

Red Beans and Rice

A marriage of legume and grain, this is a Caribbean favorite that will feed a family without leaving anyone hungry. You can substitute brown rice for extra fiber.

INGREDIENTS | SERVES 4

¼ cup diced celery

¼ cup diced onion

¼ cup diced green bell pepper

1 clove garlic, minced

1 tablespoon olive oil

¼ cup diced ham

2 cups cooked red beans

½ teaspoon dried thyme

¼ teaspoon cayenne pepper

¾ cup water

Salt, to taste

2 cups cooked white rice

1. Sauté celery, onion, green bell pepper, and garlic in olive oil.

2. Add ham, beans, thyme, cayenne pepper, water, and salt.

3. Simmer for 45 minutes. Adjust seasoning and serve over rice.

PER SERVING: Calories: 460 | Fat: 5 g | Protein: 26 g | Sodium: 122 mg | Fiber: 23 g | Carbohydrate: 79 g

Dal

Dal is a classic East Indian dish that you can easily create and enjoy in the comfort of your own home!

INGREDIENTS | SERVES 6

6 cloves garlic
¼ Scotch bonnet chili pepper
1 tablespoon olive oil
1 cup dried yellow split peas
4 cups Basic Vegetable Stock (Chapter 10) or low-sodium canned vegetable stock

Caution: Hot

Scotch bonnet chili peppers are among the hottest peppers in the world. They are comparable to habanero peppers in terms of their hotness, but they have a flavor distinct from their habanero cousin's.

1. Mince the garlic. Stem, seed, and mince the chili pepper.

2. Heat the oil to medium temperature in a medium-size saucepot; sauté the garlic and chili for 1 minute.

3. Add the peas and stock; simmer for 1 to 2 hours, until the peas are thoroughly cooked. Serve with flatbread.

PER SERVING: Calories: 143 | Fat: 1 g | Protein: 8 g | Sodium: 174 mg | Fiber: 8.5 g | Carbohydrate: 20 g

Grilled Vegetable Hero

This sandwich is sure to please your vegetarian friends.

INGREDIENTS | SERVES 6

1 eggplant
1 red pepper
1 Vidalia onion
1 tablespoon extra-virgin olive oil
6 whole-wheat wraps
3 ounces goat cheese (optional)
Freshly cracked black pepper, to taste

1. Preheat oven grill. Slice eggplant, pepper, and onion approximately 1-inch thick; toss in olive oil; place on grill and cook al dente.

2. Brush the wraps with oil. Layer the veggies on the wraps.

3. Sprinkle with cheese and pepper, and serve.

PER SERVING: Calories: 124 | Fat: 3.5 g | Protein: 3.5 g | Sodium: 154 mg | Fiber: 4 g | Carbohydrate: 20 g

Falafel Sandwich

This is a Middle Eastern classic. In many Middle Eastern countries, falafel stands are on every downtown street, as ubiquitous as McDonald's but much healthier.

INGREDIENTS | SERVES 6

1 cup dried chickpeas
½ cup chopped red onion
3 cloves garlic, peeled
1 teaspoon salt
1 teaspoon pepper
1 teaspoon ground cumin
Pinch of cayenne pepper
1 teaspoon baking powder
3 tablespoons all-purpose flour
3 tablespoons whole-wheat flour
2 cups vegetable oil
3 rounds of pita bread
6 tablespoons hummus
1 cup chopped fresh tomatoes
1 cup shredded lettuce
½ cup chopped cucumbers
6 tablespoons plain yogurt
2 tablespoons chopped fresh parsley

1. Soak the chickpeas in 3 cups of water overnight.

2. Drain the chickpeas and put them in a food processor with the red onion, garlic, salt, pepper, cumin, and cayenne pepper. Pulse until everything is combined and the texture is fine but not a paste.

3. Sprinkle the baking powder and flours over the mixture and pulse again until well combined. Refrigerate for 3 hours.

4. Heat the oil in a deep fryer or large pot to 375°F. Shape falafel mixture into small balls and fry 4 to 5 at a time. Drain on paper towels.

5. Cut the pita rounds in half and open them to create a pocket bread out of each half. For each sandwich, spread the inside of a pita pocket with hummus, stuff a few falafel into it, and top with tomatoes, lettuce, and cucumbers. Drizzle yogurt over the top and sprinkle with parsley.

PER SERVING: Calories: 607 | Fat: 42 g | Protein: 12 g | Sodium: 605 mg | Fiber: 8 g | Carbohydrate: 48 g

Two-Bean Chili Wraps

Here is a vegetarian chili that tastes great and introduces you to the soy food called tempeh. Made from fermented soybeans, tempeh is high in B vitamins and is an excellent protein substitute for saturated fatty meats.

INGREDIENTS | SERVES 6

2 tablespoons olive oil

6 cloves garlic, chopped

1 onion, chopped

2 teaspoons cumin powder

1 teaspoon turmeric

1 teaspoon cayenne pepper

16 ounces tempeh, minced

1 zucchini, chopped

1 red pepper, chopped

1 (14-ounce) can diced tomatoes

1 (15-ounce) can kidney beans, drained and rinsed

1 (15-ounce) can cannellini beans, drained and rinsed

½ cup kalamata olives, diced

Pinch of stevia

Sea salt, to taste

6 whole-grain tortillas

2 cups cooked brown rice

1 avocado, diced

Grated Romano or goat cheese (optional)

½ cup parsley, chopped

1. In a large saucepan, heat oil; sauté garlic and onion until soft.

2. Add cumin, turmeric, and cayenne; cook until roasted, 1 minute.

3. Add tempeh; cook 3 minutes.

4. Add zucchini, red pepper, and diced tomatoes; stir well.

5. Add beans and olives; stir well.

6. Add stevia and salt.

7. Cover, reduce heat, and simmer 20 minutes.

8. Lightly heat tortillas and spoon rice along center of each. Top with chili, avocado, and cheese.

9. Sprinkle with parsley, roll, and serve.

PER SERVING: Calories: 758 | Fat: 26 g | Protein: 28 g | Sodium: 685 mg | Fiber: 12 g | Carbohydrate: 72 g

What Is Stevia?

No more worries about the devastating side effects of artificial sweeteners! Finally, there is an herbal sweetener 300 times sweeter than sugar without any side effects. Stevia helps regulate blood-sugar levels and is safe for diabetics and those of you needing a safe alternative sweetener. Add a little at a time, tasting as you go to determine the right level of sweetness.

Black Bean and Plantain Burritos

These filling burritos make a luscious supper dish.
Queso fresco is a slightly salty, crumbly Mexican cheese; look for it in a Hispanic market.

INGREDIENTS | SERVES 4

¼ cup canola oil

4 (15¼-ounce) cans black beans, drained and rinsed

½ cup salsa

2 teaspoons dried oregano

2 teaspoons ground cumin

2 teaspoons ancho chili powder

2 yellow plantains, peeled

4 (9-inch) whole-wheat tortillas

½ cup queso fresco, or other white crumbly cheese

Snipped fresh cilantro, for garnish

What Are Plantains?

If you have not already sampled this banana look-alike—and banana variety— you'll find that plantains are so versatile that they can be eaten green in savory dishes, or allowed to ripen, even to turn black, and be used as a sweet accent in both sweet and savory fare. Popular in Latino and African countries, the plantain is a pleasing starchy fruit, but note: plantains are not eaten raw.

1. Heat the oil in a large skillet over medium heat and add the beans, stirring and mashing them as they cook. Stir in the salsa and the seasonings and continue cooking and mashing for about 5 minutes more.

2. Split the plantain in half lengthwise and then into quarters. Spray a nonstick skillet with nonstick cooking spray and pan-fry the plantain pieces until they are browned on both sides. Remove the plantain pieces and heat the 2 tortillas in the same skillet, spraying again as needed. When soft, place the tortillas on serving plates. Heap a portion of the beans on one side of the tortilla, place 2 pieces of plantain on the beans, and sprinkle with 2 tablespoons queso fresco; fold the tortilla into a burrito or taco shape. Repeat with the remaining ingredients.

PER SERVING: Calories: 1,041 | Fat: 23 g | Protein: 49 g | Sodium: 442 mg | Fiber: 33 g | Carbohydrate: 167 g

Meatless Meatloaf Sandwich

Use vegetable broth instead of beef to make this a vegetarian dish. However, it would not be vegan because it still has animal products—egg, cheese, and Worcestershire sauce.

INGREDIENTS | SERVES 8

1 cup reduced sodium beef broth
¾ cup kasha
¼ cup olive oil
¾ cup shredded carrots
1 cup diced onion
½ cup diced celery
¼ cup grated Parmesan cheese, plus 8 tablespoons for sandwiches
2 tablespoons chopped fresh parsley
1 tablespoon Dijon mustard
1 tablespoon Worcestershire sauce
1 egg, beaten or ¼ cup egg substitute
1 teaspoon salt
½ teaspoon pepper
1 cup finely chopped pecans, in a food processor
2 tablespoons tomato paste
1 tablespoon brown sugar
½ cup sliced red onions
16 slices of whole-wheat bread

Kasha Buckwheat Groats

Kasha is a term that means porridge, and can be made from grains such as wheat, buckwheat, and rice. It is often used to refer specifically to whole-grain buckwheat, or groats, in the United States. You can make a meaty meatloaf and add fiber with a few tablespoons of unflavored kasha.

1. Preheat oven to 350°F. Spray a loaf pan with oil.

2. Bring the beef broth to a boil in a saucepan and add the kasha. Cover, turn down the heat, and simmer for 15 minutes.

3. Add the olive oil to a sauté pan and sauté the carrots, onion, and celery in it for 5 minutes. Transfer them to a large bowl.

4. Add the Parmesan cheese, parsley, Dijon mustard, Worcestershire sauce, egg, salt, and pepper and mix together with a wooden spoon. Add the cooked kasha and pecans and combine thoroughly. Add a little beef broth if it seems too dry.

5. Press the mixture into the oiled loaf pan. Spread the tomato paste on top of the loaf, sprinkle the brown sugar over the tomato paste, and scatter the red onions across; bake 30 minutes. Remove the loaf from the loaf pan and cut into slices.

6. Per sandwich: Sprinkle 1 tablespoon Parmesan cheese on each meatless loaf slice and brown in a skillet, then sandwich it between 2 slices of bread. Add lettuce, mayonnaise, ketchup, or any other sandwich ingredients you like.

PER SERVING: Calories: 509 | Fat: 23 g | Protein: 13 g | Sodium: 867 mg | Fiber: 9 g | Carbohydrate: 65 g

Sunflower Veggie Burgers

For a vegan version of the recipe, substitute vegetable broth for beef broth and omit Worcestershire sauce, as it has a trace of anchovy flavoring. You can serve these burgers with pesto, add cheese to melt on top, and make some caramelized onions to add to the fiber.

INGREDIENTS | SERVES 8

1½ cups beef broth

½ cup water

¾ cup medium bulgur

⅓ cup dried red lentils

1½ cups chopped mushrooms

1 minced shallot

½ teaspoon celery salt

1½ teaspoons chopped fresh oregano

½ teaspoon chopped fresh thyme

1½ teaspoons chopped fresh sage

¼ teaspoon onion powder

¼ teaspoon paprika

1 teaspoon Dijon mustard

1 teaspoon kosher salt

1 cup sunflower seeds, shelled and roasted (no salt)

½ cup whole-wheat flour

2 teaspoons instant yellow miso

1 tablespoon soy sauce

1 tablespoon Worcestershire sauce

2 tablespoons bread crumbs

Olive oil

1. Put broth, water, bulgur, and lentils in a saucepan. Bring to a simmer, cover, and turn heat to low for 30 minutes. Set aside.

2. In a large bowl, combine the mushrooms, shallot, herbs, spices, mustard, salt, sunflower seeds, and whole-wheat flour.

3. Stir the miso, soy sauce, and Worcestershire sauce into the warm bulgur mixture, then add the mixture to the mushroom mixture. Stir well, then stir in the bread crumbs.

4. Measure and mold the mixture into 8 portions on a wax paper–lined sheet pan. Press down the mounds with your hand to flatten them slightly into patties. Cover with plastic wrap and refrigerate 3 hours or overnight.

5. To cook the patties, brush both sides with olive oil and cook in a nonstick pan 2 minutes per side over medium-high heat. Serve hot on buns with condiments of your choice.

PER SERVING: Calories: 177 | Fat: 8.5 g | Protein: 8 g | Sodium: 352 mg | Fiber: 4.5 g | Carbohydrate: 19 g

Veggie Burgers

These luscious treats, made with various legumes such as chickpeas, black beans, black-eyed peas, and soy, are now available everywhere in frozen form. You can make your own using the recipes in this chapter for a fresher, more hands-on approach. They are a high-fiber, nutritious lunch, dinner, or snack.

Green Lentil Salad

Green lentils are smaller and plumper than other lentils, which makes them look like the caviar of lentils. When you make this dish yourself, you can cook the lentils to your preference.

INGREDIENTS | SERVES 4

1 cup dried French green lentils

5 cups water

1 bay leaf

2 tablespoons olive oil

1 carrot, finely chopped

1 stalk celery, finely chopped

2 tablespoons minced shallots

1 teaspoon minced garlic

2 tablespoons extra-virgin olive oil

¼ cup lemon juice

1 teaspoon grated lemon zest

1 tablespoon chopped fresh thyme

1 tablespoon chopped fresh parsley

¼ teaspoon ground coriander

Salt and pepper, to taste

1. Put the lentils, water, and bay leaf in a saucepan. Bring to a boil, reduce heat, and simmer for 20 minutes. Drain in a colander, remove the bay leaf, and let the lentils cool. Put them in a large bowl and set aside.

2. Heat the olive oil in a sauté pan and cook the carrot, celery, and shallots over medium heat until tender, about 5 minutes. Add to the lentils.

3. Add the garlic, extra-virgin olive oil, lemon juice, lemon zest, thyme, parsley, coriander, salt, and pepper to the lentils. Toss to combine and chill.

4. Serve chilled or at room temperature.

PER SERVING: Calories: 390 | Fat: 14 g | Protein: 19 g | Sodium: 37 mg | Fiber: 24 g | Carbohydrate: 47 g

Iron Power

Lentils are one of the best vegetable sources of iron. They are ideal for vegetarians and help to prevent iron deficiency anemia. They are also an excellent source of protein and fiber, which allows meals to keep you satisfied for hours.

Potato and Chickpea Curry Salad

This is yet another perfect example of something that tastes wonderful and is good for you, too!

INGREDIENTS | SERVES 6

1 teaspoon olive oil

1 large yellow onion, sliced

1 cup chickpeas

1½ tablespoons curry powder

½ bulb garlic, minced

1 bay leaf

4 cups Basic Vegetable Stock (Chapter 10) or low-sodium canned vegetable stock

2 baked potatoes, cubed

¼ bunch celery, cut into small dice

1 pint cherry tomatoes, cut into halves

Kosher salt, to taste

Freshly cracked black pepper, to taste

1. Heat the oil on medium in a stockpot. Sauté the onion, then add the chickpeas, curry, garlic, and bay leaf.

2. Add the stock and simmer for 2 hours. Strain, discard the stock, and allow the peas to cool.

3. In large bowl, mix together the peas, potatoes, celery, and tomatoes. Season with salt and pepper. Serve with your favorite soup or sandwich.

PER SERVING: Calories: 352 | Fat: 2g | Protein: 12 g | Sodium: 299 mg | Fiber: 8.5 g | Carbohydrate: 45 g

Three-Bean Salad

Any number of bean types can work in this recipe—the kinds used here are the common beans used in a traditional three-bean salad.

INGREDIENTS | SERVES 6

1 large red onion

3 sprigs marjoram

¼ cup kalamata olives

1 cup green beans

½ cup cooked red kidney beans

½ cup cooked chickpeas or cannellini beans

2 tablespoons extra-virgin olive oil

½ cup balsamic vinegar

Freshly cracked black pepper, to taste

1. Thinly slice the onion and chop the marjoram. Roughly chop the olives.

2. Cook the green beans in boiling water or steam until al dente, then shock in ice-cold water and drain thoroughly.

3. Mix together all the ingredients in a large bowl. Adjust seasonings as desired.

PER SERVING: Calories: 215 | Fat: 8.5 g | Protein: 7 g | Sodium: 141 mg | Fiber: 7.5 g | Carbohydrate: 27 g

Kidney Bean and Barley Casserole

Feel free to substitute any type of bean and vegetable purée to better suit your taste.

INGREDIENTS | SERVES 6

1 teaspoon olive oil

¼ bunch celery

1 yellow onion

½ head romaine lettuce

1 cup puréed carrots

1 cup Basic Vegetable Stock (Chapter 10) or low-sodium canned vegetable stock

1 cup cooked kidney beans

½ cup cooked barley

3 sprigs thyme, leaves only

½ teaspoon dried oregano leaves

½ teaspoon chili powder

Freshly cracked black pepper, to taste

1. Preheat oven to 325°F. Grease a casserole or loaf pan with the oil.

2. Slice the celery and onion. Shred the romaine lettuce.

3. Blend together the carrot purée and stock.

4. In the prepared dish, layer the beans, celery, onion, barley, herbs, spices, and the carrot-stock mixture; cover and bake for 30 to 45 minutes. Serve topped with shredded romaine.

PER SERVING: Calories: 186 | Fat: 1.5 g | Protein: 10 g | Sodium: 131 mg | Fiber: 11 g | Carbohydrate: 33 g

Using Thyme

When using thyme for flavoring, use whole cleaned sprigs and remove after cooking. If you wish to leave the thyme in, strip the stem of its leaves and add only the leaves to your dish. Or, just use thyme as a garnish.

CHAPTER 13

Soylicious

"Sausage" Bread Pudding

Vary the berry topping to suit your taste by using raspberries, blueberries, blackberries, or strawberries. If these are not available, substitute 2 cups of your favorite seasonal fruits cut into small cubes.

INGREDIENTS | SERVES 4

1 tablespoon olive oil

1 teaspoon minced garlic

1 cup soy "sausage" meat

1 teaspoon Cajun or Creole seasoning or hot sauce to taste

2 cups low-fat milk

3 tablespoons melted butter

4 large eggs or 1 cup egg substitute

2 cups shredded low-fat Cheddar or Monterey jack cheese

3 cups cubed sourdough bread

2 cups fresh blackberries or blueberries

What Are Soy Sausages?

Made from soy proteins, soy "sausages" are available as links or as a compact product packed in a tube. In the tube, the soy meat is easy to crumble and sauté like its pork sausage counterpart; alternatively, it slices easily and pan-fries like a patty. Look for soy sausage products in a refrigerated case displayed with other vegetarian and vegan items.

1. Preheat the oven to 375°F. Lightly butter a 2-quart baking dish.

2. Heat the oil in a large skillet over medium heat and sauté the garlic for about 30 seconds. Add and crumble the soy sausage, stirring as you crumble, and season with the Cajun seasoning. Reduce the heat to low.

3. Meanwhile, beat together the milk, butter, and eggs until foamy. Stir in the cheese and sausage mixture. Put the bread into the baking dish and pour the milk mixture over the bread.

4. Bake the pudding for about 45 minutes or until puffy and golden. Serve hot with the fruit topping.

PER SERVING: Calories: 711 | Fat: 30 g | Protein: 44 g | Sodium: 971 mg | Fiber: 7 g | Carbohydrate: 39 g

Miso Soup with Soba Noodles and Fried Tofu

Japan's beloved miso soup typically contains little bits of cubed tofu.
But in this variation, tofu becomes a star player in the dish.

INGREDIENTS | SERVES 4

4 ounces dry soba noodles

3 tablespoons miso paste, or to taste

1 (9-ounce) package fried tofu, diced

1 bunch watercress, leaves only

Soy sauce, to taste

Tofu 101

Basic tofu is made by crushing dried soybeans with water, extracting the liquid to produce soy milk. This soy milk is then boiled, and a coagulant, such as a natural food acid or a salt, is added to produce curds. The resultant solid mass is then cut and packaged for sale.

1. Bring a pot of lightly salted water to a boil and cook the soba noodles; these cook quickly, so test them for doneness after about 3 minutes. Drain and toss them to separate the strands.

2. Bring 6 cups water to a boil and stir in the miso paste; start gradually so you find the right flavor for you. When it is fully dissolved, add the tofu and continue cooking until the tofu is heated. Add the watercress leaves.

3. Portion the noodles into 4 soup bowls and ladle the hot soup over the noodles. Add soy sauce, as desired, and serve.

PER SERVING: Calories: 395 | Fat: 14 g | Protein: 17 g | Sodium: 721 mg | Fiber: 3 g | Carbohydrate: 31 g

Fit Cream of Broccoli Soup

Silken tofu makes an excellent substitute for dairy cream or milk in this simple, tasty soup. Top with toasted pine nuts for that extra crunchy flavor.

INGREDIENTS | SERVES 8

2 heads of broccoli

½ onion, chopped

2 cloves garlic, minced

1 tablespoon extra-virgin olive oil

½ cup fresh parsley, minced

6 cups Basic Vegetable Stock (Chapter 10) or low-sodium canned vegetable stock

3 tablespoons white or yellow miso

1 (12-ounce) package silken tofu

Sea salt, to taste

Freshly ground white pepper, to taste

Miso

Miso is a Japanese culinary staple that is made by fermenting rice, barley, and/or soybeans with salt and a unique fungus. The final product is a thick paste that can be used for sauces, spreads, soups, and even for pickling meats or vegetables. This seasoning is high in protein and many B vitamins.

1. Cut the florets off the broccoli stems; peel and chop.

2. In a large heavy saucepan, sauté the onion and garlic in oil until just tender; add half the parsley, setting the rest aside to use as garnish.

3. Add the stock and broccoli; bring to a boil; reduce heat and simmer until broccoli is tender, about 15 minutes.

4. Remove a small amount of broth to a bowl and dissolve the miso in it. Return it to the soup pot and stir; remove pot from heat.

5. Crumble silken tofu into broth; use a hand-wand mixer to purée until smooth. An alternative is to ladle the soup into a blender in batches and purée until smooth.

6. Add salt and pepper to taste; serve either warm or chilled, topped with toasted pine nuts and minced parsley.

PER SERVING: Calories: 112 | Fat: 2 g | Protein: 9 g | Sodium: 342 mg | Fiber: 5 g | Carbohydrate: 14 g

Cellophane "Chicken" Noodle Salad

In the traditional Thai version of this salad, cooks use fish sauce instead of soy sauce and use ground pork, shrimp, and/or chicken for the meat.

INGREDIENTS | SERVES 4

4 ounces cellophane, or bean thread, noodles, softened in hot water for 20 minutes

1 (6-ounce) package soy "chicken" strips, optional

½ cup thinly sliced scallions

½ cup fresh cilantro leaves

1 to 2 tablespoons crushed red pepper

2 tablespoons lime juice

2 tablespoons soy sauce

1 tablespoon pickled garlic, chopped

1. Drain the soaked and softened noodles and cut them into serving pieces. Put the noodles, "chicken" strips if using, scallions, cilantro leaves, and crushed red pepper into a serving bowl.

2. Mix together the lime juice, soy sauce, and pickled garlic and toss with the salad ingredients.

PER SERVING: Calories: 114 | Fat: 0 g | Protein: 1.5 g | Sodium: 465 mg | Fiber: 0.5 g | Carbohydrate: 27 g

A Super-Hero Wrap-Up

This is such a versatile carry-all for nutrients that you can switch filling ingredients around to suit your palate. While the filling ingredients are only suggestions, try to stick to the amounts suggested, or the wrap may spill out all the goodies.

INGREDIENTS | SERVES 1

1 tablespoon olive oil

1 tablespoon minced garlic, or to taste

3 ounces soy "chicken" strips

¼ red onion, thinly sliced

1 (10-inch) whole-wheat wrap

3 tablespoons plain low-fat yogurt, preferably the thick Greek yogurt

2 tablespoons chopped fresh dill weed

½ cup julienned cucumber

½ cup julienned red pepper

1. Heat the oil in a large skillet over medium heat. Sauté the garlic, "chicken" strips, and red onion for 3 to 4 minutes or until the onion wilts slightly. Set aside to cool.

2. Heat the wrap for 30 to 40 seconds per side in a nonstick skillet or according to package directions. Set aside.

3. Toss the "chicken" mixture with the yogurt, dill weed, cucumber, and red pepper. Spread the wrap out flat and top with this mixture. Roll up as desired.

PER SERVING: Calories: 430 | Fat: 21 g | Protein: 21 g | Sodium: 603 mg | Fiber: 7.5 g | Carbohydrate: 39 g

Golden West Chili

This chili, which is as bright and sunny as a day in California, can be altered to suit your taste. Just keep the proportions about the same. Serve this with fresh flour tortillas.

INGREDIENTS | SERVES 6

3 tablespoons canola oil

1 large onion, diced

12 ounces ground soy "meat" crumbles

1 tablespoon chili powder, or more to taste

1 (15-ounce) can golden hominy

1 (15½-ounce) can canary beans, drained and rinsed

1 (15½-ounce) can pigeon peas, drained and rinsed

1 cup green salsa

1 cup Mexican beer, or more as needed

Salt and freshly ground black pepper, to taste

3 tomatillos, chopped, for garnish

Grated cheese, for garnish

Chopped fresh cilantro, for garnish

Diced avocados, for garnish

Toasted pumpkin seeds, for garnish

1. Heat the oil in a large saucepan over medium heat and sauté the onion until partially golden, about 5 minutes. Add the soy crumbles and continue cooking for 3 or 4 more minutes. Stir in the chili powder. Add the hominy, beans, pigeon peas, salsa, and beer and stir well.

2. Reduce the heat to medium-low and continue cooking and stirring about 8 minutes more. Season with salt and pepper. Serve in individual bowls, garnishing as desired.

PER SERVING: Calories: 562 | Fat: 12 g | Protein: 32 g | Sodium: 342 mg | Fiber: 19 g | Carbohydrate: 79 g

What Is Hominy?

If you are not from the South or have never eaten the Mexican classic posole, you may not be familiar with the white corn kernel known as hominy. Made from dried corn kernels that have been treated chemically, hominy has a pleasant texture and mild taste. In the Southwest and in Mexico, larger-kernel hominy is available and is known as posole. The smaller hominy is sold canned in most supermarkets; look for the larger variety at a Latino market.

Asian Soy Chili

For a totally Asian meal, consider serving this chili over hot steamed jasmine rice.

INGREDIENTS | SERVES 4

3 tablespoons canola oil

1 large onion, diced

1½ tablespoons minced garlic, or to taste

1½ tablespoons minced fresh ginger

1 tablespoon black bean–garlic paste

6 ounces soy "meat" crumbles

1 (10-ounce) package fresh edamame, rinsed

1 cup crumbled silken firm tofu

1 cup vegetable broth, or more as desired

1 tablespoon soy sauce, or more to taste

1 teaspoon toasted sesame oil, or more to taste

1 teaspoon crushed red pepper, or more as desired

Toasted soybeans, for garnish

Sliced scallions, for garnish

Diced firm tofu, for garnish

1. Heat the oil in a large saucepan over medium heat and sauté the onion, garlic, and ginger for 2 to 3 minutes or until fragrant. Stir in the black bean–garlic paste and the soy crumbles. Sauté for about 4 minutes.

2. Reduce the heat to medium-low. Stir in the edamame, tofu, broth, soy sauce, sesame oil, and crushed red pepper. Cook and stir for about 10 minutes. Serve in individual bowls, garnishing as desired.

PER SERVING: Calories: 333 | Fat: 21 g | Protein: 21 g | Sodium: 470 mg | Fiber: 6.5 g | Carbohydrate: 15 g

The Taste of Tofu

Tofu has very little taste on its own. It relies on seasoning and marinades to bring out its true colors. Therefore, tofu can be adapted to any type of dish imaginable. Its presence will give the dish a powerful protein and phytochemical infusion.

Meatless Cabbage Rolls

Also known as stuffed cabbage, depending on where you come from, high-fiber cabbage is stuffed with lean meat or, in this case, soy "meat" crumbles, with more fiber in the whole grains and brown rice.

INGREDIENTS | SERVES 4; SERVING SIZE 3 ROLLS

12 large cabbage leaves

2 cups cooked brown rice

½ cup currants

¼ cup toasted hazelnuts

½ cup minced onion

½ cup celery, chopped

¾ teaspoon salt

Pepper, to taste

2 cups soy meat crumbles

1 tablespoon olive oil

2 cups tomato sauce

2 garlic cloves, finely minced

1 tablespoon brown sugar

1. Blanch the cabbage leaves in boiling water for 4 minutes. Remove and lay flat on a tray. Chill in the refrigerator.

2. Combine the cooked brown rice, currants, hazelnuts, onion, celery, salt, and pepper in a bowl. Add soy crumbles and mix well. Remove cabbage leaves from the refrigerator and blot with paper towels. Place about ¼ cup soy meat mixture on each cabbage leaf. Fold in sides and then roll up leaf to completely enclose filling.

3. Heat the olive oil in a skillet. Add the tomato sauce, garlic, and brown sugar and stir to combine.

4. Place the cabbage rolls in the tomato sauce, seam sides down. Spoon some of the sauce over the rolls, cover, and cook over medium-low heat for 60 minutes. Reduce heat to low and simmer for an additional 20 minutes, adding a little water if needed. Serve hot.

PER SERVING: Calories: 758 | Fat: 18 g | Protein: 32 g | Sodium: 951 mg | Fiber: 15 g | Carbohydrate: 62 g

Stuffed Bell Peppers

Similar to the cabbage rolls, stuffed peppers offer lean meat, vegetables, and whole-grain fiber in the casing and the stuffing. This recipe uses soy "meat" crumbles in place of the beef. For the extra-nutrition-conscious cook: red and yellow peppers have far more vitamin C in them than the green ones.

INGREDIENTS | SERVES 6

2 large green bell peppers

2 large red bell peppers

2 large yellow bell peppers

2 cups soy "meat" crumbles

¼ cup Grape Nuts cereal

½ cup cooked brown rice

½ cup diced onion

½ cup diced carrots

½ cup diced celery

Salt and pepper, to taste

2½ cups tomato sauce

1. Preheat oven to 350°F.

2. Cut peppers in half through the stem and discard seeds, stem, and membrane. Lay pepper cups in a casserole dish.

3. Mix together the soy crumbles, cereal, rice, onion, carrots, celery, and ½ cup tomato sauce. Season mixture with salt and pepper.

4. Stuff each pepper half with a ball of soy meat mixture, mounding it on top.

5. Pour tomato sauce over tops of stuffed peppers. Cover with foil and bake 45–60 minutes.

PER SERVING: Calories: 313 | Fat: 6 g | Protein: 20 g | Sodium: 572 mg | Fiber: 9 g | Carbohydrate: 35 g

Asian Stir-Fried Rice

When cooking tofu, you need to press out the excess water, otherwise it splatters in hot oil and doesn't brown well. To do this, slice a block of tofu in half and wrap the cut pieces in layers of paper towels, changing the towels for new sheets when these get soaked.

INGREDIENTS | SERVES 4

3 tablespoons canola oil

8 ounces firm tofu, cubed

3 cloves garlic, crushed and minced

1 onion, diced

1 tablespoon minced fresh ginger, or to taste

1 cup cubed winter squash, such as butternut or kabocha

1 cup shelled edamame

1 (8-ounce) can sliced bamboo shoots, drained

2 long green chilies, thinly sliced

2 cups cooked short-grain brown rice, chilled

3 tablespoons soy sauce, or to taste

½ cup vegetable broth or water, as needed

1. Heat the oil in a large wok or skillet over medium-high heat. Add and stir-fry the tofu, cooking it until it starts to brown. Remove it from the wok and set aside.

2. Add the garlic, onion, and ginger and stir-fry for about 1 minute. Add the squash and edamame and stir-fry about 2 minutes. Add the bamboo shoots, chilies, and rice, stirring well to combine. Add the soy sauce and cover the wok, cooking the mixture for about 5 minutes or until the squash becomes tender. During the cooking, check that the mixture does not get too dry and add vegetable broth as needed, stirring it in well. Serve hot.

PER SERVING: Calories: 762 | Fat: 26 g | Protein: 32 g | Sodium: 711 mg | Fiber: 9 g | Carbohydrate: 47 g

Why Chill the Rice?

If you don't chill cooked rice for stir-frying, the grains clump together and become mushy; they are also likely to absorb too much oil during the cooking. Besides, stir-frying is a great way to use up leftover rice. This recipe calls for short-grain brown rice, which is somewhat sticky, but it provides a delicious texture and flavor for this dish. Any leftover rice will work.

Artichoke Tofu and Rice Bake

No amount is given for black pepper purposely to allow the cook to add the amount she or he prefers.

INGREDIENTS | SERVES 6

3 fresh artichokes

1 shallot

2 cloves garlic

2 teaspoons olive oil, divided

½ cup brown rice

2½ cups Basic Vegetable Stock (Chapter 10) or low-sodium canned vegetable stock

3 ounces soft tofu

1 sprig fresh tarragon

Freshly cracked black pepper, to taste

6 green olives

6 black olives

½ cup Balsamic Reduction Sauce (Chapter 17)

Helping Things Along

To help things along, prepare and halfway cook the artichokes a day ahead. Trim the top of each leaf with scissors and cut the artichokes in half lengthwise. Peel the stems and remove the prickly "choke" in the centers. Cook in boiling water for 15 minutes, then remove and let cool.

1. Prepare the artichokes (see "Helping Things Along" for prep directions) and cook them halfway in boiling water, for approximately 15 minutes; set aside. Cut the shallot into a small dice and mince the garlic.

2. Heat 1 teaspoon of the oil to low temperature in a medium-size saucepan; add the shallot and garlic and sweat for 2 minutes. Add the rice; stir for 1 minute. Add 2 cups of the stock, cover, and simmer on medium heat for 35 to 40 minutes.

3. Preheat oven to 350°F.

4. In a medium-size bowl, combine the cooked rice mixture with the tofu, tarragon, pepper, and olives. Place the artichokes in a baking dish. Stuff small amounts of the rice mix between the artichoke leaves. Pour the remaining stock into the baking dish. Drizzle the remaining oil over the top of the artichokes. Cover and bake for 20 minutes. Serve with Balsamic Reduction Sauce.

PER SERVING: Calories: 149 | Fat: 3.5 g | Protein: 4.5 g | Sodium: 392 mg | Fiber: 4.5 g | Carbohydrate: 17 g

Curried "Meatballs" in Pita

For a spicier filling, use hot mango chutney instead of the sweet and add 1 or 2 diced green chilies to the meatball mixture. If you can find them, use the Greek-style pita loaves, which are extra-large but require wrapping as these loaves don't slit open for an inner pocket.

INGREDIENTS | SERVES 2

1 tablespoon canola oil

1 cup diced tomatoes

½ cup chopped onions

1 (9-ounce) package soy "meatballs"

½ cup chopped fresh cilantro

2 tablespoons sweet mango chutney

1 tablespoon Indian curry powder

1 teaspoon ground turmeric

Salt, to taste

1 cup plain low-fat yogurt

2 large whole-wheat pita loaves, softened

1. Heat the oil in a large skillet over medium heat and sauté the tomatoes and onion until softened. Meanwhile, cut the "meatballs" in half and add them to the skillet, stirring well and cooking until they are heated through. Stir in the cilantro, chutney, curry powder, turmeric, and salt. Cook about 2 minutes more and stir in the yogurt. Cook 2 to 3 minutes more and set aside.

2. Spoon the mixture evenly into the pita pockets; alternatively, wrap the "meatballs" up in the pita, tucking one end up to prevent dripping.

PER SERVING: Calories: 543 | Fat: 19 g | Protein: 33 g | Sodium: 980 mg | Fiber: 9 g | Carbohydrate: 58 g

Soy Nut and Bean Patties

Soy nuts can be ground in a food processor, a spice grinder, or even a coffee grinder.

INGREDIENTS | SERVES 6

½ cup soy nuts

1 cup cooked beans

1 shallot

8 cloves garlic

2 ounces Parmesan cheese

1 egg or ¼ cup egg substitute

¼ cup Basic Vegetable Stock (Chapter 10) or low-sodium canned vegetable stock

1 teaspoon dried oregano

Freshly cracked black pepper, to taste

2 teaspoons olive oil

1. Preheat oven broiler.

2. Grind the soy nuts. Purée the beans in a blender. Finely dice the shallot and mince the garlic. Grate the cheese. Beat the egg.

3. Combine all the ingredients. Form the mixture into patties and cook under the broiler for 4 minutes on each side.

PER SERVING: Calories: 236 | Fat: 7 g | Protein: 16 g | Sodium: 86 mg | Fiber: 8 g | Carbohydrate: 29 g

Sweet and Sour "Meatballs" over Brown Rice

*This pleasing stir-fry brings together all the beloved flavors of a popular Chinese entrée,
but instead of pork, you use anti-inflammatory soy "meatballs."*

INGREDIENTS | SERVES 4

1 (20-ounce) can unsweetened pineapple cubes in juice

1 cup 100% pineapple juice

½ cup water

⅓ cup soy sauce

¼ cup white vinegar

3 tablespoons granulated sugar

2 tablespoons cornstarch

2 teaspoons sesame oil

2 tablespoons canola oil

1 (9-ounce) package soy "meatballs"

1 red pepper, seeded and diced

1 zucchini, diced

1 bunch scallions, sliced on the diagonal

2 teaspoons minced garlic

1 cup cashews

2 cups cooked brown rice

1. Drain the pineapple cubes and reserve the juice. Combine the juice, water, soy sauce, vinegar, sugar, cornstarch, and sesame oil in a mixing bowl, blending well. Set aside.

2. Heat the canola oil in a large skillet or wok over medium heat. When it is hot, add the "meatballs" and stir-fry for about 2 minutes.

3. Add the pineapple cubes, red pepper, zucchini, scallions, and garlic and stir-fry for 2 minutes.

4. Pour in the pineapple juice mixture and stir well to coat all the ingredients. Cook, stirring often, for about 2 more minutes or until the sauce thickens slightly. Remove from the heat and stir in the cashews. Serve over hot brown rice.

PER SERVING: Calories: 812 | Fat: 31 g | Protein: 11 g | Sodium: 928 mg | Fiber: 5 g | Carbohydrate: 70 g

Vegetarian "Meatballs"

Although you can make a meatball-type product at home with a mixture of such ingredients as cereals, cheeses, and/or grains, most well-stocked markets offer in their specialty foods section heat-and-serve meatballs made from soy proteins. Your friends and family may never know the difference between these and the ground beef originals.

Sautéed Mixed Greens with Kielbasa "Sausage"

Bursting with flavor and nutrients, this greens medley suits a casual dinner;
offer this with a toasted baguette.

INGREDIENTS | SERVES 4

2 tablespoons olive oil

1 large onion, thinly sliced

1 (12-ounce) package Kielbasa soy "sausage," thinly sliced

1 bunch chard, rinsed and coarsely chopped

1 bunch collards, rinsed and julienned

½ cup grated Parmesan cheese

1. Heat the oil in a large stockpot over medium heat and sauté the onion and "sausage" slices until the onion turns golden.

2. Add the greens and a sprinkling of water, cover the stockpot, and steam the greens until they are wilted and tender. Sprinkle the greens with the Parmesan cheese and serve.

PER SERVING: Calories: 285 | Fat: 16 g | Protein: 21 g | Sodium: 701 mg | Fiber: 5 g | Carbohydrate: 14 g

Meatless Meatball and Bean Tortellini

For a splash of color, add some chopped-up oil-packed sun-dried tomatoes to taste. Additionally, you can boost flavors with a garnish of capers and pitted niçoise olives.

INGREDIENTS | SERVES 4

1 (12-ounce) package fresh tortellini

3 tablespoons olive oil

5 cloves garlic, minced

1 (9-ounce) package soy "meatballs"

1 (19-ounce) can cannellini, drained and rinsed

1 (14½-ounce) can roasted tomatoes

Salt and freshly ground black pepper, to taste

1. Cook the tortellini according to package directions, drain, and set aside.

2. Meanwhile, heat the oil in a large skillet over medium heat and sauté the garlic and the "meatballs" for 4 to 5 minutes. Add the cannellini and tomatoes and continue cooking until the mixture is heated through. Season with salt and pepper. Add the tortellini, stirring to combine, and serve.

PER SERVING: Calories: 571 | Fat: 20 g | Protein: 29 g | Sodium: 863 mg | Fiber: 9 g | Carbohydrate: 70 g

Crispy Chinese Cabbage with Shredded Peanut "Chicken"

You might want to accompany this salad with crispy spring rolls and a peanut dipping sauce. For variety's sake, try using crispy tofu in place of the "chicken" strips.

INGREDIENTS | SERVES 4 TO 6

5 cups shredded napa cabbage (about 1¼ pounds)

1 sweet red pepper, seeded and julienned

1 cup roasted peanuts

¾ cup fresh cilantro leaves

1 tablespoon plus ¼ cup canola oil

2 (6-ounce) packages soy "chicken" strips

1 cup shredded bamboo shoots, rinsed and drained

3 tablespoons crunchy peanut butter

3 tablespoons soy sauce

3 cloves garlic, minced

3 tablespoons rice vinegar

3 tablespoons sugar

1 to 2 teaspoons crushed red pepper

1. Put the cabbage shreds, julienned pepper, peanuts, and cilantro leaves in a large bowl. Set aside.

2. Heat 1 tablespoon oil in a large wok or skillet over medium heat and stir-fry the "chicken" strips and bamboo shoots for 1 minute. Set aside.

3. Mix the ¼ cup oil, peanut butter, soy sauce, garlic, vinegar, sugar, and crushed red pepper, whisking together to mix well. Blend the dressing ingredients with a whisk until smooth in a small bowl and set aside.

4. Add the "chicken" strips and bamboo shoots to the cabbage mixture and toss with the salad dressing to coat the ingredients well. Serve.

PER SERVING: Calories: 427 | Fat: 29 g | Protein: 20 g | Sodium: 787 mg | Fiber: 6 g | Carbohydrate: 26 g

Tofu Mac and Cheese

*If you enjoy macaroni and cheese, you'll likely love this fancier version.
The good ol' mac and cheese just won't ever be the same.*

INGREDIENTS | SERVES 6

3 heads fresh spinach

1 shallot

3 cloves garlic

3 ounces goat cheese

3 ounces firm tofu

2 tablespoons olive oil, plus extra for greasing

2½ tablespoons all-purpose unbleached flour

2 cups skim milk

3 cups cooked pasta

¼ cup chopped Spanish olives

Freshly cracked black pepper, to taste

1. Preheat oven to 350°F.

2. Steam the spinach. Mince the shallot and garlic. Crumble the goat cheese and cut the tofu into small cubes.

3. Heat the 2 tablespoons oil to medium temperature in a medium-size saucepan, then add the flour to form a roux. Whisk in the milk, and cook until thickened to make white sauce.

4. Grease a casserole pan and ladle in the white sauce. Layer the pasta, spinach, cheese, tofu, olives, shallots, garlic, pepper, and more white sauce (in that order). Continue to layer until all ingredients are used.

5. Bake, covered, for approximately 15 to 20 minutes until heated through. Uncover and brown for 5 to 10 minutes longer.

PER SERVING: Calories: 348 | Fat: 13 g | Protein: 23 g | Sodium: 366 mg | Fiber: 8.5 g | Carbohydrate: 43 g

Ma Po Tofu

This dish showcases tofu with a backdrop of plenty of garlic and ginger; you can adjust the chili heat to suit your taste, and always feel free to add more garlic. Look for the black bean garlic sauce condiment at an Asian grocery or a well-stocked supermarket. Serve this over steamed brown rice.

INGREDIENTS | SERVES 4

3 tablespoons vegetable oil

4 cloves garlic, minced

1-inch piece fresh ginger, thinly sliced

3 tablespoons black bean garlic sauce

2 tablespoons soy sauce

1 tablespoon Vietnamese garlic-chili paste, or more to taste

1 cup Basic Vegetable Stock (Chapter 10) or low-sodium canned vegetable stock

1 tablespoon cornstarch

1 tablespoon sugar

1 pound firm tofu, drained, pressed dry, and diced

6 ounces soy "meat" crumbles

2 bunches scallions, trimmed and cut on the diagonal

1. Heat a large wok or skillet over medium heat and add the vegetable oil. When it is hot, add the garlic and the ginger and stir-fry for 30 seconds. Stir in the black bean garlic sauce, the soy sauce, and the chili paste.

2. Mix the vegetable stock together with the cornstarch and sugar and stir into the wok. Stir in the tofu and the soy crumbles and stir-fry the mixture until the sauce thickens and the tofu is heated through. Add the scallions, stir-fry for 1 to 2 minutes more, and serve.

PER SERVING: Calories: 370 | Fat: 23 g | Protein: 27 g | Sodium: 699 mg | Fiber: 5 g | Carbohydrate: 18 g

Soft or Hard?

There are two main types of tofu: soft or regular tofu. Soft tofu, also known as silken tofu, has a softer consistency and will fall apart if not handled carefully. Hence, it is best used in sauces, dressings, and desserts resulting in a thick and creamy texture. Regular tofu, also called firm, is best used in stir fries, tofu bakes, or any recipes where you want the tofu to retain its shape.

Mediterranean Tofu

Because you are using silken tofu, it will partially fall apart as you stir the dish, dispersing itself throughout the mixture.

INGREDIENTS | SERVES 4

2 tablespoons canola oil

1 large sweet onion, diced

4 cloves garlic, minced

3 zucchini, thinly sliced

1 (14½-ounce) can crushed tomatoes

1 (1 pound) package silken firm tofu, cubed

1 cup pitted kalamata olives

1. Heat the oil in a large wok or skillet and sauté the onion and garlic for about 3 minutes.

2. Add the zucchini and cook 3 minutes more.

3. Add the tomatoes, tofu, and olives and cook 2 to 3 minutes more. Serve.

PER SERVING: Calories: 447 | Fat: 37 g | Protein: 21 g | Sodium: 945 mg | Fiber: 4.5 g | Carbohydrate: 17 g

Sesame Tofu

Lots of crunchy sesame seeds are the coating for these chewy, crusty marvels. You can also add a cup of cooked chopped broccoli to get your greens. Sliced raw sugar snaps make a fine garnish.

INGREDIENTS | SERVES 4 (SERVING SIZE 1½ CUPS)

1 pound fresh tofu, cubed

½ cup rice flour

Pinch of five spice powder

1 teaspoon sesame oil

1 egg, beaten or ¼ cup egg substitute

¾ cup sesame seeds

½ cup peanut oil

½ cup teriyaki sauce

4 cups cooked rice or noodles

¼ cup sliced green onions

1. Drain the tofu cubes well on paper towels.

2. Mix the rice flour with the spice powder. Mix the sesame oil with the egg.

3. Dredge the tofu in the flour mixture, then dip in the egg mixture and toss in sesame seeds to coat. Lay the tofu in a single layer and let dry for 10 minutes.

4. Heat peanut oil in a skillet and pan-fry the tofu until crispy.

5. Drain the tofu on paper towels and then toss with teriyaki sauce. Serve over rice or noodles with green onions.

PER SERVING: Calories: 891 | Fat: 53 g | Protein: 33 g | Sodium: 1,117 mg | Fiber: 6 g | Carbohydrate: 77 g

CHAPTER 14

Great Grains

Millet

This grain side dish is often mixed with ground corn, buckwheat, and other grains for added fiber and flavor. It mixes well with fruit for breakfast and is excellent for people with gluten intolerance.

INGREDIENTS | SERVES 4

2½ cups Rich Poultry Stock (Chapter 10) or low-sodium canned chicken stock
1 cup millet
2 tablespoons butter
½ teaspoon salt

1. Heat the chicken stock to boiling.

2. Sauté millet in butter for a few minutes; then add boiling chicken broth and salt. Stir and cover.

3. Turn heat to low and simmer 25 minutes. Turn off heat and let stand, covered, for 5 minutes.

PER SERVING: Calories: 250 | Fat: 7.5 g | Protein: 7.5 g | Sodium: 698 mg | Fiber: 4.5 g | Carbohydrate: 37 g

Kasha Buckwheat Groats

Kasha refers to toasted buckwheat kernels that can be purchased whole, cracked, or ground. This whole grain is high in fiber, protein, B vitamins, and potassium. It imparts a nutty taste and unique texture to salads, soups, and stews.

INGREDIENTS | SERVES 4

1 tablespoon olive oil
1 cup whole kasha
2 cups chicken broth
½ teaspoon salt

1. Heat the olive oil in a skillet over medium-high heat and sauté the kasha in it for 3 minutes.

2. Add the chicken broth and salt and bring to a boil. Cover, turn heat to low, and simmer for 15 minutes.

3. Take the pan off the heat and let it sit with the cover on for 10 minutes. Serve warm.

PER SERVING: Calories: 180 | Fat: 4.5 g | Protein: 6.5 g | Sodium: 572 mg | Fiber: 4 g | Carbohydrate: 31 g

Quinoa with Sautéed Garlic

This is the type of recipe that can become a staple in your kitchen—quick, easy, and a very delicious way to prepare any type of grain. Of course, anything tastes great tossed with olive oil and garlic!

INGREDIENTS | SERVES 6

1 cup quinoa

2 cups water, Basic Vegetable Stock (Chapter 10) or low-sodium canned vegetable stock

½ teaspoon sea salt

½ medium onion

6 cloves garlic

¼ cup extra-virgin olive oil

A Gluten Substitute

For gluten-intolerant individuals, quinoa is a good substitute for gluten-based grains such as couscous, a refined wheat product that also cooks quickly and is found in many Middle Eastern recipes. Quinoa is available in grain, flour, bread, and pasta form in many natural-foods stores.

1. Place the quinoa in a metal strainer; rinse well under running water. Drain; add to a heavy saucepan with water or stock and sea salt.

2. Chop onion; add to quinoa.

3. Cover and bring to a boil over medium-high heat; reduce heat and simmer until all water has been absorbed, about 15–20 minutes.

4. Meanwhile, slice the garlic lengthwise along the clove and set aside.

5. Heat oil in a small skillet; sauté garlic until just crisp, but not yet brown. Remove from heat.

6. When quinoa is done, pour garlic and oil over quinoa; toss gently. Serve as a side dish or top with stir-fried beans and vegetables for a main dish.

PER SERVING: Calories: 193 | Fat: 11 g | Protein: 4 g | Sodium: 200 mg | Fiber: 2 g | Carbohydrate: 21 g

Polenta

Polenta is a dish made from boiled whole-grain yellow or white cornmeal. Polenta is very diverse, since it can be boiled, fried, baked, grilled, microwaved, and served morning, noon, or night.

INGREDIENTS | SERVES 6

1 cup skim milk

2 cups favorite low-sodium stock

½ cup cornmeal

¼ cup grated cheese (optional)

Freshly cracked black pepper, to taste

Bring the milk and stock to a boil over medium heat in a saucepan. Slowly whisk in the cornmeal a bit at a time; stir frequently until cooked, approximately 15 minutes until mixture is the consistency of mashed potatoes. Remove from heat, add the cheese, and season with pepper.

PER SERVING: Calories: 57 | Fat: 0.5 g | Protein: 2.5 g | Sodium: 68 mg | Fiber: 1 g | Carbohydrate: 11 g

Udon Noodle Slaw

Make this dish ahead and chill it for an easy and refreshing supper or light lunch. This is one cooked pasta that you'll want to drain and rinse off in cold water. Otherwise, you'll find starch clings to the strands.

INGREDIENTS | SERVES 4

1 (1 pound) package fresh udon noodles

6 ounces broccoli slaw

3 tablespoons pickled ginger

⅓ cup low-sodium soy sauce

2 tablespoon brown rice vinegar

1 tablespoon toasted sesame oil

1 tablespoon low-fat mayonnaise

1 tablespoon sugar

1. Bring a large pot of water to a boil and cook the noodles for about 1 minute. Drain and rinse in cold water. Set aside to cool slightly.

2. Add the broccoli slaw and the ginger to a salad bowl. Mix together the soy sauce, vinegar, sesame oil, mayonnaise, and sugar, stirring to combine well. Add the noodles to the bowl and toss the mixture together until well combined. Add the dressing and toss again.

PER SERVING: Calories: 181 | Fat: 4 g | Protein: 7.5 g | Sodium: 784 mg | Fiber: 1 g | Carbohydrate: 31 g

Quinoa-Parsley Tabbouleh

*Make sure to seed the tomatoes for easier digestion,
and also to prevent excess liquid from making your tabbouleh soggy.*

INGREDIENTS | SERVES 6

1 cup quinoa

2 cups water, Basic Vegetable Stock
(Chapter 10) or low-sodium canned
vegetable stock

½ teaspoon sea salt

1 cup fresh parsley

3 green onions

1 cup plum tomatoes

1 clove garlic

¼ cup extra-virgin olive oil

Juice of 1 fresh lemon

Sea salt, to taste

High-Protein Meal

Quinoa makes this traditional Middle Eastern dish high in protein. Add some veggies
and a bean dish to round out the protein
profile of this meal. It is also light enough
to serve as a side dish with fish, chicken, or
beef.

1. In a heavy saucepan, combine quinoa, water or stock, and sea salt; bring to a boil.

2. Reduce heat and simmer until all water is absorbed, about 15–20 minutes.

3. When quinoa is done, spoon into a large bowl and allow to cool.

4. While the grain is cooling, mince parsley and green onions; set aside.

5. Halve tomatoes lengthwise; scoop out seeds into a measuring cup or small bowl.

6. Chop tomatoes into small pieces; add to parsley and green onions.

7. Press and mince garlic; whisk it together in a small bowl with oil, lemon juice, and sea salt.

8. Strain and discard tomato seeds; add tomato liquid to lemon dressing.

9. Add parsley, green onion, and tomatoes to quinoa; toss well.

10. Add lemon dressing; mix well to combine all ingredients. Adjust seasonings with salt if needed.

PER SERVING: Calories: 196 | Fat: 11 g | Protein: 4.5 g | Sodium: 207 mg | Fiber: 2.5 g | Carbohydrate: 22 g

Quinoa-Apple Salad

Although you may not think to combine fruits and vegetables,
in this instance the combination of tastes works perfectly together.

INGREDIENTS | SERVES 8

⅓ cup quinoa
1 cup water
1 bunch mesclun greens, rinsed
2 apples, cut into pieces
1 red pepper, chopped
¼ cup olive oil
⅛ cup apple cider vinegar
2 cloves garlic
1 tablespoon agave syrup
2 pitted dates
⅛ teaspoon cinnamon
2 tablespoons water
1 cup chopped walnuts

Agave Syrup

Agave syrup is a low-glycemic sweetener made from the sap of the blue agave plant. Blue agave is higher in fructose-producing carbohydrates than other types of agave and is considered to be the finest in the world. Quality-brand tequilas are also produced from the blue agave plant.

1. Rinse quinoa in cool running water.

2. Combine water and quinoa in a saucepan.

3. Cover, bring to a boil, and simmer on low heat until all water is absorbed.

4. Meanwhile, rinse and dry greens and set aside.

5. Core and chop apple. Remove seeds from pepper and chop; set aside.

6. In a food processor, purée oil, vinegar, garlic, agave, dates, and cinnamon.

7. Add water; thin to dressing consistency.

8. Pour dressing around bottom of a large salad bowl.

9. Place mesclun in bowl. Add peppers, apples, cooled quinoa, and walnuts.

10. Toss well before serving.

PER SERVING: Calories: 219 | Fat: 17 g | Protein: 3.5 g | Sodium: 4 mg | Fiber: 2.5 g | Carbohydrate: 16 g

Quinoa–Black Bean Salad

The longer a grain salad marinates, the better the flavors are absorbed by the ingredients. Make it the night before and take some to work for lunch the next day.

INGREDIENTS | SERVES 8

1 cup quinoa

2 cups water

½ teaspoon sea salt

1 carrot

2 green onions

⅓ cup pumpkin seeds

½ cup parsley leaves

1 (14-ounce) can black beans

Juice of 1 lemon

1 clove minced garlic

2 tablespoons apple cider vinegar

3 tablespoons extra-virgin olive oil

½ teaspoon salt

Toasting Pumpkin Seeds

Raw pumpkin seeds can be toasted in a dry skillet over medium-low heat. Keep them moving around by shaking the pan from time to time or stirring them with a wooden spoon. You'll know they are done when they've stopped popping or turned a golden brown.

1. In a medium saucepan, combine quinoa, water, and ½ teaspoon sea salt. Cover, bring to a boil, reduce heat to low, and simmer until all water is absorbed, about 20 minutes.

2. When done, spoon into a large bowl and allow to cool.

3. Meanwhile, grate carrot, slice onions, toast pumpkin seeds, mince parsley, and rinse canned beans.

4. When quinoa is cool, add carrot, green onions, pumpkin seeds, parsley, and black beans; mix well.

5. In a small bowl, whisk together lemon, garlic, vinegar, oil, and salt.

6. Add vinaigrette; mix completely and allow to marinate a few minutes before serving.

PER SERVING: Calories: 347 | Fat: 11 g | Protein: 17 g | Sodium: 311 mg | Fiber: 9.5 g | Carbohydrate: 48 g

Bulgur-Stuffed Zucchini

Bulgur has a strong nutty flavor that adds to the flavor of the stuffing.

INGREDIENTS | SERVES 6

1 shallot

1 medium tomato

3 cloves garlic

2 leeks

3 small zucchini

2 teaspoons extra-virgin olive oil

1 cup bulgur wheat

½ cup dry white wine

3 cups water, Basic Vegetable Stock (Chapter 10) or low-sodium canned vegetable stock

½ bunch fresh mint

½ bunch fresh parsley

1 teaspoon grated lemon zest

Bulgur Versus Brown Rice

Bulgur wheat and brown rice are both whole grains, but bulgur offers a nutritional edge over brown rice. Bulgur not only offers fewer calories and less fat, but more than twice the fiber in comparison to brown rice.

1. Preheat oven to 375°F.

2. Finely dice the shallot and tomato. Mince the garlic and thinly slice the leeks. Cut the zucchini in half lengthwise and place the halves in a microwave-safe dish, cut side down. Pour in just enough water to cover the bottom of the dish and par-cook in the microwave for 1 to 2 minutes on high heat; let cool slightly.

3. Heat the oil to medium temperature in a medium-size stockpot. Add the shallot, garlic, and bulgur; toss in the oil until slightly brown, about 5 minutes. Add the leeks and let them wilt in the mixture. Pour in the wine and let reduce for about 1 minute.

4. Add the stock and simmer for approximately 15 minutes, until the bulgur is thoroughly cooked.

5. Meanwhile, chop the mint and parsley. When the bulgur is cooked, remove from heat and stir in the tomato, lemon zest, mint, and parsley.

6. Spoon the mixture into the zucchini halves and place on baking sheet; bake in the oven until the zucchini is reheated, about 5 to 8 minutes.

PER SERVING: Calories: 70 | Fat: 2 g | Protein: 2 g | Sodium: 10 mg | Fiber: 2.5 g | Carbohydrate: 12 g

Squash-Blossom Polenta

You can add additional edible flowers to this recipe for more color.
Adding ½ cup fresh or frozen corn kernels will increase the texture and fiber.

INGREDIENTS | SERVES 4

4 cups water
1 teaspoon salt
1 cup coarse-ground yellow cornmeal
2 tablespoons butter
1 cup chopped zucchini squash blossoms

Know Your Edible Flowers

Bean blossoms have a sweet, beany flavor. Nasturtiums have a wonderfully peppery flavor similar to watercress. Violets, roses, and lavender lend a sweet flavor to salads or desserts. Bright yellow calendulas are an economical alternative to expensive saffron, though not quite as pungent.

1. Put water and salt in a saucepan and bring to a boil. Reduce heat to medium-low. Gradually add cornmeal and stir constantly until it has thickened, about 15 minutes.

2. Stir in butter, then add the chopped squash blossoms.

3. Serve immediately for soft polenta, or pour into a greased 9" × 13" baking dish and let cool. When cool, it can be cut into squares or triangles and grilled, sautéed, or baked.

PER SERVING: Calories: 162 | Fat: 7 g | Protein: 2.5 g | Sodium: 651 mg | Fiber: 2.5 | Carbohydrate: 24 g

Kale Stuffed with Basmati Rice

Never use the center stalk of the kale in any recipe. It is too tough to eat.

INGREDIENTS | SERVES 6

1 head kale
1 red bell pepper
1 leek
1 tablespoon olive oil
1½ cups basmati rice
¼ cup sunflower seeds
3 cups stock
3 sprigs thyme, leaves only
¼ teaspoon ground cardamom seeds
½ teaspoon ground cumin
Freshly cracked black pepper, to taste

1. Steam the kale. Finely dice the red pepper. Thinly slice the whole leek.

2. Heat the oil in a large saucepan and sauté the pepper and leek for approximately 1 minute. Add the rice and sunflower seeds; toss for 1 minute. Add the stock, thyme, and spices; cover and simmer for 10 to 15 minutes, until the rice is cooked.

3. Lay out the kale leaves, spoon on the rice mixture, and fold into rolls. Serve either at room temperature or heated slightly in a 375°F oven.

PER SERVING: Calories: 228 | Fat: 4.5 g | Protein: 5 g | Sodium: 23 mg | Fiber: 4 g | Carbohydrate: 43 g

Wild Rice Stir-Fry with Snow Peas and Broccolini

With its delicate nutty flavor and sturdy texture,
wild rice makes a delicious base for any number of different add-in ingredients.

INGREDIENTS | SERVES 6

3 tablespoons vegetable oil, or more if needed

4 cloves minced garlic

1 tablespoon minced fresh ginger

3 cups cooked wild rice

¼ pound snow peas, rinsed and trimmed

1 bunch broccolini, cooked until crisp-tender and chopped

1 (8-ounce) can water chestnuts, drained

1 bunch scallions, sliced

½ cup water mixed with 1 tablespoon cornstarch

5 tablespoons hoisin sauce

3 tablespoons soy sauce

Whole cashews, for garnish

1. Heat the oil in a large wok over medium to medium-high heat. Add the garlic, ginger, and wild rice and stir-fry for about 1 minute. Add the snow peas, broccolini, and water chestnuts and stir-fry for 3 to 4 minutes more, adding more oil if needed. Add the scallions, water-cornstarch slurry, hoisin sauce, and soy sauce. Reduce the heat to medium-low and cover the wok for 2 to 3 minutes.

2. Uncover the wok and stir the mixture for 2 more minutes or until the vegetables are tender. Spoon onto serving plates, garnish with cashews, and serve.

PER SERVING: Calories: 283 | Fat: 8 g | Protein: 10 g | Sodium: 608 mg | Fiber: 4.5 g | Carbohydrate: 46 g

Wild Rice Is Not a Rice?

Despite its name, wild rice is not a rice but rather is a grass native to the Great Lakes region. Typically, the rice requires thorough rinsing and lengthy cooking to tenderize the grains. But some markets now sell pre-cooked wild rice in vacuum-sealed foil packets that requires only a few moments of reheating to ready it for the table.

Tabbouleh Salad

This whole-grain salad is made from bulgur wheat, which is simply whole-wheat berries that have been steamed, dried, cracked, and rehydrated. It absorbs the flavors of spices, aromatic vegetables, and meats.

INGREDIENTS | SERVES 6

½ cup medium bulgur wheat

1½ cups water

⅓ cup lemon juice

2 tablespoons chopped fresh mint

1 teaspoon salt

1 teaspoon pepper

¼ cup extra-virgin olive oil

1 cup chopped fresh parsley

½ cup chopped green onions

2 large tomatoes, diced

1 tablespoon minced garlic

1. Soak the bulgur in the water for at least 2 hours.

2. Drain the excess water and put the bulgur in a large bowl.

3. Add the remaining ingredients to the bulgur and mix well.

4. Let sit at room temperature for 60 minutes or refrigerate overnight.

5. Serve chilled or at room temperature.

PER SERVING: Calories: 138 | Fat: 9 g | Protein: 2.5 g | Sodium: 399 mg | Fiber: 3.5 g | Carbohydrate: 13 g

Prepare Your Own Bulgur

If you soak 2 cups of wheat berries in 4 cups of water overnight, you can make your own bulgur the next day. Drain the wheat berries, simmer them in 4 cups of water for 60 minutes, and drain. Dry the wheat berries on a baking sheet pan in a 250°F oven for 45 minutes or until dry. Chop up the dried, cooked wheat berries in a food processor and store in a large jar.

Barley-Vegetable Casserole

Since this recipe is high in carbohydrates, accompany it by a large fresh green salad for a well-balanced meal.

INGREDIENTS | SERVES 6

1 large yellow onion
1 leek
1 carrot
1 beet
1 parsnip
¼ bunch cilantro
1 tablespoon olive oil
1 cup barley
½ teaspoon ground cumin
1 quart Basic Vegetable Stock (Chapter 10)
 or low-sodium canned vegetable stock
Freshly cracked black pepper, to taste

1. Preheat oven to 350°F.

2. Slice the onion and leek. Peel and finely dice the carrot, beet, and parsnip. Chop the cilantro.

3. Combine all the ingredients in a large casserole dish greased with oil. Cover tightly and bake for 60 minutes.

PER SERVING: Calories: 182 | Fat: 2 g | Protein: 5 g | Sodium: 303 mg | Fiber: 7.5 g | Carbohydrate: 32 g

Whole-Wheat Pasta

This fresh pasta needs only a brief 3 to 5 minutes cooking time in boiling water. If you don't have a pasta machine, you can hand-roll the dough to achieve a rustic version of this high-fiber pasta.

INGREDIENTS | SERVES 2

½ cup whole-wheat flour
½ cup flour
½ teaspoon salt
1 egg, beaten
2 teaspoons water

To Buy or Not to Buy?

If you are interested in adding a variety of fibrous grains and flours to your diet, it's worthwhile to get yourself a pasta machine. They are very simple and fun to use. Kids are more likely to eat pastas that have spinach and whole grains in them if they are involved in making them.

1. Combine flours and salt. Make a well in the center.

2. Combine egg and water. Pour into the well in the flour mixture. Gradually bring the flour into the egg with a fork to form a dough. Knead dough for 10 minutes. Wrap in plastic.

3. Let rest 45 minutes before rolling with a pasta machine.

PER SERVING: Calories: 253 | Fat: 3 g | Protein: 10 g | Sodium: 615 mg | Fiber: 4.5 g | Carbohydrate: 46 g

Lasagna Florentine

The term Florentine is used in classic French and Italian cuisine to refer to a dish containing spinach. Seasonings such as nutmeg, lemon juice, and lemon zest all marry well with spinach.

INGREDIENTS | SERVES 8

5 cups tomato sauce

1 (1-pound) box whole-wheat lasagna noodles, cooked

3 eggs

16 ounces ricotta cheese

2 cups mozzarella cheese, shredded

2 cups chopped cooked spinach

½ cup chopped fresh parsley

Salt and pepper, to taste

½ cup grated Parmesan cheese

Spinach and Florentine

The cheeses and spinach are a high-protein and high-fiber combination. Fresh baby spinach is delicious and easy to deal with in the kitchen. You can also substitute arugula for spinach. If you want to get very aromatic, try adding some chopped watercress to the spinach.

1. Preheat oven to 350°F. Oil a baking dish and spread 1 cup tomato sauce on the bottom. Cover the sauce with a layer of cooked noodles.

2. In a bowl, combine the eggs, ricotta, and 1 cup mozzarella cheese until well blended. Stir in the spinach, parsley, salt, and pepper.

3. Spread half of the ricotta mixture over the noodles in the pan, then top the ricotta with a layer of noodles. Ladle 2 cups of the tomato sauce over the noodles and top with another layer of noodles.

4. Spread the remaining ricotta mixture over the noodles. Top with another layer of noodles. Ladle the remaining tomato sauce over the noodles.

5. Scatter the remaining mozzarella cheese over the sauce, then sprinkle the Parmesan cheese over it. Bake for 75 minutes.

PER SERVING: Calories: 497 | Fat: 16 g | Protein: 31 g | Sodium: 246 mg | Fiber: 9 g | Carbohydrate: 58 g

Whole-Wheat Bread

This is a basic loaf of bread that can be used for sandwiches or toast or used to make stuffing and croutons. The fiber is in the wheat flour. Throw in 2 ounces of wheat germ to give it even more fiber and nutrition.

INGREDIENTS | SERVES 8

1 packet yeast

3 tablespoons sugar

1⅓ cups warm water

3 tablespoons soft butter

1 teaspoon salt

¼ teaspoon baking powder

1¾ cups all-purpose flour

1¾ cups whole-wheat flour

From Whole-Wheat to Whole-Grain Bread

You can add all kinds of grains to your whole-wheat bread. Mix in some ground corn, millet, wheat bran flakes, ground soy or soy flour, and malt. You can sweeten the bread with honey, maple syrup, or red bean paste. This amplifies the flavors, and the grainy texture makes fabulous toast, French toast, and sandwiches. Giving your body what it needs is not that hard; it simply takes a little time and thought.

1. Combine yeast, ½ teaspoon sugar, and ⅓ cup water in a bowl. Let sit for 5 minutes.

2. In a mixing bowl, combine remaining water, butter, remaining sugar, salt, and baking powder. Mix in the all-purpose flour, followed by the yeast mixture, mixing with an electric mixer. Add the whole-wheat flour and knead with dough hook for 10 minutes.

3. Turn dough into an oiled bowl. Cover and set in a warm place. Let rise for 1 to 2 hours until doubled in bulk.

4. Punch down dough, then shape into a cylinder and place in an oiled loaf pan. Cover and let rise in a warm place for 90 minutes until doubled in size.

5. Preheat oven to 350°F. Uncover and bake for 40 minutes.

PER SERVING: Calories: 250 | Fat: 5 g | Protein: 7 g | Sodium: 337 mg | Fiber: 4.5 g | Carbohydrate: 45 g

Whole-Wheat Biscuits

*You can make breakfast sandwiches with these hearty biscuits
to get a jump start on your daily fiber requirements.*

INGREDIENTS | SERVES 8

1½ cups all-purpose flour

1½ cups whole-wheat flour

4½ teaspoons baking powder

1½ teaspoons salt

1 tablespoon sugar

6 tablespoons cold butter

1¼ cups buttermilk

1. Preheat oven to 400°F.

2. Combine flours, baking powder, salt, and sugar in a mixing bowl.

3. Cut butter into small pieces and add to dry ingredients. Mix butter into dry ingredients with a pastry cutter or your fingers. Add buttermilk and mix with a wooden spoon to form the dough.

4. Roll dough on a floured board to 1-inch thickness. Cut circles with a 2–3-inch round cookie cutter or drinking glass. Place rounds on a baking sheet and bake for 12 minutes.

PER SERVING: Calories: 262 | Fat: 9.5 g | Protein: 7 g | Sodium: 568 mg | Fiber: 3.5 g | Carbohydrate: 40 g

Multigrain Dinner Rolls

Whole-wheat flour, rolled oats, and sunflower seeds make up the multiple grains in these fiber-rich dinner rolls. They are delicious with butter, herbed olive oil, or cream cheese.

INGREDIENTS | SERVES 12

1 packet yeast

3 tablespoons warm water

1 cup warm milk

2½ ounces melted butter

1 teaspoon salt

1 egg, beaten

3 tablespoons sugar

2 cups all-purpose flour

1¾ cups whole-wheat flour

¼ cup rolled oats

1 egg, beaten

½ cup sunflower seeds

Oats and Type 2 Diabetes

Oat products contain long-chain starches called beta glucans. Recent research suggests that beta glucans may help type 2 diabetics better manage their blood sugar levels. Better blood sugar control results in better inflammatory control.

1. Combine yeast and water and let sit for 5 minutes to proof.

2. Add milk, butter, salt, egg, and sugar to the yeast mixture. Mix well.

3. Stir in the all-purpose flour with a wooden spoon or the paddle attachment of an electric stand mixer. Gradually add whole-wheat flour and rolled oats. Knead with a dough hook for 10 minutes. Put dough in an oiled bowl, cover and let rise in a warm place for 90 minutes.

4. Punch down dough, divide into 12 pieces, and roll each piece in a ball. Place dough balls on a greased baking sheet. Cover and let rise until doubled, about 60 minutes.

5. Preheat oven to 350°F. Uncover rolls, brush with egg, and sprinkle with sunflower seeds. Bake for 15 minutes.

PER SERVING: Calories: 253 | Fat: 9 g | Protein: 8 g | Sodium: 255 mg | Fiber: 4 g | Carbohydrate: 37 g

Whole-Wheat Hamburger Buns

These buns are a good way to add more fiber to a cheeseburger or veggie burger.
They also make good sandwich rolls for mixed deli meats.
The ginger adds a lot of flavor as well as some anti-inflammatory qualities to this meal.

INGREDIENTS | SERVES 6

1 packet yeast
3 tablespoons sugar
Pinch of dried ginger
1⅓ cups warm water
3 tablespoons soft butter
1 teaspoon salt
¼ teaspoon baking powder
1¾ cups all-purpose flour
1¾ cups whole-wheat flour
1 egg, beaten

How's Your Yeast?

Wondering if your yeast is still alive and kicking? Mix a little sugar and water together with the yeast. If the yeast is still viable it will ferment the sugar into ethanol. Visually you will see the mixture bubble and foam. This is frequently referred to as proofing the dough.

1. Combine yeast, ½ teaspoon sugar, ginger, and ⅓ cup water in a bowl. Let sit for 5 minutes.

2. In a mixing bowl, combine remaining water, butter, remaining sugar, salt, and baking powder. Mix in the all-purpose flour and then the yeast mixture, mixing with an electric mixer. Add whole-wheat flour. Knead with a dough hook for 10 minutes.

3. Turn dough into an oiled bowl. Cover and let rise in a warm place for 1 to 2 hours until doubled in bulk.

4. Punch down dough, then divide into 6 pieces, and shape into buns. Cover and let rise in a warm place for 1½ hours until doubled in size.

5. Preheat oven to 350°F. Uncover buns, gently brush with egg, and bake for 20 minutes.

PER SERVING: Calories: 345 | Fat: 7 g | Protein: 10 g | Sodium: 460 mg | Fiber: 6 g | Carbohydrate: 61 g

Whole-Wheat Pizza Dough

*Making your own pizza dough is fun and rewarding, and this recipe helps
bring more fiber into your diet than standard pizza dough.*

INGREDIENTS | SERVES 8

1 package yeast
½ cup warm water
½ teaspoon sugar
1½ cups all-purpose flour
1 ounce olive oil
½ cup cool water
1½ teaspoons salt
1 cup whole-wheat flour

Whole-Wheat Pizza Dough

Once you've made it, you'll wonder why
anyone would want to use all-purpose flour
for pizza dough. The nutty flavor of the
whole wheat, the added B vitamins, and
the crisp texture give you much more nutrition for the same amount of effort. Plus,
you can top a whole-wheat pizza base with
anything you like, from a white topping of
cheeses to a red one with fresh tomatoes.

1. Combine yeast with the warm water, sugar, and ½ cup
   all-purpose flour. Let sit 10 minutes.

2. Add olive oil, cool water, salt, and 1 cup all-purpose
   flour. Combine with a wooden spoon.

3. Add the whole-wheat flour and mix to form dough.

4. Knead dough on a floured board for 5 minutes,
   adding flour as needed to prevent sticking.

5. Cover dough and set aside in an oiled bowl. Let
   dough rise in a warm place for 60 minutes. Punch
   down dough and divide in half. Roll the halves into
   balls and let rise, covered, for 60 minutes. Roll or
   stretch dough into pizza rounds.

6. Preheat the oven to 400°F. Bake the pizza on a pizza
   stone or cookie sheet for 12–15 minutes.

PER SERVING: Calories: 173 | Fat: 4 g | Protein: 5 g |
Sodium: 438 mg | Fiber: 3 g | Carbohydrate: 30 g

Shallot-Walnut Herb Bread

This flavorful loaf is perfect with a cheese plate, fruit, and paté. The excellent fiber comes from whole-wheat flour, shallot, and walnuts. The fresh sage and thyme add color and flavor but not a great deal of fiber.

INGREDIENTS | SERVES 8

1 packet yeast

3 tablespoons maple syrup

1⅓ cups warm water

3 tablespoons walnut oil

1 teaspoon salt

¼ teaspoon baking powder

1¾ cups all-purpose flour

1¾ cups whole-wheat flour

1 shallot, minced

½ cup chopped walnuts

1 tablespoon minced fresh sage

1 tablespoon minced fresh thyme

The Ins and Outs of Walnut Oil

Walnut oil is best used in cold dishes, since heating this oil can produce a bitter taste and destroy the beneficial antioxidants. Walnut oil can be more expensive than other oils, but it is a great source of the inflammation-busting omega-3 fatty acids.

1. Combine yeast, ½ teaspoon maple syrup, and ⅓ cup water in a bowl. Let sit for 5 minutes.

2. In a mixing bowl combine remaining water, walnut oil, remaining maple syrup, salt, and baking powder. Mix in the all-purpose flour, then the yeast mixture with an electric mixer. Add the whole-wheat flour, shallot, walnuts, and herbs. Knead with a dough hook for 10 minutes.

3. Turn dough into an oiled bowl. Cover and let rise for 1 to 2 hours until doubled in bulk in a warm place.

4. Punch down dough, then shape into a cylinder and place in an oiled loaf pan. Cover and let rise in a warm place for 90 minutes until doubled in size.

5. Preheat oven to 350°F. Uncover bread and bake for 40 minutes.

PER SERVING: Calories: 307 | Fat: 11 g | Protein: 8 g | Sodium: 294 mg | Fiber: 5 g | Carbohydrate: 47 g

Cinnamon-Swirl Raisin Bread

Toast this bread for breakfast for a healthy start to a long workday or spread blue cheese and drizzle honey on toast points with Poached Pears. The whole-wheat flour gives you both protein and fiber, and the raisins add some iron with a little sweetness on top.

INGREDIENTS | SERVES 8

1 packet yeast

3 tablespoons sugar

1⅓ cups warm water

3 tablespoons soft butter

1 teaspoon salt

¼ teaspoon baking powder

1¾ cups all-purpose flour

1¾ cups whole-wheat flour

1 cup raisins

3 tablespoons cinnamon

1. Combine yeast, ½ teaspoon sugar, and ⅓ cup water in a bowl. Let sit for 5 minutes.

2. In a mixing bowl, combine remaining sugar, remaining water, butter, salt, and baking powder. Mix in the all-purpose flour and then the yeast mixture with an electric mixer. Add the whole-wheat flour and raisins. Knead with dough hook for 10 minutes.

3. Turn dough into an oiled bowl, cover, and let rise in a warm place for 1–2 hours until doubled in bulk.

4. Punch down dough, then roll into a rectangle. Sprinkle the cinnamon over the dough, roll it into a cylinder, and place in an oiled loaf pan. Cover and let rise in a warm place for 90 minutes until doubled in size.

5. Preheat oven to 350°F. Uncover bread and bake for 40 minutes.

PER SERVING: Calories: 317 | Fat: 5 g | Protein: 8 g | Sodium: 49 mg | Fiber: 6.5 g | Carbohydrate: 63 g

Cornmeal Dumplings

These dumplings work well as a side dish or served in soup. Don't forget stews and casseroles, too! This dish is low in fat and high in inflammation-fighting ingredients.

INGREDIENTS | SERVES 6

½ cup cornmeal

½ cup whole-wheat flour

½ teaspoon curry powder

Pinch of iodized salt

1 egg white

¼ cup nonfat yogurt

¼ cup skim milk

1 teaspoon extra-virgin olive oil

1 jalapeño or serrano pepper

¼ cup cooked corn

A Spicy Anti-Inflammatory Blend

Curry is a blend of ground spices including turmeric, cumin, coriander, and cayenne. Together these spices are touted to enhance the health of the cardiovascular and immune systems.

1. Sift together the cornmeal, flour, curry powder, and salt. In a separate bowl, mix together the egg white, yogurt, milk, and oil. Combine the wet and dry ingredients.

2. Stem, seed, and mince the chili pepper; fold it into the dumpling mixture along with the corn.

3. Bring 1½ gallons of water to a boil. Drop dumplings by the teaspoonful into the water (use a spoon to scoop the dumpling mix from the bowl and another spoon to push the dumpling into the boiling water). Cook for approximately 12 to 15 minutes or until the dumplings are cooked through.

PER SERVING: Calories: 96 | Fat: 1.5 g | Protein: 4 g | Sodium: 28 mg | Fiber: 2 g | Carbohydrate: 18 g

Spelt Naan

Chickpea flour may be substituted for spelt flour if that is what you have on hand or simply prefer.

INGREDIENTS | SERVES 6

¼ cup spelt flour

½ cup all-purpose unbleached flour

¼ cup water

1 teaspoon olive oil

1. Sift together the flours, then add the water and mix all at once; let the dough rest in a warm place for at least 30 minutes.

2. Knead the dough on a slightly floured board. Roll into 8-inch circle.

3. Heat a heavy-bottomed fry pan (preferably cast iron) to medium temperature and coat the bottom of the pan with the oil; cook the naan until golden brown, then cook the other side until golden brown.

PER SERVING: Calories: 69 | Fat: 1 g | Protein: 2 g | Sodium: 1 mg | Fiber: 1 g | Carbohydrate: 13 g

CHAPTER 15

Vegetables with Vitality

Tomato Salad with Basil–Pine Nut Dressing

This recipe makes a nice addition to any summer celebration, but shy away from it if nightshade vegetables, such as tomatoes, trigger inflammation in your body.

INGREDIENTS | SERVES 6

1 large Vidalia onion

4 large ripe tomatoes

½ bunch fresh basil

¼ cup kalamata olives

⅓ cup pine nuts

6 cloves roasted garlic

Freshly cracked black pepper, to taste

3 tablespoons extra-virgin olive oil

1. Thinly slice the onion, and cut the tomatoes into large wedges; combine in a mixing bowl and drizzle with oil. Thinly slice the basil leaves and olives; set aside.

2. Dry-sauté the pine nuts (without oil) over medium heat until light brown, 1 to 2 minutes. Blend the garlic to form a paste, then add the pine nuts, basil leaves, and pepper.

3. Dollop the garlic mixture over the tomatoes and onions. Adjust seasonings to taste. To serve, place in a bowl and garnish with the olive slices.

PER SERVING: Calories: 163 | Fat: 14 g | Protein: 3 g | Sodium: 139 mg | Fiber: 1.5 g | Carbohydrate: 7.5 g

Asian Fusion Salad

This salad combines Thai and Chinese ingredients with Western baby spinach and olive oil for a tantalizing concoction.

INGREDIENTS | SERVES 4

3 tablespoons light coconut milk

3 tablespoons Thai chili sauce

2 tablespoons low-sodium soy sauce

1 tablespoon olive oil

2 cups baby spinach

1 bunch watercress, trimmed

1 (8-ounce) can sliced water chestnuts

8 sesame-flavored rice crackers, crumbled

½ cup crushed cashews

1. Combine the coconut milk, Thai chili sauce, soy sauce, and olive oil, mix well, and set aside.

2. Combine the spinach, watercress, and water chestnuts in a salad bowl, add the dressing, and toss until the leaves are well coated. Sprinkle the crushed rice crackers and cashews over top, toss again, and serve.

PER SERVING: Calories: 208 | Fat: 14 g | Protein: 5 g | Sodium: 340 mg | Fiber: 3 g | Carbohydrate: 17 g

Sunshine Salad

This is a unique and tasty combination of greens, fruit, and nuts.
It's great for a potluck dinner; keep the dressing separate and mix just before serving.

INGREDIENTS | SERVES 4

6 ounces plain low-fat yogurt

2 tablespoons low-fat sour cream

2 tablespoons low-fat mayonnaise

1 tablespoon lemon zest

¼ teaspoon red pepper flakes

⅛ teaspoon seasoned salt

6 cups baby spinach salad leaves

1 large cucumber, peeled, seeded, and sliced, about 2 cups (about ¼-inch slices, cut into half-moons)

1 cup canned mandarin oranges, drained

1 cup halved cherry tomatoes

½ cup roasted sunflower seeds

1. In a small bowl, combine the yogurt, sour cream, mayonnaise, lemon zest, red pepper flakes, and seasoned salt; mix until well blended. Taste and adjust seasoning as desired.

2. In a large bowl, combine the spinach, cucumber, oranges, cherry tomatoes, and half of the sunflower seeds. Toss with half of the dressing, adding more a bit at a time to reach desired consistency. To serve, transfer the salad to a chilled bowl and top with the remaining sunflower seeds.

PER SERVING: Calories: 239 | Fat: 12 g | Protein: 10 g | Sodium: 305 mg | Fiber: 5.5 g | Carbohydrate: 23 g

Waldorf Salad

This salad is high in fiber because of the apples with skin, celery, grapes,
and walnuts. It's delicious for the same reasons.

INGREDIENTS | SERVES 4

1 cup diced red apple, skin on

1 cup diced Granny Smith apple, skin on

1 cup diced celery

½ cup halved seedless grapes

½ cup chopped walnuts

¼ cup low-fat mayonnaise

¼ cup plain low-fat yogurt

4 butter lettuce leaves

1. Combine apples, celery, grapes, walnuts, mayonnaise, and yogurt in a bowl.

2. Spoon salad onto lettuce, either on a platter or individual plates.

3. Serve chilled.

PER SERVING: Calories: 183 | Fat: 13 g | Protein: 3.5 g | Sodium: 48 mg | Fiber: 3 g | Carbohydrate: 17 g

Jicama Salad with Mango and Black Beans

*This is a great brunch dish, easy to increase in quantity,
and it looks great served on a bed of crispy greens.*

INGREDIENTS | SERVES 4

1 cup peeled and diced jicama (about ½-inch dice)

⅓ cup diced ripe mango (about ⅓-inch dice)

½ cup canned black beans, drained and rinsed

½ cup diced red onion (about ⅓-inch dice)

⅓ cup mandarin oranges, drained

2 tablespoons fresh lime juice

2 tablespoons fresh orange juice

2 tablespoons finely chopped cilantro

¾ teaspoon seasoned salt

Freshly cracked black pepper, to taste

1. Combine the jicama, mango, black beans, red onion, and mandarin oranges in a medium-size bowl and toss to mix.

2. Mix together the lime juice, orange juice, cilantro, salt, and pepper in a bowl. Pour over the jicama mixture and toss well. Let stand at room temperature for 10 minutes to allow the flavors to blend, and serve.

PER SERVING: Calories: 121 | Fat: 0.5 g | Protein: 6 g | Sodium: 439 mg | Fiber: 5.5 g | Carbohydrate: 23 g

Apple, Ginger, and Carrot Salad

For a sweet salad use red apples, but for something more tart, to help balance out the carrots and cranberries, use the green Granny Smith variety of apple.

INGREDIENTS | SERVES 4

2 apples

Juice of ½ lemon

2 large carrots

¼ cup dried cranberries

12 walnut halves

1 teaspoon fresh ginger juice

¼ cup extra-virgin olive oil

¼ cup golden balsamic vinegar

1 teaspoon ume plum vinegar

1. Core and chop the apples. Place in a medium-size bowl; toss with lemon juice.

2. Peel and grate the carrots; add to the apples along with the cranberries and walnut halves.

3. On the fine setting, grate a 2-inch piece of fresh ginger and squeeze or press to extract the juice.

4. In a bowl, whisk together the oil, ginger juice, balsamic vinegar, and plum vinegar; pour over the apple salad. Toss to mix; serve on a bed of fresh spinach or arugula.

PER SERVING: Calories: 250 | Fat: 19 g | Protein: 2 g | Sodium: 46 mg | Fiber: 4 g | Carbohydrate: 22 g

Coleslaw

This is a mayonnaise-free version of the shredded cabbage salad classic. You'll find that the sesame oil adds a wonderful nutty flavor. You can also garnish the slaw with toasted sesame seeds.

INGREDIENTS | SERVES 4

3 cups shredded cabbage

¼ cup shredded carrot

¼ cup green onion, sliced on the bias

¼ cup canola oil

1 teaspoon sesame oil

2 tablespoons rice vinegar

1 tablespoon sesame seeds

Salt and pepper, to taste

1. Mix all ingredients together.

2. Refrigerate at least 60 minutes before serving.

> **PER SERVING:** Calories: 167 | Fat: 16 g | Protein: 1.5 g | Sodium: 50 mg | Fiber: 2 g | Carbohydrate: 6 g

Broccoli Slaw

Broccoli, carrots, raisins, and almonds add lots of fiber and flavor to this salad.

INGREDIENTS | SERVES 4

3 cups blanched broccoli florets

¼ cup shredded carrot

2 tablespoons mayonnaise

1 teaspoon Dijon mustard

1 tablespoon red wine vinegar

1 tablespoon minced shallots

¼ cup golden raisins

½ cup toasted sliced almonds

Salt and pepper, to taste

1. Mix all ingredients together.

2. Refrigerate at least 60 minutes before serving.

> **PER SERVING:** Calories: 129 | Fat: 8 g | Protein: 3 g | Sodium: 68 mg | Fiber: 1.5 g | Carbohydrate: 13 g

Roasted Kale

This is a simple recipe requiring four ingredients, and yields a crisp, chewy kale that is irresistible. You can also slice up some collard greens or Swiss chard as a substitute for kale, or mix them all together for a tasty medley.

INGREDIENTS | SERVES 2

6 cups kale
1 tablespoon extra-virgin olive oil
1 teaspoon garlic powder
1 teaspoon sea salt

Quality Sea Salt

Commercial salt is highly refined—99.5 percent is made up of sodium chloride, with additives of anticaking chemicals, potassium iodide, and sugar (dextrose) to stabilize the iodine. Instead, look for a high-quality sea salt, which is loaded with minerals, and in moderation, can actually give you energy.

1. Preheat oven to 375°F.

2. Wash and trim kale by pulling leaves off the tough stems or running a sharp knife down the length of the stem.

3. Place leaves in a medium-size bowl; toss with extra-virgin olive oil and garlic powder.

4. Roast for 5 minutes; turn kale over and roast another 7–10 minutes, until kale turns brown and becomes paper-thin and brittle.

5. Remove from oven and sprinkle with sea salt. Serve immediately.

PER SERVING: Calories: 160 | Fat: 8 g | Protein: 6 g | Sodium: 849 mg | Fiber: 4 g | Carbohydrate: 20 g

Braised Okra with Tomato

Feta cheese imparts a tangy, salty note to this recipe that is mellowed by the dry red wine. It is a delicious combination of flavors.

INGREDIENTS | SERVES 6

1½ pounds okra

8 plum tomatoes

2 shallots

4 cloves garlic

1 tablespoon olive oil

¼ cup dry red wine

½ cup Basic Vegetable Stock (Chapter 10) or low-sodium canned vegetable stock

4 sprigs oregano, leaves only

4 ounces feta cheese, crumbled

Freshly cracked black pepper, to taste

Storing Olive Oil

Olive oil should be kept away from sunlight and heat. It does not need to be refrigerated. If the oil gets too cold, it will become cloudy but will return to its normal color when it returns to room temperature.

1. Preheat oven to 375°F.

2. Remove the tops of the okra. Cut the tomatoes into wedges. Fine-dice the shallots and mince the garlic.

3. Heat the oil in a Dutch oven (or other heavy-bottomed pan with a lid) to medium-high temperature. Add the okra, shallots, and garlic; sauté for 2 minutes. Add the wine, and reduce by half. Add the stock and oregano; bring to simmer, cover and place in the oven for 15 to 20 minutes.

4. Remove from oven and add the feta and pepper. Adjust seasoning to taste, then serve.

PER SERVING: Calories: 128 | Fat: 6 g | Protein: 6 g | Sodium: 228 mg | Fiber: 4.5 g | Carbohydrate: 14 g

Braised Radicchio

Adding a dried fruit to this dish can offset the bitterness.

INGREDIENTS | SERVES 6

6 heads radicchio

2 leeks

3 cloves garlic

1 tablespoon olive oil

¼ cup dry red wine

1 cup orange juice

1 cup Basic Vegetable Stock (Chapter 10) or low-sodium canned vegetable stock

Freshly cracked black pepper, to taste

Kosher salt, to taste

Cleaning Leeks

Leeks need to be thoroughly cleaned because they collect plenty of dirt while growing. Cut off the bottom of the root and trim tops according to how much of the green will be used in the recipe. Cut in half lengthwise and submerge in cold water. Rub all of the dirt out of each layer and dry on clean towels.

1. Preheat oven to 375°F.

2. Cut the radicchio heads in half. Cut the leeks into ½-inch-wide strips. Mince the garlic.

3. Heat the oil in a heavy-bottomed roasting pan to medium temperature on stovetop. Add the radicchio, leeks, and garlic; toss for about 2 minutes.

4. Add the red wine and reduce by half (approximately 2 minutes). Add the orange juice and stock. Remove from stovetop, cover, and place in oven for 25 to 30 minutes.

5. Remove from oven and arrange in a shallow bowl. Sprinkle with pepper and salt.

PER SERVING: Calories: 84 | Fat: 2.5 g | Protein: 2.5 g | Sodium: 25 mg | Fiber: 1.5 g | Carbohydrate: 14 g

Shaved Fennel with Orange Sections and Toasted Hazelnuts

Tangelos, mandarin, or any easily sectioned citrus will work wonderfully with this recipe.

INGREDIENTS | SERVES 6

3 bulbs fennel

6 oranges

1 teaspoon hazelnuts

3 ounces fresh orange juice

2 tablespoons extra-virgin olive oil

1 tablespoon fresh orange zest

1. Finely slice the fennel bulbs. Remove the peel and pith from the oranges. With a small paring knife, remove each section of the oranges.

2. Form a mound of fennel on each serving plate and arrange the oranges on top. Sprinkle with nuts, then drizzle with the orange juice and oil. Finish with a sprinkle of zest.

PER SERVING: Calories: 171 | Fat: 5 g | Protein: 3 g | Sodium: 61 mg | Fiber: 8 g | Carbohydrate: 31 g

Wilted Spinach

Any type of stock can be used depending on your taste and preference. Raisins, dates, or any dried fruit can be substituted for the pineapple.

INGREDIENTS | SERVES 6

2 pounds fresh spinach

¼ cup almonds

¼ cup dried pineapple

¼ cup Basic Vegetable Stock (Chapter 10) or low-sodium canned vegetable stock

Freshly cracked black pepper, to taste

1. Tear the spinach into bite-size pieces. Finely chop the almonds in a food processor or with a knife. Cut the pineapple into small dice.

2. Heat a large sauté pan to medium-high heat. Pour in the stock and add the spinach and almonds all at once. Toss until the spinach is just wilted. Remove from heat and add the pineapple. Season with pepper and serve.

PER SERVING: Calories: 65 | Fat: 2.6 g | Protein: 5.5 g | Sodium: 120 mg | Fiber: 3.5 g | Carbohydrate: 9 g

Roasted Peppers

Many people don't know that peppers become very sweet when roasted.

INGREDIENTS | SERVES 6

2 tablespoons olive oil
2 green peppers
2 yellow peppers
2 red peppers
6 cloves garlic, minced
Freshly cracked black pepper, to taste
Kosher salt, to taste

1. Pour the olive oil in a stainless steel bowl. Dip the peppers in the olive oil, then roast or grill them on an open flame (reserve the bowl with the oil in it). Shock the peppers in ice water and remove the skins.

2. Julienne the peppers and add them to the bowl with the olive oil, along with the garlic, black pepper, and salt.

3. Let sit at room temperature in serving bowl until ready to serve.

PER SERVING: Calories: 76 | Fat: 4.5 g | Protein: 1.5 g | Sodium: 2.5 mg | Fiber: 2.5 g | Carbohydrate: 9 g

Roasted Asparagus

Use thicker asparagus to withstand the heat of the grill.
Be sure to remove the woody end of the stalk first.

INGREDIENTS | SERVES 6

2 bunches asparagus
1 tablespoon extra-virgin olive oil
Kosher salt, to taste (optional)
Freshly cracked black pepper, to taste

Preheat grill to medium. Toss the asparagus in the oil, then drain on a rack and season with salt and pepper. Grill the asparagus for 1 to 2 minutes on each side (cook to desired doneness). Serve immediately.

PER SERVING: Calories: 30 | Fat: 2 g | Protein: 1 g | Sodium: 1 mg | Fiber: 1 g | Carbohydrate: 2 g

Asparagus

Asparagus is low in calories and sodium, and offers numerous vitamins and minerals, most notably folate and potassium. The stalks also offer a blast of inflammation-fighting antioxidants.

Ratatouille

*There are no limits to the types of vegetables that can be added to ratatouille.
Get creative and experiment!*

INGREDIENTS | SERVES 6

1 small eggplant

1 small zucchini squash

1 small yellow squash

½ leek

1 plum tomato

1 shallot

2 cloves garlic

2 sprigs marjoram

¼ cup kalamata olives

½ teaspoon olive oil

1 cup Basic Vegetable Stock (Chapter 10)
  or low-sodium canned vegetable stock

Freshly cracked black pepper, to taste

1. Large-dice the eggplant, zucchini, yellow squash, leek, and tomato. Finely dice the shallot and garlic. Mince the marjoram and chop the olives.

2. Place all the ingredients in a saucepot and cook at low temperature for 1½ hours.

PER SERVING: Calories: 61 | Fat: 4.5 g | Protein: 1 g | Sodium: 135 mg | Fiber: 2.5 g | Carbohydrate: 6 g

Skewered Vegetables

Cover the tips of the skewers with aluminum foil to prevent them from burning.

INGREDIENTS | SERVES 6

1 medium par-baked sweet potato or
  yam

1 medium par-baked baking potato

1 yellow pepper

1 medium-size red onion

1 medium zucchini

1 sprig tarragon, leaves only

1 teaspoon olive oil

Freshly cracked black pepper, to taste

Kosher salt, to taste

1. Soak 12 wooden skewers in water for at least 4 hours.

2. Peel the potatoes and cut into 2-inch cubes. Stem and seed the pepper and cut into 2-inch squares. Cut the onion into wedges. Cut the zucchini into 2-inch chunks. Mince the tarragon.

3. Preheat grill.

4. Skewer the vegetables, alternating types. Brush them with the oil, sprinkle with pepper and salt, and grill until al dente. Sprinkle with tarragon before serving.

PER SERVING: Calories: 81 | Fat: 0.5 g | Protein: 2 g | Sodium: 16 mg | Fiber: 2 g | Carbohydrate: 16 g

Chilled Broccoli Trio

To parboil the broccoli, plunge each batch into boiling water for 3 to 5 minutes, depending on the variety. Rinse each batch under cold running water and drain very well.

INGREDIENTS | SERVES 4

2 cups broccoli florets, parboiled

2 cups chopped broccoli rabe, parboiled

2 cups chopped Chinese broccoli, parboiled

4 cloves garlic, chopped

1 cup toasted walnuts

½ cup crumbled Gorgonzola cheese

Balsamic salad dressing, as desired

Salt and fresh ground black pepper, to taste

Crushed red pepper, to taste

1. Combine the three broccolis in a mixing bowl and toss with the garlic. Chill until ready to serve.

2. Just before serving, add the walnuts, cheese, dressing, salt, pepper, and crushed red pepper. Toss well.

PER SERVING: Calories: 311 | Fat: 26 g | Protein: 12 g | Sodium: 328 mg | Fiber: 4.5 g | Carbohydrate: 12 g

Roasted Asparagus with Summer Squash and Peppers

Don't skip this warm-weather dish if you cannot find the mini sweet peppers; simply substitute red, yellow, or green bell peppers.

INGREDIENTS | SERVES 4

¼ cup olive oil

3 tablespoons balsamic vinegar

1 tablespoon minced garlic

1 pound asparagus, stem ends trimmed

1 pound mixed summer squashes, thinly sliced

1 pound mini sweet peppers, stemmed and sliced in half lengthwise

2 to 3 hot peppers, or to taste, chopped

Seasoning salt, to taste

1. Preheat the oven to 400°F.

2. Mix the olive oil, balsamic vinegar, and garlic together and set aside.

3. Place the vegetables in a roasting pan, mixing them together. Pour the olive oil mixture over the vegetables and gently mix them to coat in oil. Sprinkle the vegetables with seasoning salt.

4. Roast the vegetables uncovered for about 45 minutes or until they begin to darken; stir occasionally. Serve hot.

PER SERVING: Calories: 202 | Fat: 14 g | Protein: 4.5 g | Sodium: 7 mg | Fiber: 5.5 g | Carbohydrate: 19 g

Mediterranean Green Beans

This simple recipe can be served hot or at room temperature.
Add any leftovers to salads as a nice healthy addition.

INGREDIENTS | SERVES 4

1 pound fresh green beans, ends trimmed, cut into 1-inch pieces

2 teaspoons minced fresh rosemary

1 teaspoon lemon zest

1 tablespoon olive oil

1 tablespoon, plus ½ teaspoon kosher salt

Freshly cracked black pepper, to taste

1. Fill a medium-size saucepan with cold salted water and bring to a boil over high heat. Add the beans and cook until they are a vibrant green, just about 4 minutes.

2. Drain the beans and transfer to a large bowl. Add the remaining ingredients and toss to coat evenly. Serve warm or at room temperature.

PER SERVING: Calories: 70 | Fat: 3.5 g | Protein: 2 g | Sodium: 1,347 mg | Fiber: 3.5 g | Carbohydrate: 9 g

Vegetable Pita with Feta Cheese

Let your imagination go wild with seasonal veggies.
This simple-to-prepare pita delight is delicious and good for you, too.

INGREDIENTS | SERVES 6

1 eggplant, sliced into ½-inch pieces, lengthwise

1 zucchini, sliced into ½-inch pieces, lengthwise

1 yellow squash, sliced

1 red onion, cut into ⅓-inch rings

1 teaspoon virgin olive oil

Freshly cracked black pepper, to taste

6 whole-wheat pita bread

3 ounces feta cheese

1. Preheat oven to 375°F.

2. Brush the sliced vegetables with oil and place on a racked baking sheet. Sprinkle with black pepper. Roast until tender. (The vegetables can be prepared the night before and put in the refrigerator; reheat or bring to room temperature before roasting.)

3. Slice a 3-inch opening in the pitas to gain access to the pockets. Toast the pitas if desired. Fill the pitas with the cooked vegetables. Add cheese to each and serve.

PER SERVING: Calories: 238 | Fat: 7 g | Protein: 8 g | Sodium: 360 mg | Fiber: 6.5 g | Carbohydrate: 36 g

CHAPTER 16

Robust Roots

Browned Mixed Potato Pancakes

*This is an alternate version of the classic potato pancake.
For even more variety, try other types of potatoes when available.*

INGREDIENTS | SERVES 6

1 large sweet potato
1 large baking potato
1 tablespoon olive oil

Peel and shred the potatoes. Form into small patties. Heat a small sauté pan to medium-high heat and brush with oil. Place the potato patties in the sauté pan. Let brown on each side; serve immediately.

PER SERVING: Calories: 85 | Fat: 2 g | Protein: 1.5 g | Sodium: 15 mg | Fiber: 2 g | Carbohydrate: 15 g

Roasted Potatoes with Vegetables

This dish serves double duty as a treat for breakfast or as a side dish at dinner.

INGREDIENTS | SERVES 6

3 Idaho baking potatoes
1 sweet potato
3 carrots
1 yellow onion
½ pound button mushrooms
2 tablespoons olive oil
Freshly cracked black pepper, to taste
Kosher salt, to taste

1. Preheat oven to 400°F.

2. Large-dice the potatoes, carrots, and onion. Trim off any discolored ends from the mushrooms stems.

3. In a large bowl, mix together the olive oil, potatoes, carrots, onions, and mushrooms. Place them evenly in a roasting pan, and sprinkle with salt and pepper.

4. Roast the vegetables for 30–45 minutes, until tender. Serve warm.

PER SERVING: Calories: 240 | Fat: 5 g | Protein: 5 g | Sodium: 69 mg | Fiber: 6 g | Carbohydrate: 43 g

Roasted-Garlic Potato-Salad Lettuce Rolls

It's perfectly fine to cook red potatoes with the skin on—there's no need to peel them.

INGREDIENTS | SERVES 6

6 cooked Idaho potatoes or 12 small
  red-skinned potatoes

½ bulb roasted garlic

1 yellow onion

¼ cup extra-virgin olive oil

2 tablespoons balsamic vinegar

¼ bunch parsley, chopped

Freshly cracked black pepper, to taste

Kosher salt, to taste

1 head large-leaf lettuce

Chop the potatoes and mash them with the garlic. Mix together all the ingredients except the lettuce. Adjust seasoning to taste. Place the potato salad on lettuce leaves, then roll up.

PER SERVING: Calories: 384 | Fat: 9 g | Protein: 7 g | Sodium: 23 mg | Fiber: 6.5 g | Carbohydrate: 67 g

Fiery Indian Potatoes

This unusual potato dish is not for the faint of heart, yet it is a delicious dish and pairs well with thick plain yogurt or as an accompaniment to other vegetarian dishes. Look for the Indian red chili powder at an Indian market; otherwise, use ground cayenne.

INGREDIENTS | SERVES 6

6 large potatoes, peeled and cubed

3 tablespoons vegetable oil, or more as
  needed

5 dried red chilies, or to taste, crushed

1 tablespoon mustard seeds

1 teaspoon ground turmeric

1 teaspoon red chili powder

Salt and freshly ground black pepper, to
  taste

1 tablespoon ground coriander

1 cup chopped fresh cilantro, for garnish

1. Steam the potato cubes until just tender. Set aside.

2. Heat the oil in a large skillet or wok, and sauté the potatoes for 2 minutes. Add the chilies, mustard seeds, turmeric, chili powder, salt, and pepper and continue cooking over medium heat, stirring, until the seasonings are well mixed and the potatoes begin to brown. Stir in the coriander, garnish with the cilantro, and serve.

PER SERVING: Calories: 353 | Fat: 8 g | Protein: 7 g | Sodium: 21 mg | Fiber: 6.5 g | Carbohydrate: 64 g

Overly Stuffed Baked Sweet Potato

This robust dish offers a whopping 16 grams of fiber per potato.
Make sure you use reduced fat cheeses to keep the fat content under control.

INGREDIENTS | SERVES 4

4 large sweet potatoes

2 cups mild or hot salsa

2 cups grated low-fat Cheddar cheese

2 jalapeño peppers, diced, or more to taste, optional

2 cups cubed Monterey jack cheese

4 cups vegetarian chili

Chopped fresh cilantro, for garnish

1. Bake the sweet potatoes in a 350°F oven until tender. Remove from the oven and, when they are cool enough to handle, slit open the tops and scoop out the flesh, leaving a thin layer of flesh around the interior.

2. Mix the sweet potato flesh with the salsa, grated cheese, and jalapeño, if using. Spoon it back into the skin and dot the top with the Monterey jack cheese. Return the sweet potatoes to the oven to cook until the cheese melts.

3. Meanwhile, heat the chili, and when the cheese has melted, put the sweet potatoes on a serving plate and spoon the chili over top. Garnish with the cilantro and enjoy.

PER SERVING: Calories: 766 | Fat: 33 g | Protein: 48 g | Sodium: 1,834 mg | Fiber: 15 g | Carbohydrate: 71 g

Potato Gnocchi

To obtain the optimum flavor, toss the cooked gnocchi in a sauté pan with the sauce for 1 to 2 minutes.

INGREDIENTS | SERVES 6

1 medium potato

¾ cup whole-wheat flour

¾ cup all-purpose flour

2 egg whites

¼ cup Basic Vegetable Stock (Chapter 10) or low-sodium canned vegetable stock

Pinch of iodized salt (optional)

1 teaspoon olive oil

2 cups Fresh Tomato Sauce (Chapter 17)

2 ounces Romano cheese

3 large basil leaves

Freshly cracked black pepper, to taste

Pasta Dishes

Pasta is a common staple in the Italian diet. Many variations can be created by the substitution of ingredients and with the shape of the pasta. Gnocchi is no exception. It can be prepared in diverse ways as well.

1. Peel the whole potato and boil until thoroughly cooked, about 20 minutes.

2. Using a dough hook set at low speed (or your hands), mix together the potato, flours, egg whites, stock, salt, and oil for 1 minute until all the ingredients are thoroughly incorporated; let the dough rest for approximately 1 hour.

3. Roll out the dough using both hands to form a long ½-inch-thick "rope," then slice into 1-inch-long pieces. Place the pasta in salted boiling water and cook until al dente, then drain.

4. Heat the sauce. Grate the cheese and thinly slice the basil. To serve, ladle the sauce over the top of the gnocchi, then sprinkle with black pepper, cheese, and basil.

PER SERVING: Calories: 217 | Fat: 3 g | Protein: 9 g | Sodium: 92 mg | Fiber: 5 g | Carbohydrate: 39 g

Parsnip Curry

Related to carrots, parsnips are even more fibrous and have a stronger, nutty flavor. Look for thinner parsnips, since fatter ones tend to have a thick, woody core that should be cut out.

INGREDIENTS | SERVES 4

3 tablespoons canola oil

2 minced cloves garlic

1 tablespoon grated gingerroot

1 teaspoon minced fresh red chili pepper

6-inch lemongrass stalk, thinly sliced

1 cup diced onion

⅓ cup tomato paste

1½ cups light coconut milk

½ cup Rich Poultry Stock (Chapter 10) or low-sodium canned chicken stock

2 pounds parsnips, peeled and cubed

3 tablespoons light soy sauce

1 teaspoon grated lime zest

3 tablespoons fresh lime juice

2 tablespoons chopped cilantro

4 cups steamed brown rice

1. Put the oil in a large pot and turn the heat to medium. Add the garlic, ginger, red chili pepper, lemongrass, and onion and sauté for 10 minutes.

2. Stir in the tomato paste well, then add the coconut milk, chicken broth, and parsnips. Bring to a boil, then reduce and simmer for about 15 minutes, until the parsnips are tender.

3. Add the soy sauce, lime zest, lime juice, and cilantro. Stir and remove from heat. Pour the curry into a soup tureen or large serving bowl.

4. Put the steamed brown rice on a serving platter and serve it with the curry.

PER SERVING: Calories: 1,184 | Fat: 35 g | Protein: 11 g | Sodium: 537 mg | Fiber: 18 g | Carbohydrate: 97 g

A Healthy Coconut

Pure coconut milk can pack a powerful punch in the fat department, especially its contribution of saturated fat. Light coconut milk will impart the unique taste of coconut without the added calories and fat. Also, be aware that the saturated fat found in coconut milk is plant-based unlike that found in meats and other non-plant foods high in fat. As with all things in life, moderation is key.

Baked Acorn Squash

"Fork tender" means that a fork easily pierces the cooked food; it feels soft.

INGREDIENTS | SERVES 6

3 acorn squashes
1 cup Rich Poultry Stock (Chapter 10) or
   low-sodium canned chicken stock
1 teaspoon curry powder
Freshly cracked black pepper, to taste
Kosher salt, to taste

Season the Seeds

To make a great garnish for this dish, season the squash seeds with some salt, pepper, and curry powder, then toast them in the oven or on the stovetop.

1. Preheat oven to 350°F.

2. Cut the squashes in half and remove the seeds. Place the squashes in a baking dish cut side up and pour in the stock. Sprinkle with the curry powder, pepper, and salt; bake, covered, for 45 minutes.

3. Uncover, baste with pan juices, and bake uncovered for another 15 minutes or until fork tender.

PER SERVING: Calories: 89 | Fat: 0 g | Protein: 2 g | Sodium: 99 mg | Fiber: 3 g | Carbohydrate: 23 g

Oven-Steamed Spaghetti Squash

Another serving option would be to lightly spray squash with olive oil and brown quickly under a broiler.

INGREDIENTS | SERVES 6

2 spaghetti squashes
1 cup water
¼ cup olive oil
Freshly cracked black pepper, to taste

Oven Steaming

Oven steaming is a convenient method of healthy food preparation without the hassle of having to watch over a pot on top of the stove.

1. Preheat oven to 350°F.

2. Cut the squashes in half; remove and discard the seeds. Place the squashes cut side down in a baking dish and pour in the water. Cover the baking dish with a lid or aluminum foil. Steam in the oven for 45 minutes to 1 hour, until fork tender.

3. Remove from oven and let cool slightly. Scrape out the insides of the squashes, spooning the flesh into a serving bowl. Drizzle with olive oil and sprinkle with pepper.

PER SERVING: Calories: 121 | Fat: 9.5 g | Protein: 1 g | Sodium: 23 mg | Fiber: 0 g | Carbohydrate: 9 g

Vegetable Terrine

To spice up this dish, add a poblano chili pepper in place of one of the red bell peppers.

INGREDIENTS | SERVES 6

1 medium-size baked sweet potato

1 large par-baked baking potato

1 medium-size yellow onion

3 red bell peppers

1 large eggplant

4 cloves garlic

1 head escarole

2 tablespoons olive oil

1 tablespoon curry powder

Freshly cracked black pepper, to taste

¼ cup chopped unsalted cashew nuts

1. Preheat oven to 375°F.

2. Peel and mash the sweet potato. Peel and slice the baking potato into 1-inch thick slices. Thickly slice the onion. Cut the peppers in half and remove the seeds. Slice the eggplant lengthwise into 1-inch slices. Mince the garlic. Steam the escarole until wilted.

3. Brush the onion, peppers, and eggplant with the oil, then sprinkle with curry and black pepper; roast in oven until al dente, approximately 10 to 20 minutes.

4. Grease a loaf pan with the remaining oil. Line the pan with the eggplant, allowing the slices to drape up and over the sides of the pan. Then layer the remainder of the ingredients and sprinkle with remaining curry and drizzle with oil. Fold over the eggplant slices to seal the terrine.

5. Seal tightly with plastic wrap and place something heavy on top to press the ingredients firmly together. Refrigerate for at least 4 hours.

6. Cut into 2-inch slices to serve.

PER SERVING: Calories: 173 | Fat: 7.5 g | Protein: 4 g | Sodium: 20 mg | Fiber: 5 g | Carbohydrate: 25 g

Citrus-Steamed Carrots

Figs are the fruit of gods and goddesses. Enjoy the pleasure yourself!

INGREDIENTS | SERVES 6

1 pound carrots
1 cup orange juice
2 tablespoons lemon juice
2 tablespoons lime juice
3 fresh figs
1 tablespoon extra-virgin olive oil
1 tablespoon capers

1. Peel and julienne the carrots. In a pot, combine the citrus juices and heat on medium-high. Add the carrots, cover, and steam until al dente. Remove from heat and let cool.

2. Cut the figs into wedges. Mound the carrots on serving plates and arrange the figs around the carrots. Sprinkle the olive oil and capers on top, and serve.

PER SERVING: Calories: 93 | Fat: 2.5 g | Protein: 1.5 g | Sodium: 94 mg | Fiber: 3 g | Carbohydrate: 18 g

CHAPTER 17

Death-Defying Sauces, Dressings, and Rubs

Walnut-Parsley Pesto

Walnuts add a significant blast of omega-3 fatty acids to this delicious pesto.

INGREDIENTS | SERVES 4

½ cup walnuts

8 cloves garlic

1 bunch parsley, roughly chopped

¼ cup olive oil

Freshly cracked black pepper, to taste

Kosher salt, to taste

1. Chop the walnuts in a food processor or blender. Add the garlic and process to form a paste. Add the parsley; pulse into the walnut mixture.

2. While the blender is running, drizzle in the oil until the mixture is smooth. Add pepper and salt to taste.

PER SERVING: Calories: 229 | Fat: 23 g | Protein: 3 g | Sodium: 6 mg | Fiber: 1 g | Carbohydrate: 4 g

Pesto for All

Most people are familiar with traditional pesto, which is made with basil and pine nuts, but many prefer this variation with parsley and walnuts.

Basil–Pine Nut Pesto

You can also add ¼ cup of Parmesan or Romano cheese—mix it in by hand after you have removed the sauce from the processor or blender.

INGREDIENTS | SERVES 4

½ cup pine nuts

8 cloves garlic

¼ bunch basil, chopped

¼ cup olive oil

Freshly cracked black pepper, to taste

Kosher salt, to taste

1. Chop the pine nuts in a food processor or blender. Add the garlic and process to form a paste. Add the basil; pulse into the pine nut mixture.

2. While the blender is running, drizzle in the oil until the mixture is smooth. Add pepper and salt to taste.

PER SERVING: Calories: 223 | Fat: 22 g | Protein: 4.5 g | Sodium: 2 mg | Fiber: 1 g | Carbohydrate: 4 g

Fresh Tomato Sauce

Quick-cooked fresh tomato sauce has wonderful flavor and many uses. If you are short on time, grab a can of low-sodium tomato sauce as a substitute.

INGREDIENTS | SERVES 32

2 large yellow onions

1 shallot

8 cloves garlic

20 fresh plum tomatoes

10 large fresh basil leaves

3 sprigs fresh oregano leaves

¼ bunch fresh parsley

1 tablespoon olive oil

½ cup dry red wine

Freshly cracked black pepper, to taste

2 tablespoons cold unsalted butter (optional)

1. Dice the onions and mince the shallot and garlic. Chop the tomatoes and herbs.

2. Heat the oil in a large stockpot. Add the onions, shallots, and garlic. Sauté lightly for approximately 2 to 3 minutes, then add the tomatoes. Toss the tomatoes in the onion mixture for approximately 3 minutes. Add the wine and let it reduce for approximately 10 minutes.

3. Add the herbs and spices. Add the butter, if desired. Adjust seasonings to taste, then remove from heat and serve.

PER SERVING: Calories: 18 | Fat: 0.5 g | Protein: 0.5 g | Sodium: 3 mg | Fiber: 0.5 g | Carbohydrate: 2.5 g

Thai Peanut Sauce

This is a great sauce for grilled or broiled chicken or beef skewers. It will keep in the refrigerator, covered, for up to a week. Bring to room temperature before serving.

INGREDIENTS | SERVES 4

2 tablespoons water

¼ cup creamy peanut butter

2 tablespoons tamari

1 teaspoon red pepper flakes

2 teaspoons sesame oil

2 tablespoons chopped unsalted peanuts, for garnish (optional)

1. Place all the ingredients (except the peanuts) in the bowl of a food processor fitted with a metal blade or in a blender (or blend by hand with a sturdy whisk); cover and process until smooth. Add a little more water if necessary to adjust the consistency.

2. Place the sauce in a small serving bowl and garnish with the chopped peanuts.

PER SERVING: Calories: 145 | Fat: 13 g | Protein: 6 g | Sodium: 502 mg | Fiber: 1.5 g | Carbohydrate: 4.5 g

Demi-Glacé Reduction Sauce

Demi-glacé sauces are a central part of the Mediterranean cuisine.
The term glacé refers to a reduction of stock to a quarter of its original amount.

INGREDIENTS | YIELDS 4 CUPS

1 gallon stock (vegetable, poultry, beef, seafood, etc)

Place the stock in a large, shallow saucepan; boil on high heat until reduced to a quarter of the original amount.

PER SERVING: Calories: 272 | Fat: 0 g | Protein: 48 g | Sodium: 8,864 mg | Fiber: 0 g | Carbohydrate: 16 g

Balsamic Reduction Sauce

To get the very best flavor, it is worth purchasing a high-quality vinegar instead of going for the cheaper kinds.

INGREDIENTS | SERVES 16

1 quart balsamic vinegar (or other vinegar)
2 tablespoons cold unsalted butter (optional)

Heat the vinegar in a large, shallow pan on medium-high. Allow the mixture to boil until reduced to 1 cup. Cut the butter into thin pats and whisk them into the reduced vinegar to aid in thickening.

PER SERVING: Calories: 60 | Fat: 0 g | Protein: 0 g | Sodium: 0g | Fiber: 0 g | Carbohydrate: 16 g

Asian Chili Aioli

This easy sauce goes great with dishes with an Asian flair. You can adjust the heat by increasing or decreasing the amount of Asian chili sauce.

INGREDIENTS | SERVES 2

¼ cup low-fat mayonnaise
2 tablespoons Asian chili sauce
1 teaspoon tamari

Combine all the ingredients in a small bowl and mix until blended. Refrigerate until ready to serve.

PER SERVING: Calories: 69 | Fat: 5 g | Protein: 0.5 g | Sodium: 201 mg | Fiber: 0.5 g | Carbohydrate: 5 g

Red Pepper Coulis

Coulis can be made using any fruit or vegetable.
To add variety, experiment with the addition of herbs and spices.

INGREDIENTS | SERVES 8

6 red peppers
1 tablespoon olive oil
Kosher salt, to taste
Freshly cracked black pepper, to taste

1. Preheat oven to 375°F.

2. Toss the peppers with the oil in a bowl. Place the peppers on a racked sheet pan and put in the oven for 15 to 20 minutes, until the skins blister and the peppers wilt.

3. Remove from oven and immediately place peppers in a glass container with a top. Let sit for 5 minutes, then peel off the skin. Stem, seed, and dice the peppers.

4. Place the red peppers in a blender and purée until smooth. Season with black pepper and salt.

PER SERVING: Calories: 39 | Fat: 1.5 g | Protein: 0.5 g | Sodium: 1.5 mg | Fiber: 1.5 g | Carbohydrate: 6 g

Sweet-and-Sour Relish

This recipe is a nice side with any spicy dish.

INGREDIENTS | SERVES 8

1 European cucumber
Zest and juice of 1 lime
1 teaspoon honey
1 teaspoon vinegar

Peel and dice the cucumber. Mix together all the ingredients, and chill.

PER SERVING: Calories: 9 | Fat: 0 g | Protein: 0.5 g | Sodium: 1 mg | Fiber: 0.5 g | Carbohydrate: 2 g

Difference in Cucumbers

The main difference between European cucumbers and regular cucumbers is that European cucumbers have no seeds. They also taste a bit sweeter. To substitute regular cucumbers for European, simply remove the seeds.

Cranberry Chutney

This condiment makes a perfect match with smoked turkey, so use it when you make sandwiches. Add it to brown rice for a major fiber fix. You can serve it on the side when you are carving a pork roast.

INGREDIENTS | SERVES 12

¾ cup sugar
¾ cup cider vinegar
3 cups fresh cranberries
½ cup dried cranberries
½ cup chopped dried pears
½ cup diced sweet onion
1 teaspoon grated gingerroot
½ teaspoon white pepper
¼ teaspoon ground cloves

1. Combine the sugar and vinegar in a nonreactive saucepan and heat over low until sugar dissolves.

2. Add the fresh and dried cranberries, dried pears, and sweet onion to the pan along with the ginger, white pepper, and cloves.

3. Turn the heat up and simmer for 30 minutes, stirring occasionally.

4. Remove from heat and refrigerate in a covered container.

PER SERVING: Calories: 99 | Fat: 0 g | Protein: 0 g | Sodium: 2 mg | Fiber: 2 g | Carbohydrate: 25 g

Mango Chutney

This fruity, cool chutney is a nice accompaniment to spicy dishes. To peel a ripe mango, you can slide a spoon, bottom side up, under the skin to remove it easily, without damaging the fruit.

INGREDIENTS | SERVES 8

3 mangoes
1 red onion
½ bunch fresh cilantro
1 teaspoon fresh lime juice
½ teaspoon freshly grated lime zest
Freshly cracked black pepper, to taste

Peel and dice the mangoes and onion. Chop the cilantro. Mix together all the ingredients in a medium-size bowl and adjust seasonings to taste.

PER SERVING: Calories: 56 | Fat: 0 g | Protein: 1 g | Sodium: 1.5 mg | Fiber: 1.5 g | Carbohydrate: 13 g

Apple Chutney

Try this as a side for pork dishes instead of applesauce. It also is wonderful with hearty winter squash.

INGREDIENTS | SERVES 4

2 cups ice water
1 tablespoon fresh lemon juice
3 Granny Smith apples
1 shallot
3 sprigs fresh mint
1 tablespoon freshly grated lemon zest
¼ cup white raisins
½ teaspoon ground cinnamon

1. Combine the water and lemon juice in a large mixing bowl. Core and dice the unpeeled apples and place them in the lemon water.

2. Thinly slice the shallot and chop the mint.

3. Thoroughly drain the apples, then mix together all the ingredients in a medium-size bowl.

PER SERVING: Calories: 80 | Fat: 0g | Protein: 0.5 g | Sodium: 2 mg | Fiber: 2.5 g | Carbohydrate: 21 g

Curried Vinaigrette

A great flavor for simple salads that accompany Indian-flavored entrées.
This is also a nice sauce on grilled chicken breasts served on greens.

INGREDIENTS | SERVES 8

¼ cup seasoned rice wine vinegar

⅓ cup fresh lemon juice

Sugar substitute equal to 1 teaspoon granulated sugar (optional)

1 teaspoon grated fresh ginger

1 clove minced garlic

½ teaspoon salt

½ teaspoon freshly cracked black pepper

2 teaspoons curry powder

½ teaspoon dry mustard

⅔ cup quality vegetable oil

Combine the vinegar, lemon juice, sugar substitute (if using), ginger, garlic, salt, pepper, curry powder, and mustard in a container or jar with a cover and shake vigorously to combine. Add the oil and shake until emulsified. Alternatively, combine all the ingredients in a food processor and process until creamy. Use immediately or refrigerate overnight. Bring to room temperature before using.

PER SERVING: Calories: 165 | Fat: 18 g | Protein: 0 g | Sodium: 146 mg | Fiber: 0 g | Carbohydrate: 1 g

Citrus Vinaigrette

This vinaigrette works well on summer salads and grilled or sautéed fish.
You can also use it as a marinade for chicken or fish.

INGREDIENTS | SERVES 8

⅓ cup combined lemon and orange juice

Sugar substitute equal to 1 teaspoon granulated sugar (optional)

½ tablespoon lemon zest

½ tablespoon orange zest

½ teaspoon salt

½ teaspoon freshly cracked black pepper

⅔ cup extra-virgin olive oil

Combine the lemon and orange juice, sugar substitute (if using), zests, salt, and pepper in a container or jar with cover and shake vigorously to combine. Add the oil and shake until emulsified. Alternatively, combine all the ingredients in a food processor and process until creamy. Use immediately or refrigerate overnight. Bring to room temperature before using.

PER SERVING: Calories: 165 | Fat: 18 g | Protein: 0 g | Sodium: 146 mg | Fiber: 0 g | Carbohydrate: 1 g

Savory Marinade for Meats, Fish, and Poultry

A basic flavorful marinade great for chicken, beef, and pork.
It also works well on grilled vegetables to accompany the entrée.

INGREDIENTS | SERVES 6

⅔ cup red wine vinegar

⅓ cup vegetable oil

2 tablespoons Dijon mustard

2 tablespoons Worcestershire sauce

2 cloves garlic, minced

1 tablespoon chopped fresh parsley

¼ teaspoon paprika

⅛ teaspoon ground black pepper

1 bay leaf broken into pieces

Combine all the ingredients in a glass bowl and mix well.

PER SERVING: Calories: 123 | Fat: 12 g | Protein: 0 g | Sodium: 62 mg | Fiber: 0 g | Carbohydrate: 3 g

Tropical Marinade

The acid from the pineapple juice and this aromatic blend of spices
make this a delicious marinade for poultry.

INGREDIENTS | SERVES 12

⅔ cup pineapple juice

⅓ cup vegetable oil

2 cloves garlic, minced

¼ teaspoon paprika

1 teaspoon ground cumin

¼ teaspoon ground ginger

⅛ teaspoon ground nutmeg

⅛ teaspoon ground allspice

⅛ teaspoon ground black pepper

Combine all the ingredients in a glass bowl and mix well. Reserve about ½ cup of the unused marinade and simmer for about 4 minutes to use as a glaze to finish the chicken just before serving.

PER SERVING: Calories: 63 | Fat: 6 g | Protein: 0 g | Sodium: 0.5 mg | Fiber: 0 g | Carbohydrate: 2 g

Savory Cuban Marinade

The citrus tang blended with the spice mix is a great combination for grilled meats and fish.

INGREDIENTS | SERVES 6

¼ cup chopped scallions

⅛ cup chopped garlic

½ cup freshly squeezed orange juice

¼ cup freshly squeezed lime juice

¼ cup olive oil

2 teaspoons kosher salt

½ teaspoon cayenne

1 teaspoon ground cumin

1 teaspoon dried oregano

2 tablespoons chopped fresh cilantro

½ cup vegetable stock

1 teaspoon orange zest

1 teaspoon lemon zest

Combine all the ingredients in a glass bowl and mix well.

PER SERVING: Calories: 97 | Fat: 9 g | Protein: 0.5 g | Sodium: 2 mg | Fiber: 1 g | Carbohydrate: 4 g

Turkish Rub

This rub works well with chicken or pork chops. For best results, pan-sauté or oven-roast the meat.

INGREDIENTS | SERVES 4

2 tablespoons chopped fresh mint

3 cloves garlic, minced

1 tablespoon grated fresh ginger

1 teaspoon ground cinnamon

1 teaspoon ground cumin

Freshly cracked black pepper, to taste

Combine all the ingredients in a small bowl and mix thoroughly.

PER SERVING: Calories: 6 | Fat: 0 g | Protein: 0 g | Sodium: 1 mg | Fiber: 0.5 g | Carbohydrate: 1.5 g

South-of-the-Border Rub

This dry rub packs a punch with the bite of the chili powder and red pepper.
To spread more easily, add a few teaspoons of water or stock.

INGREDIENTS | SERVES 4

2 tablespoons chili powder

3 cloves garlic, minced

2 tablespoons chopped fresh cilantro

¼ teaspoon ground red pepper

1 teaspoon ground cumin

Combine all the ingredients in a small bowl and mix thoroughly.

PER SERVING: Calories: 15 | Fat: 0.5 g | Protein: 0.5 g | Sodium: 39 mg | Fiber: 1.5 g | Carbohydrate: 3 g

From Dressings to Drinks

If you have leftover limes or lemons from making dressing or vinaigrettes, they're great additions to iced tea or water. Slice them up and remove any visible seeds. Lay them in a single layer on a tray lined with parchment paper and freeze. Store them in the freezer in a sealable plastic bag.

Creole Rub

You can double or triple this recipe and use it as a spice blend whenever you want a fiery kick for any
dish—goes great with seared ahi tuna, roasted pork, or chicken.

INGREDIENTS | SERVES 4

2 tablespoons paprika

2 teaspoons garlic powder

2 teaspoons onion powder

1 teaspoon dried thyme

1 teaspoon dried oregano

1 teaspoon ground red pepper

1 teaspoon ground black pepper

Combine all the ingredients in a small bowl and mix thoroughly. Store excess rub in an airtight container at room temperature for up to 3 months.

PER SERVING: Calories: 23 | Fat: 0 g | Protein: 1 g | Sodium: 3 mg | Fiber: 1 g | Carbohydrate: 5 g

Spicy Jerk Dry Rub

This is an authentic Jamaican jerk seasoning mix. It's used in the islands to season salads and soups and also to flavor meats, fish, and poultry.

INGREDIENTS | SERVES 4

2 teaspoons chili powder

1½ teaspoons ground allspice

½ teaspoon ground cinnamon

¼ teaspoon ground nutmeg

½ teaspoon cayenne pepper

Pinch ground cloves

Pinch garlic powder

1 tablespoon seasoned salt

1 tablespoon onion powder

Freshly ground black pepper, to taste

Combine all the ingredients in a small bowl and mix to combine. Store in an airtight jar at room temperature.

PER SERVING: Calories: 7 | Fat: 0 g | Protein: 0 g | Sodium: 695 mg | Fiber: 0.5 g | Carbohydrate: 1.5 g

Simple Herb Rub

This is a delicate rub that is appropriate for fish or chicken. For best results, pan-sauté or oven-roast the chicken.

INGREDIENTS | SERVES 4

3 tablespoons chopped fresh parsley

2 teaspoons chopped fresh thyme

3 cloves garlic, minced

2 tablespoons chopped fresh basil

¼ teaspoon ground red pepper

Combine all the ingredients in a small bowl and mix thoroughly.

PER SERVING: Calories: 5 | Fat: 0 g | Protein: 0 g | Sodium: 2 mg | Fiber: 0 g | Carbohydrate: 1 g

Italian Rub

Use a few teaspoons of wine to give it more of a pastelike consistency.
Pan-sautéing or oven-roasting the meat works best.

INGREDIENTS | SERVES 4

3 tablespoons chopped fresh parsley

2 tablespoons chopped fresh basil

2 cloves garlic, minced

2 teaspoons grated lemon zest

½ teaspoon dried thyme

½ teaspoon dried oregano

½ teaspoon ground black pepper

Combine all the ingredients in a small bowl and mix thoroughly.

PER SERVING: Calories: 4 | Fat: 0 g | Protein: 0 g | Sodium: 2 mg | Fiber: 0 g | Carbohydrate: 1 g

Yogurt Cheese

This requires overnight refrigeration, and the fresh flavor of the yogurt produces an equally light cheese, which has many uses.

INGREDIENTS | SERVES 6

32 ounces nonfat plain yogurt

½ bulb garlic, minced

Freshly cracked black pepper, to taste

½ bunch parsley, chopped

Mix together all the ingredients. Place the mixture in a colander lined with cheesecloth, then place the colander in a large bowl to catch the whey. Refrigerate overnight. When you are ready to serve, remove the colander from the refrigerator and dispose of the whey and cheesecloth. Slice and serve.

PER SERVING: Calories: 91 | Fat: 0.5 g | Protein: 9.5 g | Sodium: 120 mg | Fiber: 0 g | Carbohydrate: 13 g

Compound Butter

You can use parchment paper instead of plastic wrap or wax paper.
Use any herbs and spices that are on hand.

INGREDIENTS | SERVES 32

1 pound unsalted butter
1 bunch parsley, chopped
8 cloves garlic, minced
Freshly cracked black pepper, to taste
Kosher salt, to taste

Uses for Flavored Butters

In addition to serving flavored butter with crusty bread at the table, you can use it in the kitchen while cooking. For example, place a slice on top of the item you are preparing or getting ready to serve and it will melt, imparting its flavor to the dish. Compound butter is also good to serve with light poached dishes.

1. Allow the butter to soften at room temperature.

2. In a medium-size bowl, thoroughly mix together the parsley, garlic, and butter. Season with pepper and salt to taste.

3. Spread onto wax paper or plastic wrap, and wrap tightly. Freeze completely, then slice into small pats.

PER SERVING: Calories: 23 | Fat: 0.5 g | Protein: 1 g | Sodium: 3 mg | Fiber: 1.5 g | Carbohydrate: 5 g

CHAPTER 18

Disappearing Desserts and Snacks

Chocolate–Peanut Butter Smoothie

*This is the perfect recipe for when you want an instant chocolate
fix with a little calcium and healthy fats on top.*

INGREDIENTS | SERVES 2

2 cups dairy or nondairy milk

1 large frozen banana

2 heaping tablespoons peanut butter

1 heaping tablespoon unsweetened
chocolate powder

Sprinkle of the sweetener of choice
(optional)

1. Combine ingredients in a blender; purée until smooth.

2. Divide between two glasses; serve immediately.

PER SERVING: Calories: 319 | Fat: 12 g | Protein: 15 g |
Sodium: 147 mg | Fiber: 5 g | Carbohydrate: 44 g

Cantaloupe Sorbet

*This is delicious served with a bit of low-fat whipped cream.
The addition of berries will boost the fiber and enhance the eye appeal.*

INGREDIENTS | SERVES 12

½ cup sugar

¼ cup water

3 cups cantaloupe purée

¼ cup lemon juice

1. Combine sugar and water in a saucepan and heat just
   until sugar dissolves. Remove from heat and chill.

2. Combine chilled sugar syrup, cantaloupe purée, and
   lemon juice.

3. Freeze in an ice-cream freezer according to
   manufacturer's instructions. If you don't have one, you can
   freeze the mixture in a 9" × 13" pan. Break it into chunks,
   process in a food processor, and return to the freezer in
   the pan. Repeat the processing after the mixture has
   frozen again to make a smooth, scoopable sorbet.

PER SERVING: Calories: 64 | Fat: 0 g | Protein: 1 g |
Sodium: 14 mg | Fiber: 1 g | Carbohydrate: 16 g

Low-Calorie Whipped Cream

Regular whipped cream can be high in calories and fat, especially the saturated-type. Try this easy recipe for making healthy whipped cream in the comfort of your own home.

INGREDIENTS | SERVES 6

1 (5-ounce) can evaporated milk
1 teaspoon unflavored gelatin
2 tablespoons cold water
2 tablespoons sugar
3 tablespoons vegetable oil

1. Get the milk really cold by placing it in a shallow container in the freezer until crystals begin to form.

2. Place the gelatin and water in a dish without mixing. Place this dish in a container of hot water until the gelatin dissolves. Once it has dissolved, remove the dish from the hot water, stir and allow it to cool.

3. Beat the chilled milk until it forms stiff peaks. Then gradually add the sugar and oil. Finally, add the gelatin mixture. Continue beating until stiff peaks form again.

4. Cover and place in the freezer for 10 minutes, then transfer to the refrigerator.

5. When you are ready to serve, stir the cream so it is not quite as stiff. You can make this 2 to 3 days ahead of time as long as you keep it covered in the refrigerator.

PER SERVING: Calories: 111 | Fat: 9 g | Protein: 2 g | Sodium: 25 mg | Fiber: 0g | Carbohydrate: 7 g

Strawberry Sorbet

Try this with a slice of chocolate cake or add it to a glass of lemonade.

INGREDIENTS | SERVES 12

½ cup sugar

¼ cup water

3 cups strawberry purée

¼ cup lemon juice

Sorbet or Sherbet?

Sherbet (not sherbert, as it's often mispronounced) includes milk. It's like a watery ice cream. Sorbets, Italian ices, and granites are all related, giving you a great fruity chill-down on a hot day or after an evening meal. If they are puréed, they will have less fiber, but you can always serve them with berries, cut-up peaches, or whatever is in season.

1. Combine sugar and water in a saucepan and heat just until sugar dissolves. Remove from heat and chill.

2. Combine chilled sugar syrup, strawberry purée, and lemon juice.

3. Freeze in an ice-cream freezer according to manufacturer's instructions. If you do not have an ice-cream machine, transfer the sorbet mixture to a freezer-safe bowl or container. Cover tightly with plastic wrap, foil or an airtight cover. Place the container in the freezer and allow the mixture to freeze for 2 hours. Remove from the freezer and beat with a hand mixer to break up the ice crystals that are beginning to form. Cover and place back in the freezer. Freeze for 2 more hours. Remove from the freezer and beat again with a hand mixer. The sorbet should be thick but too soft to scoop. If it is not thick enough, return it to the freezer for additional freezing time. Beat again with a hand mixer once the desired consistency is achieved.

PER SERVING: Calories: 64 | Fat: 0 g | Protein: 0 g | Sodium: 1 mg | Fiber: 1 g | Carbohydrate: 13 g

Mango-Ginger Ice

Select ripe mangoes, preferably the flat yellow varieties available seasonally. Mangoes have a subtle sweet flavor that works well with fresh ginger—a truly inflammation-fighting combination.

INGREDIENTS | SERVES 4

Juice of 3 limes

1 tablespoon freshly grated fresh ginger

3 ripe mangoes, peeled and sliced

1 teaspoon fresh lime zest

1 cup sugar syrup (see sidebar)

Simple Sugar Syrup

To make sugar syrup: Combine 3 cups water and 2 cups granulated sugar in a saucepan and cook over medium-low heat until the sugar dissolves entirely and the mixture turns slightly syrupy. Set aside to cool. Save leftovers for another use.

Combine the ingredients in the container of a blender and process until smooth. Chill the mixture and churn according to manufacturer's directions. Scoop the mixture into a container and freeze.

PER SERVING: Calories: 346 | Fat: 0.5 g | Protein: 1.5 g | Sodium: 55 mg | Fiber: 3 g | Carbohydrate: 94 g

Chocolate Fudge Mousse with Coffee Whipped Cream

You can use instant coffee crystals to make the coffee.
Use parfait glasses or wineglasses with a wide bowl for a formal presentation.

INGREDIENTS | SERVES 4

1 package sugar-free, fat-free instant chocolate fudge pudding mix

2 cups cold skim milk

Low-Calorie Whipped Cream (Chapter 18)

1 tablespoon double-strength brewed coffee, chilled

Fresh strawberry slices

1. Combine the pudding mix and milk in a medium-size mixing bowl. Use an electric mixer to beat for about 1½ minutes, until smooth. Equally divide the mixture between 4 parfait cups. Set aside for 5 to 7 minutes.

2. Prepare the low-calorie whipped cream. Stir in the coffee and mix just until blended. Refrigerate until ready to serve.

3. To serve, top the pudding with equal amounts of coffee whipped cream. Served chilled. Garnish with fresh strawberries, if desired.

PER SERVING (WITHOUT WHIPPED CREAM): Calories: 68 | Fat: 0.5 g | Protein: 4 g | Sodium: 167 mg | Fiber: 0.5 g | Carbohydrate: 12 g

Citrus Sherbet

Sherbet can be made with any fruit, as long as you have the right ratio of liquid, egg whites, and sugar.

INGREDIENTS | SERVES 8

4 Valencia oranges
2 ruby red grapefruits
1 key lime
1¼ cups granulated sugar
⅓ cup water
3 egg whites
¼ teaspoon cream of tartar
¼ teaspoon salt
Edible orchid or mint leaves, for garnish

1. Juice the oranges, grapefruits, and lime, then measure out 3 cups of unfiltered juice and set aside.

2. In a saucepan, combine the sugar and water. Bring to a boil, stirring until the sugar dissolves. Cook to 238°F (soft ball on a candy thermometer).

3. Meanwhile, beat the egg whites with the cream of tartar and salt until stiff. Slowly pour the hot syrup into the bowl with the egg whites, continuing to beat at high speed until the mixture is stiff and glossy (approximately 5 minutes).

4. Stir in the juices, then pour into a shallow pan. Freeze until almost firm, then return to the bowl. Beat again until blended. Return to the container for scooping or smaller serving dish and freeze.

5. To serve: Remove from freezer, allowing 15 minutes before serving. Scoop and garnish.

PER SERVING: Calories: 200 | Fat: 0 g | Protein: 3.5 g | Sodium: 97 mg | Fiber: 3.5 g | Carbohydrate: 50 g

Strawberry Parfait

This is a simple preparation that takes full advantage of those luscious ripe strawberries of summer.

INGREDIENTS | SERVES 4

1 cup strawberries, rinsed, dried, and hulled

1½ cups nondairy whipped topping (such as Cool Whip), thawed

½ cup light, sugar-free strawberry preserves

4 whole strawberries

Fresh mint leaves, for garnish

1. Slice the strawberries lengthwise and divide equally between 4 chilled martini glasses or ramekins.

2. Combine the whipped topping with the preserves in a medium-size mixing bowl and stir until evenly blended. Dollop the mixture on top of the fruit or use a piping bag to top each with a rosette. Garnish each with a whole strawberry and a fresh mint leaf.

PER SERVING: Calories: 81 | Fat: 1 g | Protein: 1g | Sodium: 11 mg | Fiber: 2 g | Carbohydrate: 24 g

Crunchy Peach Parfait

Be sure to choose yogurt containing the Live and Active Cultures seal. Researchers are finding that yogurt and its cultures may have a beneficial effect on the immune system, reduce cholesterol levels, and reduce the risk of certain chronic diseases such as colon cancer.

INGREDIENTS | SERVES 1

1 cup plain low-fat yogurt

½ teaspoon vanilla extract

1 tablespoon maple syrup

6 walnut halves

1 cup fresh sliced peaches

½ cup granola

Working with Yogurt

Mixing yogurt in a blender can cause it to break down and become liquefied. Instead, either whisk it gently or fold the yogurt into the mixture when incorporating it into most recipes.

1. Spoon yogurt into a small bowl; add vanilla and maple syrup; mix well.

2. Lightly chop walnuts into large pieces; set aside.

3. In a long-stemmed parfait glass, begin with a layer of yogurt, then sliced peaches, and finally the granola. Repeat layering to top of glass.

4. Sprinkle walnuts on top and serve chilled.

PER SERVING: Calories: 580 | Fat: 18 g | Protein: 21 g | Sodium: 308 mg | Fiber: 8 g | Carbohydrate: 93 g

Fresh Fruit and Meringue

This recipe works well with soft fruits, such as blackberries, blueberries, and raspberries. It's a perfect ending to a picnic or a sweet, light finish to any summer lunch.

INGREDIENTS | SERVES 12

6 egg whites
½ cup granulated sugar
¼ teaspoon cream of tartar
2 cups chopped fresh fruit
¼ teaspoon freshly grated lemon zest
½ pound chopped almonds
3 tablespoons honey

1. Preheat oven to 200°F.

2. Line a baking sheet with parchment paper or spray with cooking spray.

3. In a copper or stainless steel bowl, beat the egg whites, sugar, and cream of tartar until stiff. Bake in oven for 5 to 6 hours, until dry, crispy, and lightly golden.

4. Serve with fresh seasonal fruit. Sprinkle with lemon zest, almonds, and honey.

PER SERVING: Calories: 184 | Fat: 9.5 g | Protein: 6.5 g | Sodium: 33 mg | Fiber: 3 g | Carbohydrate: 21 g

Caramelized Pears with Toasted Almonds

Use pears that are ripe but still firm. Overly ripe pears will cook too quickly.

INGREDIENTS | SERVES 4

3 pears, ripe but firm, quartered, cored, and thinly sliced
1 packed tablespoon brown sugar
2 tablespoons sliced almonds
½ cup low-fat vanilla yogurt
Fresh mint leaves, for garnish

1. Clean and oil broiler rack. Preheat to medium-high.

2. Fan the pear slices in concentric circles in a shallow ovenproof dish. Sprinkle the brown sugar over the pears.

3. Broil until the sugar is caramelized, but not burned, about 4 to 5 minutes. Sprinkle the almonds on top and broil for 1 more minute, until golden.

4. To serve, divide the pears among 4 serving plates. Top each with equal parts of the yogurt and garnish with mint leaves. Serve immediately.

PER SERVING: Calories: 146 | Fat: 2 g | Protein: 2 g | Sodium: 23 mg | Fiber: 5 g | Carbohydrate: 32 g

Walnut Biscotti

This is a delicious basic cookie that's not too sweet.
You can intensify the almond flavor in this recipe by adding a spoonful of almond extract.

INGREDIENTS | SERVES 10

1 egg or ¼ cup egg substitute
¼ cup sugar
¾ teaspoon baking powder
Pinch of salt
½ cup all-purpose flour
¼ cup whole-wheat flour
½ cup toasted walnuts, chopped

Biscotti

Biscotti means "twice baked" in Italian. It starts out like a sweet bread and then, cut into slices and rebaked, turns into a delicious cookie with endless variations. Various dried fruits, different kinds of nuts, and other flavorings spike biscotti. You can throw in seeds to add to the crunch and fiber.

1. Preheat oven to 350°F. Grease a baking sheet pan or line it with parchment.

2. Whip the egg and sugar together with an electric mixer until light yellow in color and very fluffy.

3. In a separate bowl combine the baking powder, salt, and flours. Add dry mixture to the egg mixture and combine to make a smooth dough. Stir in walnuts.

4. Scrape dough out onto the prepared baking sheet pan and form it into a broad, flat log using wet fingers. Bake for 30 minutes, remove from oven, and cool for 5 minutes. Turn the oven down to 275°F.

5. Cut the log into ½-inch wide slices and place the slices back on the baking sheet, cut sides facing up. Bake 15 minutes, turn cookies over, and bake 10 minutes more. Cool on a rack.

PER SERVING: Calories: 97 | Fat: 4 g | Protein: 3 g | Sodium: 11 mg | Fiber: 1 g | Carbohydrate: 13 g

Cranberry-Pistachio Biscotti

This is a festive cookie to have around holiday time, studded with red and green.
Your guests will get an inconspicuous fiber infusion from the nuts and cranberries.
Offer low-fat eggnog to get an extra protein and calcium punch.

INGREDIENTS | SERVES 10

2 ounces unsalted butter, softened

¼ cup sugar

1 egg or ¼ cup egg substitute

½ teaspoon vanilla

¼ teaspoon grated nutmeg

1 teaspoon baking powder

Pinch of salt

½ cup all-purpose flour

½ cup whole-wheat flour

½ cup shelled pistachios

¼ cup dried cranberries, chopped

1. Preheat oven to 350°F. Grease a baking sheet pan.

2. Cream the butter and sugar with an electric mixer. Add egg and vanilla and beat to incorporate.

3. In a separate bowl combine the nutmeg, baking powder, salt, and flour. Add this dry mixture to the egg-butter mixture and combine to make a smooth dough. Stir in pistachios and cranberries.

4. Scrape dough out onto the prepared baking sheet pan and form it into a broad, flat log using wet fingers. Bake for 30 minutes, remove from oven, and cool for 5 minutes. Turn the oven down to 275°F.

5. Cut the log into ½-inch-wide slices and place the slices back on the baking sheet, cut sides facing up. Bake 15 minutes, turn cookies over, and bake 10 minutes more. Cool on a rack.

PER SERVING: Calories: 153 | Fat: 8 g | Protein: 3.5 g | Sodium: 13 mg | Fiber: 1.5 g | Carbohydrate: 18 g

Sunflower Seed Shortbread

These delicate cookies are simple to make, and you'll enjoy the nutty, crunchy fiber content of whole-wheat flour and sunflower seeds. They are wonderful as an after-school snack or at teatime to give your friends a fiber boost!

INGREDIENTS | SERVES 12

½ cup butter, softened
¼ cup sugar
½ teaspoon vanilla
¾ cup all-purpose flour
½ cup whole-wheat flour
½ teaspoon salt
1 egg white
½ cup toasted sunflower seeds, shelled

Seedless

The sunflower seed is actually the fruit of the sunflower. The edible portion of the sunflower seed is referred to as the sunflower kernel. Regardless of its name, sunflower seeds provide essential fatty acids, amino acids (the building blocks of proteins), and cholesterol-lowering phytosterols.

1. Preheat oven to 325°F.

2. Combine butter and sugar in a bowl and mix with a wooden spoon or electric mixer until slightly fluffy but not whipped.

3. Add vanilla and mix well.

4. Add flours and salt and mix to form a smooth dough.

5. Press dough into a 9-inch pie plate, and brush the dough with the egg white. Sprinkle the sunflower seeds on top of the dough, press in, and bake for 20 minutes. Remove from oven and cut into 12 wedges immediately. Let cool.

PER SERVING: Calories: 162 | Fat: 11 g | Protein: 3 g | Sodium: 104 mg | Fiber: 1.5 g | Carbohydrate: 15 g

Wheat-Free Brownies

These are the perfect substitute brownie for individuals with gluten or egg allergies. The key to making these chewy is the brown rice flour. The silken tofu replaces the oil and keeps the fat grams way down.

INGREDIENTS | SERVES 8

1½ cups brown rice flour

1 cup unsweetened cocoa powder

¼ teaspoon sea salt

1 (10-ounce) package soft silken tofu

1 teaspoon orange extract

1 teaspoon vanilla extract

½ cup barley malt

½ cup maple syrup

1 cup low-fat soy or rice milk

⅔ cup walnuts, chopped

1. Preheat oven to 350°F.

2. In a medium-size bowl, combine flour, cocoa, and salt.

3. In a blender, purée tofu, orange extract, vanilla extract, barley malt, maple syrup, and milk.

4. Stir tofu mixture into flour mixture; add walnuts; mix well.

5. Pour into a lightly oiled 8" × 8" baking dish; bake for 30 minutes.

PER SERVING: Calories: 324 | Fat: 11 g | Protein: 10 g | Sodium: 110 mg | Fiber: 6.5 g | Carbohydrate: 53 g

Chocolate Substitutes

When a recipe calls for chocolate, use dark chocolate (usually less sugar) or— even better—cocoa powder. To substitute for 1 ounce of unsweetened chocolate, use 3 tablespoons dry cocoa plus 2 tablespoons sugar plus 1 tablespoon vegetable oil such as canola oil.

Almond Cookies

*Great alone or with a fruit dessert. Store in an airtight container.
For a crispy texture, put in a low-temperature oven for 1 or 2 minutes.*

INGREDIENTS | SERVES 24

Sugar substitute for baking equal to 7
  tablespoons granulated sugar

3 egg whites, at room temperature

½ cup finely ground blanched almonds

⅓ cup cake flour

1 teaspoon Cointreau or 1 tablespoon
  orange juice or frozen orange juice
  concentrate

¼ teaspoon vanilla extract

Sweet Tooth

Adding sweet spices such as cinnamon,
nutmeg, or cardamom will enhance the
perception of sweetness in your desserts.

1. Preheat oven to 425°F. Oil two 17" × 14" baking sheets, or line with parchment paper.

2. In a large bowl, stir together the sugar substitute and egg whites until the whites are frothy and the sugar substitute is dissolved. Add the remaining ingredients and whisk until the batter is somewhat smooth.

3. Place rounded teaspoon-size dollops of dough on the prepared baking sheets, leaving a 1-inch space between each cookie.

4. Bake in the oven for 5 to 6 minutes or until the edges turn golden. Remove from oven and transfer the cookies to a wire rack. Let cool completely.

PER SERVING: Calories: 20 | Fat: 1 g | Protein: 1 g |
Sodium: 8 mg | Fiber: 0 g | Carbohydrate: 2 g

Apricot–Chocolate Chip Squares

These cookies are easy and have the added crunch of granola and cashews.
Pack these instead of trail mix when you go camping or to the park.
These are so loaded with vitamins, protein, and fiber that you will be able to go on and on for miles.

INGREDIENTS | SERVES 18

1 cup unsalted butter, softened
¾ cup brown sugar
¾ cup sugar
3 eggs or ¾ cup egg substitute
1 teaspoon vanilla
1¼ cups all-purpose flour
1 cup whole-wheat flour
½ teaspoon salt
2 teaspoons baking soda
1 cup chocolate chips
1 cup chopped dried apricots
2 cups granola
1 cup chopped cashews

1. Preheat oven to 375°F.

2. Cream the butter, brown sugar, and sugar with an electric mixer until fluffy.

3. Add eggs and vanilla and combine well. Scrape the sides of the bowl.

4. Mix the flour, salt, and baking soda together in a bowl. Add it to the butter mixture, stirring well to combine into a smooth dough. Stir in chocolate chips, dried apricots, granola, and cashews.

5. Press dough into a foil-lined 15½" × 10½" × 1" baking pan and bake for 20 minutes. Cool on a rack and cut into squares.

PER SERVING: Calories: 390 | Fat: 19 g | Protein: 5.5 g | Sodium: 120 mg | Fiber: 2.5 g | Carbohydrate: 53 g

Energy Oat Bars

Rice syrup is a thick, mild sweetener that helps bind the bars together. It has a low glycemic index, meaning it won't spike your blood sugar. If you want a sweeter bar, substitute ½ cup of agave or maple syrup or honey.

INGREDIENTS | SERVES 20

¾ cup rice syrup

1½ cups toasted almond or peanut butter

1 teaspoon vanilla extract

½ cup flaxseed meal

⅓ cup unsweetened coconut

½ cup rolled oats

⅓ cup raisins

⅓ cup chopped walnuts

1. In a large, heavy saucepan, heat rice syrup on low until thin and runny, about 2 minutes.

2. Add almond butter and vanilla; stir well.

3. Remove from heat. Stir in remaining ingredients; mix well.

4. Spoon into an 8" × 8" casserole pan; spread; slice into 20 pieces.

5. Cover and chill in the refrigerator or freezer.

PER SERVING: Calories: 225 | Fat: 14 g | Protein: 7.5 g | Sodium: 10 mg | Fiber: 3 g | Carbohydrate: 21 g

Sesame Seed Cookies

These delicate cookies are a type of lace cookie, full of delicious and fiber-rich sesame seeds. The seeds add a touch of protein. These cookies are also elegant enough for dessert, topped with a low-fat ice cream.

INGREDIENTS | SERVES 15

4½ teaspoons honey

1½ tablespoons butter

½ cup powdered sugar

1 tablespoon water

½ cup sesame seeds

Pinch of salt

2 tablespoons flour

1. Stir the honey, butter, powdered sugar, and water together in a saucepan. Turn the heat to medium and bring to a boil. Boil for 1 minute and remove from heat.

2. Stir in the sesame seeds, salt, and flour. Let cool.

3. Preheat oven to 350°F. Line baking sheets with parchment paper.

4. Roll the cookie dough into balls, and place them 4 inches apart from each other on the prepared baking sheets.

5. Bake for 8 minutes, then let cool on racks.

PER SERVING: Calories: 64 | Fat: 3.5 g | Protein: 1 g | Sodium: 12 mg | Fiber: 0.5 g | Carbohydrate: 8 g

Oatmeal-Raisin Chewies

Spelt flour is an excellent substitute for wheat flour, and can be tolerated by some people with allergies or an intolerance to wheat, but is still problematic for those with a gluten allergy, such as celiac disease.

INGREDIENTS | SERVES 8

1½ cups rolled oats

¾ cup spelt flour

⅛ teaspoon sea salt

½ cup chopped walnuts

½ cup raisins

1 teaspoon cinnamon

2 tablespoons canola oil, divided

⅓ cup agave or maple syrup

½ teaspoon vanilla extract

1 cup cold spring water

1. Preheat oven to 375°F.

2. In a large bowl, mix oats, flour, salt, walnuts, raisins, and cinnamon. Add 1½ tablespoons canola oil slowly, making sure to coat oats well with oil.

3. Slowly stir in syrup and vanilla. Add water; mix until batter becomes thick.

4. Oil baking sheets with 1 teaspoon of canola oil. Using a tablespoon, spoon batter onto an oiled baking sheet.

5. Pat down each spoonful into patties about 2 inches across and ¼ inch thick and ½ inch apart. The cookies will not spread, because there is no leavening agent.

6. Place cookies in oven and bake 25 minutes, or until golden brown.

7. Cool cookies slightly before removing from pan with a spatula. Cool completely before serving.

PER SERVING: Calories: 314 | Fat: 11 g | Protein: 8 g | Sodium: 42 mg | Fiber: 5 g | Carbohydrate: 49 g

Pine Nut and Almond Macaroons

The Marsala adds a delicious taste element to these delectable cookies.
Prepare a platter of these cookies for your next brunch.

INGREDIENTS | SERVES 11

¼ cup Marsala wine

3 tablespoons dried currants

½ cup toasted slivered almonds

½ cup toasted pine nuts

Sugar substitute for baking equal to ½ cup granulated sugar

1 tablespoon all-purpose flour

1 large egg white

⅛ teaspoon almond extract

½ cup untoasted pine nuts

1. Preheat oven to 350°F. Line a large cookie sheet with foil.

2. In a small, heavy saucepan, cook the Marsala and currants over medium heat until the liquid evaporates, about 5 minutes.

3. In a food processor, finely grind the almonds, the toasted pine nuts, the sugar substitute, and flour. In a separate bowl, mix together the egg white and almond extract. Add the egg mixture to the food processor with the nuts and blend until the dough forms into a ball.

4. Place the dough in a bowl and mix in the currants. Shape the dough into ¾-inch balls. Roll the balls in the untoasted pine nuts to cover, pressing gently so the nuts adhere.

5. Flatten the balls into 1½-inch rounds and place on the prepared cookie sheet, making sure that they are spaced at least 1 inch apart. Bake until golden brown, about 15 minutes. Let cool slightly and remove from foil using a metal spatula.

PER SERVING: Calories: 107 | Fat: 8 g | Protein: 4.5 g | Sodium: 7 mg | Fiber: 1 g | Carbohydrate: 5 g

Savory Israeli Couscous Carrot Cake

The flavors of the nutty couscous and the sweet carrots make a wonderful combination. To prevent overbrowning of the top of the cake, cover it with foil halfway through the cooking time.

INGREDIENTS | SERVES 6

1½ teaspoons olive oil

6 carrots

1 shallot

2 sprigs rosemary, leaves only

1 egg or ¼ cup egg substitutes

1 egg white

1 cup cooked couscous

¼ cup skim milk

1½ cups whole-wheat flour

½ teaspoon baking powder

¼ teaspoon iodized salt

1. Preheat oven to 375°F. Brush a layer-cake pan with a quarter of the oil.

2. Peel and grate the carrots. Mince the shallot.

3. Combine the carrots and shallots with the rosemary, eggs, couscous, the remaining oil, and the milk. In a separate bowl, sift together the flour, baking powder, and salt.

4. Place in the prepared cake pan and bake for 45 minutes.

PER SERVING: Calories: 210 | Fat: 2.5 g | Protein: 9 g | Sodium: 222 mg | Fiber: 8 g | Carbohydrate: 41 g

Blackberry Cobbler

This recipe can also be made from raspberries, blueberries, cherries, or a combination, which is sometimes called jumbleberry. The berry juice soaks into the biscuits, giving them enormous flavor. The whole wheat in the biscuits adds protein and fiber.

INGREDIENTS | SERVES 8

1 recipe Whole-Wheat Biscuits (Chapter 14), unbaked

8 cups blackberries

¼ cup flour

¾ cup sugar

¼ cup cream

1. Preheat oven to 350°F.

2. Prepare biscuit dough recipe, cut biscuit circles out, and set them aside.

3. Toss the blackberries, flour, and sugar together, then put the mixture into a 9" × 11" baking dish.

4. Bake the blackberries for 25 minutes, remove from oven, and place the unbaked biscuits on top of the hot berries.

5. Brush the biscuit tops with cream and return the cobbler to the oven to bake for another 25 minutes. Serve warm.

PER SERVING: Calories: 266 | Fat: 6 g | Protein: 4 g | Sodium: 275 mg | Fiber: 8 g | Carbohydrate: 50 g

Quick Apple Crisp

There is nothing like the taste of maple syrup, apples, and cinnamon heated together and baked—an American classic the whole family will enjoy. Serve warm with a scoop of low-fat vanilla ice cream or by itself.

INGREDIENTS | SERVES 8

5 large red apples
½ cup raisins
½ cup apple juice
Juice of 1 lemon
¼ cup maple syrup
1 teaspoon cinnamon powder
2 cups raw oats (not instant)
½ cup walnuts
¼ teaspoon sea salt
1 teaspoon vanilla extract
⅓ cup canola oil
⅔ cup maple syrup

Maple Syrup

Maple syrup is made from the sap of the sugar black or red maple tree. The tree is first tapped (pierced), which allows the sap to run out freely. The clear, tasteless sap is then boiled down to evaporate the water, giving it the characteristic maple flavor and amber color, with a sugar content of 60 percent.

1. Preheat oven to 350°F.

2. Peel, core, and slice the apples. Layer in a 9" × 12" baking pan with the raisins.

3. In a small bowl, whisk together the apple juice, lemon juice, ¼ cup maple syrup, and cinnamon; pour over the apples.

4. To make the topping, process the oats in a food processor until almost flour consistency.

5. Add the walnuts and sea salt to the oats; pulse to lightly chop. Pour the mixture into a large bowl.

6. In a medium-size bowl, whisk together the vanilla extract, oil, and ⅔ cup maple syrup.

7. Pour the liquid mixture over the oats; use a wooden spoon to combine. You may need to use your hands to mix well enough to coat the oats and walnuts.

8. When done, spoon the mixture over the top of the apples. Bake 30 minutes, or until apples are tender and topping is a golden brown.

9. Allow to cool slightly before serving.

PER SERVING: Calories: 459 | Fat: 17 g | Protein: 8 g | Sodium: 7 mg | Fiber: 7 g | Carbohydrate: 73 g

Raspberry-Rhubarb Crisp

This crisp can be baked ahead of time and reheated later, or even served cold with cream poured over it. The berries and almonds will give you fiber. It's best to reheat the dessert to revive the crispy topping.

INGREDIENTS | SERVES 8

Crisp
6 cups chopped rhubarb stalks, red part only
¼ cup flour
1 cup sugar
2 cups raspberries

Topping
1 cup ground almonds
¼ cup rolled oats
1½ cups flour
½ cup brown sugar
¼ cup sugar
1 teaspoon cinnamon
½ teaspoon salt
¾ cup unsalted butter, cut in chunks

1. Preheat oven to 350°F.

2. Toss the rhubarb with ¼ cup flour and 1 cup sugar. Add the raspberries, toss gently, and then put the mixture into a 9" × 11" inch baking dish. Set aside.

3. In a bowl combine the almonds, oats, 1½ cups flour, brown sugar, sugar, cinnamon, and salt. Add the butter chunks and mix to a sandy consistency with an electric mixer. You can tell the topping is ready if it clumps together when you squeeze it in the palm of your hand.

4. Cover the raspberry-rhubarb mixture evenly with the topping and bake for 60 minutes or until the juices start to bubble up and thicken.

5. Remove the crisp from the oven and cut around the sides to loosen. Cut into squares and serve warm with ice cream.

PER SERVING: Calories: 544 | Fat: 24 g | Protein: 7.5 g | Sodium: 158 mg | Fiber: 6.5 g | Carbohydrate: 79 g

Nectarine-Cherry Tart with Oat Crumble Topping

Drizzle the warm tart with heavy cream for an extra special treat.

INGREDIENTS | SERVES 6

2 large ripe nectarines, unpeeled and thinly sliced

2 cups fresh or frozen pitted cherries

½ cup firmly packed brown sugar

3 tablespoon instant tapioca

1 tablespoon firm butter, diced

1 teaspoon vanilla extract

1 (9-inch) deep-dish pie crust

1 cup old-fashioned rolled oats

1 cup toasted walnut pieces

½ cup brown sugar

3 tablespoons flour

¼ cup butter

1. Preheat the oven to 350°F.

2. Toss the nectarine slices and cherries together, then add ½ cup brown sugar and tapioca. When this mixture is well combined, add the butter and vanilla extract. Spoon the mixture into the pie crust.

3. For topping: combine the oats, walnuts, ½ cup brown sugar, flour, and butter and mix until crumbly. Sprinkle over the filling and press down.

4. Bake until topping is brown, about 30 minutes. Serve warm.

PER SERVING: Calories: 676 | Fat: 32 g | Protein: 10 g | Sodium: 323 mg | Fiber: 6 g | Carbohydrate: 94 g

Whole Oats and Raisins

A very simple recipe you will make over and over again. Children love oats made this way and so will you. You can cook them on the stove all day or use a 1.5-quart slow cooker and make your life a whole lot easier.

INGREDIENTS | SERVES 4

1 cup whole-oat groats

Pinch of sea salt

⅓ cup raisins

5 cups water

½ teaspoon cinnamon powder

½ cup toasted walnuts

Maple syrup, to taste

Splash of milk

1. Before going to bed, combine oats, salt, raisins, water, and cinnamon in a 1.5-quart slow cooker. Turn on low; let cook overnight.

2. In the morning, chop walnuts. Stir oats and spoon ½ cup into individual bowls.

3. Top with walnuts, a drizzle of maple syrup, and a splash of milk.

PER SERVING: Calories: 280 | Fat: 11 g | Protein: 7.5 g | Sodium: 6 mg | Fiber: 6 g | Carbohydrate: 43 g

Raspberry-Almond Turnovers

Delicious for breakfast but also a good dessert or snack, these turnovers are a versatile part of the high-fiber diet repertoire. If you are a weekend warrior, make a double recipe and freeze them in individual plastic bags for use later in the week.

INGREDIENTS | SERVES 4

1 cup sliced almonds

1 sheet puff pastry, thawed in the refrigerator

1 egg white for brushing the pastry and final turnovers

4 teaspoons almond paste

1 cup frozen raspberries

4 teaspoons sugar

2 teaspoons cornstarch

1 tablespoon wheat germ

2 tablespoons powdered sugar

Puff Pastry

Unfortunately, you can't buy whole-grain puff pastry, but you can fill it with fruit and nuts for wonderful turnovers. Wheat germ is also an excellent source of vitamins and fiber, and can be added to everything from meatloaf to pancake batter.

1. Preheat the oven to 400°F. Grind half of the almonds in a food processor. Set aside.

2. Roll the puff pastry into an 11" × 11" square on a floured surface. Cut the square into four smaller squares. Paint the egg white on the pastry squares.

3. Put a teaspoon of almond paste in the middle of each square, layer ¼ cup raspberries on top, then sprinkle the ground almonds, sugar, cornstarch, and wheat germ over the berries.

4. Fold each square over to make a triangle to encase the filling. Press down on the outer edges with your fingers or a fork to seal.

5. Brush the egg white on the turnovers and sprinkle them with the remaining sliced almonds and powdered sugar. Bake for 10 minutes, turn the oven down to 350°F, and continue baking for about 10–15 minutes longer. Let cool before eating.

PER SERVING: Calories: 283 | Fat: 18 g | Protein: 8 g | Sodium: 47 mg | Fiber: 6 g | Carbohydrate: 26 g

Sample Anti-Inflammation Diet Menu

	Breakfast	Morning Snack	Lunch	Afternoon Snack	Dinner
Sunday	Organic strawberries 1 Raisin Bran Muffin (Chapter 9) Low-fat milk Hard-boiled egg	Peach Yogurt Smoothie (Chapter 9)	Two-Bean Chili Wrap (Chapter 12) Pretzels Baby carrots Low-fat milk	Pineapple Trail mix (dry-roasted almonds, dried pineapple, raisins)	Broiled Swordfish Kebab (Chapter 11) Citrus-Steamed Carrots (Chapter 16) Millet (Chapter 14)
Monday	Morning Sunshine Smoothie (Chapter 9) Apple Bread (Chapter 9) Low-fat milk	Watermelon Low-fat yogurt	Grilled Vegetable Hero (Chapter 12) Baked potato chips Almonds	Strawberry-Banana Smoothie (Chapter 9)	Apricot-Stuffed Pork Tenderloin (Chapter 11) Roasted Potatoes with Vegetables (Chapter 16)
Tuesday	Quinoa Breakfast Congee (Chapter 9) Organic blueberries Low-fat milk	Grapefruit Oatmeal-Raisin Scone (Chapter 9)	Curried Shrimp Salad in a Papaya (Chapter 11) Cinnamon-Swirl Raisin Bread (Chapter 14)	Peach Low-fat yogurt	Zesty Pecan Chicken and Grapes (Chapter 11) Oven-Steamed Spaghetti Squash (Chapter 16) Multigrain Dinner Rolls (Chapter 14)
Wednesday	Fruit-Stuffed French Toast (Chapter 9) Low-fat milk	Fresh Fruit Kebabs with Vanilla Yogurt Sauce (Chapter 9)	Lentil and Walnut Chili (Chapter 10) Sliced cucumbers Baked tortilla chips	Papaya Zucchini Bread (Chapter 9) Low-fat milk	Salmon with Anchovy-Caper Vinaigrette (Chapter 11) Mediterranean Green Beans (Chapter 15) Couscous

	Breakfast	Morning Snack	Lunch	Afternoon Snack	Dinner
Thursday	Edamame Omelet (Chapter 9) Cornmeal Grits (Chapter 9) Low-fat milk	Honeydew Melon Rice cake and peanut butter	Tofu Mac and Cheese (Chapter 13) Low-fat yogurt	Pear Energy Oat Bars (Chapter 18)	Turkey Breast Piccata (Chapter 11) Wilted Spinach (Chapter 15) Wild rice Low-fat milk
Friday	Breakfast Fruit Bars (Chapter 9) Cantaloupe Scrambled egg Low-fat milk	Organic apple Low-fat cheese and crackers	A Super-Hero Wrap-Up (Chapter 13) Popcorn Low-fat milk	Organic grapes Hummus Whole-wheat crackers	Asian Salmon Patties (Chapter 11) Succotash (Chapter 12) Brown rice
Saturday	Blackberry Buckwheat Flapjacks (Chapter 9) Mango Low-fat milk	Organic Nectarine Graham crackers with peanut butter	Meatless Meatloaf Sandwich (Chapter 12) Baby carrots Low-fat milk	Plum	Harvest Stew (Chapter 10) Multigrain Dinner Rolls (Chapter 14) Field green salad with vinaigrette dressing Low-fat milk

▼ ANTI-INFLAMMATORY EATING AND LIFESTYLE GUIDELINES

Food Group	Total Daily Amounts	Breakfast	Snack	Lunch	Snack	Dinner
Grains	6+ servings	1 serving	1 serving	2 servings	1 serving	2 servings
Fruits	2½ cups	1 cup	1 cup	1 cup	1 cup	
Vegetables	3½ cups			1–2 cups	1 cup	2 cups
Meat and Beans	5–7 servings	1 serving	1 serving	2 servings	1 serving	2 servings
Low-Fat Dairy	2–3 servings	1 serving		1 serving		1 serving
Fish Oils	250–500 mg EPA and DHA if you consume 2–3 servings of fatty fish per week.					
	1,000 mg EPA and DHA if you do not consume fatty fish.					
Vitamin D3	1,000 IU/day					
Exercise	5+ days per week including cardiovascular, strengthening, and flexibility exercise					

Glossary

Adipose Tissue

A kind of body tissue containing stored fat that serves as a source of energy; it also cushions and insulates vital organs.

Advanced-Glycation End Products (AGEs)

Substances produced when a chemical reaction occurs in the body between sugar and protein or fats resulting in the production of pro-inflammatory substances.

Alpha-Linolenic Acid (ALA)

A type of omega-3 fatty acid found in plants that can be converted into docosahexaenoic acid (DHA) and eicosapentaenoic acid (EPA).

Android Obesity

A type of obesity in which fat is localized around the waist and upper body; it is most common in men and post-menopausal women; apple-shaped fat distribution.

Alzheimer's Disease

A progressive, degenerative disease marked by a loss of cognitive ability over a ten- to fifteen-year period.

Antioxidants

Substances found in fruits, vegetables, and vegetable oils that are thought to protect cells from the damaging effects of oxidation.

Arachidonic Acid (AA)

A polyunsaturated fatty acid found in cell membranes, and the brain and muscles.

Atherosclerosis

A disease marked by narrowing and hardening of the arteries.

Autoimmune Disorder

A condition that occurs when the immune system mistakenly attacks and destroys healthy body tissue.

Beta-Amyloid Proteins

A protein that accumulates in the brain, leading to plaque development and subsequent memory loss, dementia, and Alzheimer's disease.

Biomarker

A biochemical feature found in the blood that can be used to measure the progress of disease or the effects of a treatment.

Body Mass Index (BMI)

A number calculated from a person's weight and height, and used to estimate body fatness.

Bran

The outer covering of a grain rich in fiber.

C-Reactive Protein

A protein produced in the liver and found in the blood after an injury, infection, or inflammation. A biomarker of inflammation.

Cancer

A group of diseases involving uncontrolled cell division leading to growth of abnormal tissue.

Coronary Heart Disease (CHD)

A narrowing of the small blood vessels that supply blood and oxygen to the heart.

Cortisol

A hormone produced in the body in response to stress that helps to restore homeostasis in the body.

Cyclooxygenase Enzymes (COX)

An enzyme that is responsible for formation of inflammation and pain-producing prostaglandins.

Diabetes

A group of metabolic diseases in which a person has chronically elevated blood sugar levels, either because the body does not produce insulin or the body's cells do not respond to insulin.

Docosahexaenoic acid (DHA)

An omega-3 fatty acid found in fatty fish in high concentrations.

Eicosanoid

Any of a class of compounds derived from polyunsaturated fatty acids and involved in the inflammatory response.

Eicosapentaenoic acid

An omega-3 fatty acid found in fatty fish in high concentrations.

Endosperm

The starchy portion of a grain found in refined grains and whole grains. The food supply of a grain.

Enzyme

A protein that speeds up chemical reactions in living organisms.

Erythrocyte Sedimentation Rate (ESR)

A blood test used to detect inflammation in the body.

Flavonoids

Plant chemicals with antioxidant and anti-inflammatory properties.

Fibrinogen

A protein produced in the liver that is elevated when inflammation is present in the body.

Free Radicals

Damaging substances that possess an unpaired electron and attempt to become stable by stealing electrons from other compounds in the body. Smoking, pollution, poisons, and other environmental contaminants increase the presence of free radicals in the body. Can damage cells, proteins, and DNA by altering their chemical structure.

Germ

The reproductive portion of a grain that can potentially grow into a plant. An important component of whole grains rich in essential fatty acids, vitamin E, folate, and other B vitamins.

Glycemic Index

A measure of the effects of carbohydrates on blood sugar levels.

Gynoid Obesity

A type of obesity in which fat is localized around the hips, buttocks, and thighs; it is most common in women; pear-shaped fat distribution.

High-Density Lipoprotein (HDL)

Healthy packages of fats that carry cholesterol from the body tissues to the liver. "Good" cholesterol.

Hyperglycemia

High blood glucose (sugar) levels.

Inflammation

The process by which the body's white blood cells and chemicals protect you from infection and foreign substances such as bacteria and viruses.

Insulin

A hormone that allows cells, most notably the liver, muscle, and adipose tissue, to take up glucose from the blood.

Insulin Resistance

A condition where the hormone insulin becomes less effective at lowering blood glucose levels.

Interleukin-6 (IL-6)

A protein that stimulates the inflammatory response.

Leukocyte Count

A blood measurement used to assess white blood cells in the body.

Lipoprotein-Associated Phospholipase (Lp-PLA2)

An enzyme produced by white blood cells and often bound to LDL cholesterol that causes production of pro-inflammatory substances.

Low-Density Lipoprotein (LDL)

Lethal packages of fats that carry cholesterol from the liver to the body tissues; "bad" cholesterol.

Lupus

Chronic inflammatory autoimmune disorder that affects the skin, joints, kidneys, and other organs.

Monounsaturated Fatty Acids

Healthy unsaturated fatty acids found in oils such as olive oil, canola oil, and high-oleic safflower and sunflower oils.

Non-Steroidal Anti-Inflammatory Drugs (NSAIDs)

Medications used to treat inflammation, pain, and fever.

Nuclear Factor-KB (NF-KB)

A protein that plays a key role in regulating the immune response to infection.

Omega-3 Fatty Acids

Healthy essential fatty acids that make hormones required for controlling inflammation. Can be found in fish oil and certain plant/nut oils.

Omega-6 Fatty Acids

Essential fatty acids that lead to the secretion of hormones that can contribute to a number of chronic diseases when consumed in excess. Can be found in many processed foods, vegetable oils, and meats.

Oxidation

When free radicals take an electron away from another molecule to pair with their single free electron.

Partially Hydrogenated Fats

Chemically modified unsaturated fats commonly found in refined, processed foods which promote a variety of chronic diseases.

Phytochemicals

A wide variety of substances produced by plants that have antioxidant effects in the body.

Polyphenols

An antioxidant phytochemical that tends to prevent or neutralize the damaging effects of free radicals.

Probiotics

Living microorganisms commonly consumed in fermented foods such as yogurt that have beneficial health effects.

Pro-Inflammatory Substances

A substance capable of producing inflammation.

Prostaglandins

A group of hormone-like substances that are involved in management of blood pressure and inflammation.

Refined Grains

Grain products that have been significantly modified from their natural composition and often lack the bran and germ portions of the original grain.

Rheumatoid Arthritis (RH)

An autoimmune disorder that leads to chronic inflammation of the joints and surrounding tissues.

Saturated Fatty Acids

Unhealthy fats that are solid at room temperature, and can lead to elevated LDL cholesterol levels.

Tau Proteins

A protein found in the neurons of the brain that can contribute to Alzheimer's disease when it becomes chemically modified.

Trans Fatty Acids

Unhealthy fats manufactured from unsaturated fatty acids during a process called hydrogenation.

Waist Circumference

The distance around your natural waist, which can be used to determine the location of fat storage in the body.

White Blood Cells (WBC)

Cells of the immune system involved in protecting the body against infectious disease and foreign invaders.

Whole Grains

Healthy cereal grains that contain all of their original components including the bran, germ, and endosperm.

Resource Guide

American Cancer Society (ACS)

The ACS website is aimed at providing consumers with important information to help them stay well and get well after a cancer diagnosis.
www.cancer.org

American College of Allergy, Asthma and Immunology

Provides information for patients and professionals, and links to other websites.
www.acaai.org

American Council on Exercise (ACE)

ACE is a nonprofit organization committed to enriching quality of life through safe and effective physical activity.
www.acefitness.org

American Diabetes Association (ADA)

The ADA's mission is to prevent and cure diabetes to improve the lives of all people affected by diabetes. This website provides objective and credible information regarding diabetes, its risk factors, signs and symptoms, complications, and treatment.
www.diabetes.org

American Dietetic Association

The American Dietetic Association is the world's largest organization of food and nutrition professionals. Its website provides trustworthy, science-based food and nutrition information.
www.eatright.org

American Heart Association

Provides information on a wide variety of topics related to heart health, heart disease prevention, and treatment of a variety of heart-related diseases and conditions.
www.heart.org

The American Institute of Stress

Website dedicated to exploring the multitudinous and varied effects of stress on our health and quality of life.
www.stress.org

Harvard School of Public Health: The Nutrition Source

A nutrition source maintained by the Department of Nutrition at the Harvard School of Public Health providing excellent nutrition and health-related information for consumers.
www.hsph.harvard.edu/nutritionsource

Interactive Menu Planner

A menu planner maintained by the National Institutes of Health. The interactive menu planner is designed to guide daily food and meal choices based on one day's calorie allowance. It may be used in advance to plan a meal, or at the end of a day to add up total calories, as well as fat and carbohydrates, consumed.
http://hp2010.nhlbihin.net/menuplanner/menu.cgi

MyPyramid Tracker

MyPyramid Tracker is an online dietary and physical activity assessment tool that provides information on your diet quality, physical activity status, related nutrition messages, and links to nutrient and physical activity information.
www.mypyramidtracker.org

National Sleep Foundation

This informative site features information on sleep disorders, healthy sleep support and advocacy, and online resources on sleep.
www.sleepfoundation.org

President's Challenge

President's Challenge helps people of all ages and abilities increase their physical activity and improve their fitness through research-based information, easy-to-use tools, and friendly motivation.
www.presidentschallenge.org

Shape Up America! Nutrition and Fitness Center

The purpose of the Shape Up America! website is to educate the public on the importance of the achievement and maintenance of a healthy body weight through the adoption of increased physical activity and healthy eating.
www.shapeup.org

United States Department of Agriculture: Center for Nutrition Policy and Promotion (CNPP)

Visit USDA government-sponsored website for the 2010 Dietary Guidelines for Americans. The CNPP's mission is to improve the health of Americans by developing and promoting dietary guidance that links scientific research to the nutrition needs of consumers.
www.cnpp.usda.gov/DGAs2010

U.S. Food and Drug Administration (FDA)

Provides information for consumers and professionals in the areas of food safety, supplements, and medical devices, as well as links to other sources of nutrition and food information.
www.fda.gov

U.S. Food and Nutrition Information Center

Provides a variety of materials relating to the Dietary Guidelines, food labels, and many other topics, with extensive links.
www.nal.usda.gov/fnic

U.S. National Physical Activity Plan

The National Physical Activity Plan, launched in May 2010, is a far-reaching set of policies, programs, and initiatives aimed at increasing the level of physical activity, improving health, preventing disease, and enhancing the quality of life in Americans.
www.physicalactivityplan.org

Standard U.S./Metric Measurement Conversions

VOLUME CONVERSIONS

U.S. Volume Measure	Metric Equivalent
⅛ teaspoon	0.5 milliliters
¼ teaspoon	1 milliliters
½ teaspoon	2 milliliters
1 teaspoon	5 milliliters
½ tablespoon	7 milliliters
1 tablespoon (3 teaspoons)	15 milliliters
2 tablespoons (1 fluid ounce)	30 milliliters
¼ cup (4 tablespoons)	60 milliliters
⅓ cup	90 milliliters
½ cup (4 fluid ounces)	125 milliliters
⅔ cup	160 milliliters
¾ cup (6 fluid ounces)	180 milliliters
1 cup (16 tablespoons)	250 milliliters
1 pint (2 cups)	500 milliliters
1 quart (4 cups)	1 liter (about)

WEIGHT CONVERSIONS

U.S. Weight Measure	Metric Equivalent
½ ounce	15 grams
1 ounce	30 grams
2 ounces	60 grams
3 ounces	85 grams
¼ pound (4 ounces)	115 grams
½ pound (8 ounces)	225 grams
¾ pound (12 ounces)	340 grams
1 pound (16 ounces)	454 grams

OVEN TEMPERATURE CONVERSIONS

Degrees Fahrenheit	Degrees Celsius
200 degrees F	100 degrees C
250 degrees F	120 degrees C
275 degrees F	140 degrees C
300 degrees F	150 degrees C
325 degrees F	160 degrees C
350 degrees F	180 degrees C
375 degrees F	190 degrees C
400 degrees F	200 degrees C
425 degrees F	220 degrees C
450 degrees F	230 degrees C

BAKING PAN SIZES

American	Metric
8 x 1½ inch round baking pan	20 x 4 cm cake tin
9 x 1½ inch round baking pan	23 x 3.5 cm cake tin
1 x 7 x 1½ inch baking pan	28 x 18 x 4 cm baking tin
13 x 9 x 2 inch baking pan	30 x 20 x 5 cm baking tin
2 quart rectangular baking dish	30 x 20 x 3 cm baking tin
15 x 10 x 2 inch baking pan	30 x 25 x 2 cm baking tin (Swiss roll tin)
9 inch pie plate	22 x 4 or 23 x 4 cm pie plate
7 or 8 inch springform pan	18 or 20 cm springform or loose bottom cake tin
9 x 5 x 3 inch loaf pan	23 x 13 x 7 cm or 2 lb narrow loaf or pate tin
1½ quart casserole	1.5 litre casserole
2 quart casserole	2 litre casserole

Index

Note: Page numbers in **bold** indicate recipe category lists.

We Have

EVERYTHING®

on Anything!

With more than 19 million copies sold, the Everything® series has become one of America's favorite resources for solving problems, learning new skills, and organizing lives. Our brand is not only recognizable—it's also welcomed.

The series is a hand-in-hand partner for people who are ready to tackle new subjects—like you!

For more information on the Everything® series, please visit *www.adamsmedia.com*

The Everything® list spans a wide range of subjects, with more than 500 titles covering 25 different categories:

Business	History	Reference
Careers	Home Improvement	Religion
Children's Storybooks	Everything Kids	Self-Help
Computers	Languages	Sports & Fitness
Cooking	Music	Travel
Crafts and Hobbies	New Age	Wedding
Education/Schools	Parenting	Writing
Games and Puzzles	Personal Finance	
Health	Pets	